Stock Options:
BEYOND THE BASICS

Third Edition

Stock Options:
BEYOND THE BASICS

Third Edition

Edited by Scott S. Rodrick

The National Center for Employee Ownership
Oakland, California

This publication is designed to provide accurate and authoritative information regarding the subject matter covered. It is sold with the understanding that the publisher is not engaged in rendering legal, accounting, or other professional services. If legal advice or other expert assistance is required, the services of a competent professional should be sought.

Stock Options: Beyond the Basics, 3rd ed.
Editing and design by Scott S. Rodrick

The National Center for Employee Ownership
1736 Franklin Street, 8th Floor
Oakland, CA 94612
(510) 208-1300
(510) 272-9510 (fax)
E-mail: *nceo@nceo.org*
Web site: *http://www.nceo.org/*

First edition published September 1999
Second edition August 2000
Third edition January 2003

ISBN: 0-926902-81-4

Contents

Preface

More and more companies are realizing that their employees are their most important asset. To attract, retain, and reward employees, many companies use stock options and related plans, often in "broad-based" programs that include most or even all employees. Our standard introductory guide for company owners, managers, and advisors is *The Stock Options Book*, which covers a multitude of issues relating to stock options and stock purchase plans.

This book goes one step beyond *The Stock Options Book* with extensive information on crucial issues such as administration, securities laws, and divorce. It is not a comprehensive overview like *The Stock Options Book* but rather is more selective and detailed. It is not meant to be an introduction to the field or to be a guide to all advanced issues.

We hope you find this book useful and that it inspires you to become more involved with stock plans. To read about the other information resources that we at the National Center for Employee Ownership (NCEO) offer, including many other publications on stock plans, communicating stock options to employees, and creating an ownership culture, visit our Web site at *www.nceo.org* or see the back of this book.

Third Edition (January 2003)

With the third edition, this book has been completely reorganized: the former chapter 1 is gone, having been expanded and updated to become a wholly separate book (the new version of *The Stock Options Book*); the accounting material has been similarly removed to be replaced with material published elsewhere; several other chapters have been removed; new chapters have been added on state securities laws, divorce, and underwater options; chapter 6 now focuses solely on death and has been updated; and all the remaining chapters and the glossary have been updated as needed.

Administering an Employee Stock Option Plan

Mark A. Borges

*I*N RECENT YEARS, stock options have become the most popular non-cash means for compensating employees. While many corporations have historically granted stock options to their senior management as an integral component of their executive compensation programs, a growing number of companies now grant stock options at various levels within the organization. Moreover, broad-based employee stock option programs that award stock options to all or substantially all employees, long used by smaller businesses, are now being adopted by larger corporations as well.

Befitting their popularity, employee stock options are also one of the most comprehensively regulated forms of equity compensation. A multitude of complex and, at times, confusing tax, corporate, and securities laws affect the adoption, implementation, operation, and administration of employee stock option plans. These laws are supplemented by an array of other provisions, ranging from the detailed requirements of the national securities exchanges to the general common-law principles of contracts. While the terms and conditions of individual employee stock option programs vary from company to company, the characteristics of

The Securities and Exchange Commission, as a matter of policy, disclaims responsibility for any private publication or statement by any of its employees. The views expressed herein are those of the author and do not necessarily reflect the views of the Commission or of the author's colleagues upon the staff of the Commission.

all employee stock options are heavily influenced by the various rules that govern their use.

The laws, regulations, and other principles governing employee stock options are well-documented elsewhere. Less understood are the administrative considerations that arise in maintaining an employee stock option program. This chapter discusses the more common administrative aspects of employee stock options.

Establishing the Plan

When a company decides to implement an employee stock option program, management will typically arrange for the preparation of an appropriate plan document. Typically, the plan's structure, as well as its specific terms and conditions, will be determined in consultation with the company's legal counsel, accountants, and outside compensation or benefits specialists. Factors taken into consideration in designing the plan will include the cost to the company and to proposed participants, the potential liquidity for participants, and the income tax and financial accounting consequences arising from the operation of the plan.

Most plans allow for the grant of both nonqualified stock options and incentive stock options. This permits flexibility in granting appropriate options to selected employees, while effectively limiting the total number of shares of stock available for granting under the stock option program. (The rules governing incentive stock options stipulate that the stock option plan must state the maximum number of shares of stock available for grant under the plan.) Generally, the company's legal counsel will prepare the plan documents. Once management has approved the stock option program, it will be presented to the company's board of directors for consideration and adoption. Because under the corporate laws of most states, the board has the responsibility for all issuances of the company's stock, board approval is generally required before the implementation of an employee stock option plan.

Following adoption by the board of directors, an employee stock option plan is customarily submitted to the company's shareholders for approval. Shareholder approval may be a requirement under state corporate law, the company's charter documents, or the rules of the stock exchange on which the company's securities are traded (if the company's stock is traded on a national exchange) or listed (if the company's stock is traded over the counter). Even where shareholder approval is not required, there may be distinct advantages to obtaining shareholder approval of the stock option plan. The preferential tax treatment afforded by the Internal Revenue Code (the "Code") to incentive stock options is available only if the plan has been approved by the company's shareholders. In addition, the exclusion from the deduction limit of Section 162(m) of the Code for "performance-based" compensation requires that a compensation plan or arrangement be approved by shareholders. In addition, compliance with certain provisions of the federal securities laws may be made easier if the stock option plan has been approved by shareholders.

Granting Options

Policies and Procedures

Many companies establish formal policies and procedures to facilitate the efficient administration of their employee stock option plans. Formal policies enhance the plan administrator's ability to operate the plan consistent with the company's objectives for the stock option program. They also enable the plan administrator to resolve problems arising during the administration of the plan. Formal guidelines for processing stock option grants can serve as an effective means for ensuring that all company procedures are properly followed.

A comprehensive stock option plan policy should address:

- How option recipients are to be determined.
- How the size of stock option grants (number of shares) are to be determined.
- Which type of stock options to grant: incentive stock options (ISOs) or nonqualified stock options (NSOs).
- How often stock options are to be granted.
- How the vesting schedule is to be determined.
- How stock option grants are handled in special situations.

A written procedure should address the following:

- The company's internal approval process.
- The grant transaction recordation.
- The grant agreement preparation and completion process.
- Inter-departmental communications.

Plan Participation

Under an employee stock option plan, both the selection of recipients and the timing of grants are typically reserved to the discretion of the board of directors. Companies use a wide variety of different approaches and policies for determining which employees should receive stock options. In some instances, only members of senior management are eligible to receive stock options. Other companies will grant stock options to all managers. Still other companies grant stock options to all employees, regardless of their job descriptions.

Some companies grant stock options to all newly hired employees, while others grant options only to employees who have completed a specified term of service with the company. Stock options are frequently used as a form of merit bonus, in combination with or in lieu of a salary increase or in conjunction with a promotion. It is not uncommon for a company to make periodic (for example, annual) uniform stock option grants to all employees.

Number of Shares Granted

Under an employee stock option plan, the number of shares of stock to be granted under option to each employee is typically determined by the board of directors. Companies use a wide variety of different approaches and/or policies for determining the size of a stock option grant. Typically, a company will establish guidelines for determining the number of shares of stock to be granted in each stock option. The number of shares of stock may be determined on an employee-by-employee basis, by job classification, or based on the company's overall performance over a specified period of time. The number of shares of stock may also be determined as a percentage of the employee's annual salary.

Internal Approval Process

In order to grant stock options, generally a company will find it beneficial to establish internal approval procedures. The exact nature of these procedures will vary from company to company. In any event, the procedures should address such matters as who will be recommended for a stock option grant, what the size of the grant will be, and whether any special terms and conditions will be incorporated into the grant. These decisions are usually made by the human resources department and/or other benefits personnel, possibly with input from various management-level employees. For example, in the case of newly hired employees, the hiring manager may provide the first level of stock option grant approval. For merit grants, an employee's direct supervisor may provide the stock option grant recommendation.

Next, all grants, regardless of origin, will be incorporated into a formal proposal to be submitted to the company's board of directors for review and approval. If the board of directors has delegated responsibility for stock option grants to a subcommittee of the board, such as a stock option committee or the compensation committee, the recommendations will be considered and approved. Alternatively, the committee may make its own recommendations, which will be submitted to the full board for review and final approval. Stock option grants generally become effective as of the date of board action.

Grant Agreement

Most companies document a stock option grant by preparing a grant agreement. The grant agreement for a stock option is a written document that specifies the terms and conditions of the stock option grant. The grant agreement typically contains the following:

- The correct name of the employee (the "optionee").
- The effective date of the stock option grant.
- The type of stock option (ISO or NSO).
- The number of shares of stock covered by the option.
- The option price.
- The vesting schedule for the shares that the option covers.
- The expiration date of the stock option.

In addition, the agreement usually sets out the procedures the optionee must observe to exercise the stock option, the permissible forms of payment of the option price, and other related matters. Since the agreement usually will also set out the obligations of the optionee in connection with the receipt and/or exercise of the stock option as well as any restrictions imposed on the option or the option shares, most companies require that the optionee sign the grant agreement. A company should set a time limit within which an optionee must sign and return the grant agreement; the company should address whether there is to be a penalty for failure to return an executed agreement.

When the grant of the stock option is formally approved, multiple copies (at least two) of the grant agreement usually will be given to the employee for signature. One copy is to be retained by the employee for his or her records. The plan administrator should include a copy in the employee's file, and, if desired, a third copy should be sent to the company's legal counsel.

Other documents may be distributed along with the grant agreement. A copy of the stock option plan, a summary thereof, or a plan "prospectus" is usually provided to the employee. This may be required by federal and/or state securities laws. Additionally, it may be helpful to distribute such items as a form of stock option exercise notice, an escrow agreement (if appropriate), and a question-and-answer memorandum or fact sheet that answers the most frequently asked questions about stock options and contains instructions on exercise procedures.

Vesting

Generally, an employee earns the right to exercise his or her stock option and purchase the option shares over a specified period of time. (Occasionally, a company will permit an employee to exercise his or her stock option at any time after the date of grant, subject to a right of repurchase in favor of the company should the employee leave the company before a specified date.) The process of earning the option shares is commonly referred to as "vesting." The vesting period set forth in the grant agreement is commonly referred to as the "vesting schedule."

Stock options typically are not exercisable immediately upon grant, but become exercisable either in one lump sum after a specified period of time or in cumulative increments. Generally, a vesting schedule will provide that at the completion of designated intervals, a predetermined percentage or ratio of the option shares are earned and become available for purchase by the employee. These interim dates are called "vesting dates." Typically, vesting is measured from the date a stock option is granted; however, some companies measure vesting from the date the employee was hired or commenced providing services to the company.

A company will adopt a vesting schedule that best suits the incentive or other objectives of its stock option plan. Many stock option plans provide for annual vesting schedules; that is, the option shares will vest in equal annual installments over a period of several years (typically, three, four, or five years). In certain parts of the U.S., daily, monthly, or quarterly vesting schedules are used. Occasionally, option shares will vest upon the achievement of specified company performance goals, such as earnings-per-share, revenue, or profitability targets.

Term

When a stock option is granted, the grant agreement will specify the date the right to purchase the option shares will expire. This period of time within which the stock option must be exercised is referred to as the "option term." Typically, stock option terms range between five to ten years from the date the option is granted. Occasionally, the expiration date of a stock option will be measured from the date the option shares vest. Once the stock option term has expired, the employee may no longer purchase the option shares.

In the case of an incentive stock option, the maximum permitted option term is ten years. If the employee owns stock possessing more than 10% of the total combined voting power of all classes of the company's outstanding stock, the maximum permitted option term for an ISO is five years.

Special Situations

From time to time, procedural questions may arise in connection with a stock option grant, such as how fractional shares of stock are to be allocated under the vesting schedule for the option. Most companies do not wish to show fractional shares vesting on a vesting date and will either drop or round the fractional amount. If the fraction is dropped, it is merely allocated to a later vesting period until the aggregate amount equals a whole share. If the fraction is rounded, it is usually rounded to the nearest whole share, and, if rounded down, the fractional amount is allocated to a later period until a whole share can be shown.

Exercising Options

Policies and Procedures

Consistent with the efficient administration of their employee stock option plans, many companies establish formal policies and procedures in connection with the exercise of their employee stock options. Formal guidelines for processing stock option exercises can serve as an effective means for ensuring that all company procedures are properly followed.

A comprehensive stock option plan policy should address:

- When the option shares may be exercised.
- The determination of the exercise date.
- How applicable withholding taxes are to be calculated and collected.
- The different treatment for directors and officers subject to Section 16 of the Securities Exchange Act of 1934. (Section 16 regulates the trading of their own companies' securities by key corporate insiders, such as officers and directors, by requiring such insiders to publicly disclose their transactions in their companies' securities and to turn over to their companies any profits realized from "short-swing" trading activities.)
- Permissible exercise methods.
- Exercise limits.

A written procedure should address:

- The required documents for processing the exercise.
- The tasks of the plan administrator.
- Transfer agent communications.
- Broker communications (if applicable).
- Inter-departmental communications.

Exercisability

An employee's right to exercise a stock option will be governed by the terms of the grant agreement. Where the stock option is exercisable only as the option shares vest, the employee will be able to exercise the option only on or after the vesting date. Alternatively, where the stock option is exercisable before vesting, the employee will be able to exercise the option at any time during its term. Generally, the date of exercise will be considered to be the date on which the plan administrator receives both an executed stock option exercise notice and payment of the total option exercise price for the number of option shares being purchased.

Notice of Exercise

To purchase the shares of stock underlying a stock option, the employee must follow the procedures established by the company for exercising the option. Typically, these procedures will be set forth in the employee's grant agreement. At a minimum, these procedures will require that the employee provide written notice to the company stating his or her intentions.

To exercise a stock option, the employee will complete and sign a stock option exercise notice identifying the stock option being exercised and indicating the number of option shares that the employee intends to purchase. The exercise notice may also indicate how the employee intends to pay for the option shares. Most stock option plans require a written exercise notice as a prerequisite to a valid exercise in order to establish the exercise date and document the employee's intent to exercise.

The stock option exercise notice may also contain other information, such as (1) specific representations and/or statements by the employee deemed necessary by the company to ensure compliance with all required federal and/or state securities laws, (2) information relevant to the form of payment that the employee has selected to pay the total required option exercise price for the number of option shares being purchased, (3) specific statements pertaining to the tax withholding obligations of the employee, if any, arising in connection with the exercise, or (4) specific statements regarding any restrictions and/or conditions imposed on the option shares.

Generally, the stock option exercise notice must be submitted to the plan administrator or other designated representative of the company in person, or by registered or certified mail, return receipt requested, before the expiration date of the stock option, accompanied by full payment of the total required option exercise price for the number of option shares being purchased and any other required documents. Where the optionee is not a local employee, alternate procedures may be in place for the delivery of the stock option exercise notice and payment of the option exercise price (such as by facsimile transmission).

Where the stock option is being exercised by means of a broker's "same-day-sale" exercise (see below), additional documents may have to be executed by the employee in order to complete the transaction.

Many companies have eliminated much of the paperwork associated with stock option exercises by implementing electronic "self-service" exercise programs. Through these programs, employees are able to exercise their stock options via a Web site or an automated telephonic system. Readily available from many securities brokerage firms, these systems eliminate most of the manual data entry associated with option exercises and can also reduce the number of employee inquiries about exercise procedures.

Methods of Payment

An employee stock option plan may provide for a variety of methods for exercising a stock option—that is, for paying the purchase price for the option shares. These payment methods include cash (usually in the form of a check), stock swaps, brokers' "same-day sales," and use of a promissory note. Some plans also permit the delivery of already-owned shares of stock or the withholding of option shares from the stock option exercise to satisfy the withholding tax obligation arising from the exercise. Company policy should set out the methods available to the employee and the relevant guidelines for each.

Cash Exercises   The most commonly used form of payment for a stock option exercise is cash. At the time of exercise, the employee is required to remit the total required option exercise price for the option shares being purchased plus any withholding taxes due to the company. Generally, payment will be made in the form of a check made payable to the company. The company should decide whether a cashiers' check is required for payment or whether a personal check is acceptable, whether separate checks are required for the total option exercise price and the taxes due, and the permissible time period for remitting payment.

Stock Swaps   When an employee elects to exercise a stock option by means of a stock swap, he or she is surrendering already-owned shares of stock to pay the total required option exercise price for the option shares being purchased. The surrendered shares are usually valued at the fair market value of the company's stock on the date of exercise. Typically, the employee will be permitted to engage in a stock swap exercise only if the stock option plan expressly authorizes the delivery of already-owned shares of stock as a permissible payment method. The surrendered shares are either held by the company as treasury shares or retired by the company and revert to the status of authorized but unissued shares.

Directors and officers subject to Section 16 of the Securities Exchange

Act of 1934 may, if certain requirements have been satisfied, engage in a stock swap without the transaction giving rise to either a "purchase" or "sale" for purposes of the "short-swing profits" recovery provision of Section 16(b).

For accounting purposes, the surrender of already-owned shares of stock to pay the total required exercise price for the exercise of an employee stock option may trigger the recognition of a compensation expense for financial accounting purposes. Under the present accounting standards, where the surrendered shares are not "mature," the stock swap will be considered the functional equivalent of the cash settlement of a stock appreciation right, resulting in a new measurement date for the option and ultimately the recognition of an expense equal to the difference between the option exercise price and the fair market value of the company's stock on the date of exercise. For shares of stock to be considered "mature," the shares must have been held by the employee for at least six months before the date of exercise. Because of this accounting position, most companies prohibit employees from engaging in "pyramid" exercises. A "pyramid" exercise is a form of stock swap in which an employee uses the unrealized appreciation in a small number of shares of stock to conduct a series of successive stock swaps to exercise a stock option in full.

Reload Stock Options   Some stock option plans provide for the grant of so-called "reload" stock options in connection with stock swap exercises. Essentially, a reload option feature provides that upon a stock swap exercise, the employee will receive an automatic grant of a new stock option at the then-current fair market value of the company's stock for a number of shares of stock equal to the number of already-owned shares surrendered to the company to complete the stock swap exercise.

Brokers' "Same-Day-Sale" Exercises   A "same-day-sale" exercise is a means by which an employee can finance the exercise of a stock option by immediately selling through a securities brokerage firm that number of option shares from the stock option being exercised necessary to satisfy the payment of the total required option exercise price for the option shares being purchased plus any withholding taxes due to the company.

Generally to effect a "same-day-sale" transaction, an employee will first contact the plan administrator and indicate his or her decision to exercise a vested stock option. At that time, the employee will be advised of the securities brokerage firm or firms used by the company for these transactions and asked to select a broker (if the employee does not already use one of the brokerage firms included on the company's list). The employee will also complete the required forms for a standard stock option exercise (typically, a stock option exercise notice) and the additional forms necessary for a "same-day-sale" exercise (such as a set of irrevocable instructions to the company, a stock transfer power, a Form W-9, and, if a brokerage account needs to be established, a new account form and/or a margin agreement form).

Once the forms have been completed and the plan administrator has confirmed that the employee does, in fact, have sufficient option shares to cover the proposed transaction, the exercise notice and the irrevocable instructions (which may be integrated into a single document) will be immediately transmitted to the securities brokerage firm. The securities brokerage firm will also be instructed as to how many option shares are to be sold (either just enough to cover the total required option exercise price for the transaction and any associated withholding taxes or some greater number, up to all, of the option shares).

Following the sale, the company is notified of the sale price so that the required withholding taxes, if any, can be calculated. This figure is then transmitted to the securities brokerage firm so that it can divide the sales proceeds between the company and the employee.

Generally, within the settlement period (currently three business days), the securities brokerage firm will remit to the company the portion of the sales proceeds necessary to cover the total required option exercise price for the option shares being purchased and any applicable withholding taxes due to the company. This amount is usually paid by check, by wire transfer, or through a deposit into the company's account at the securities brokerage firm.

Typically, the company will not instruct its transfer agent to deliver a share certificate for the "same-day-sale" to the securities brokerage firm until payment of the option exercise price has been made. Upon receipt of the certificate, the transaction will be completed and the balance of the sale proceeds, less brokerage commissions, is remitted to the employee.

A company may make formal arrangements with one or more securities brokerage firms to facilitate "same-day-sale" exercises. Not only do such arrangements simplify the administration of these programs, they also enable the transactions to be completed more expeditiously. Sometimes referred to as "captive broker" programs, the company will keep the securities brokerage firm or firms updated on outstanding stock options and vested shares, thereby enabling the employee to contact the brokerage firm directly when he or she wants to exercise a stock option. To further simplify the administration of these transactions, some companies will establish an "omnibus" account with one or more securities brokerage firms and transfer a block of shares to the account for the purpose of ensuring that sufficient shares are available to deliver upon the settlement of the sale.

For income tax purposes, it is important for a company to satisfy itself as to when the option exercise is deemed to occur in the context of a "same-day-sale" transaction—either the date that the stock option exercise notice is submitted or the date that payment of the total required option exercise price is received. To the extent that these are different dates, the amount of income realized from the exercise, if any, and the applicable withholding taxes may vary. In addition, the determination may result in a difference between the exercise date and the sale date, thereby resulting in variations between the amount of gain reported by the company and by the securities brokerage firm. Companies employ various techniques to ensure that payment of the option exercise price is received or credited for the employee's benefit on the earliest possible date, such as providing in their stock option plans that delivery of the appropriate paperwork for a "same-day-sale" exercise will be an acceptable payment method or by arranging for immediate payment by, or receipt of a short-term "loan" from, a securities brokerage firm. The resolution of this matter for an individual company generally will be based upon the provisions of the company's stock option plan and/or the grant agreement, as well as by any applicable provisions of state corporate law.

Except as discussed below, directors and officers subject to Section 16 of the Securities Exchange Act of 1934 may participate in these "same-day-sale" exercise programs. As affiliates of the company, however, they are subject to certain restrictions not imposed on regular employees. For example, such "same-day-sale" exercise transactions may be restricted to the company's trading "window period." As affiliates, their sales of company stock also must be made in compliance with the conditions of Securities Act Rule 144, the resale exemption from the registration requirements of the Securities Act of 1933 that imposes certain conditions on any sale of securities by a company's directors and officers. In addition, in some circumstances, a "same-day sale exercise" may be viewed as involving either an extension of credit or an arrangement for the extension of credit in the form of a personal loan by the company, which is prohibited under the Securities Exchange Act of 1934. Effective July 30,

2002, this prohibition precludes the directors and executive officers of companies that are subject to the reporting requirements of the Exchange Act from engaging in certain types of "same-day-sale" exercises. Accordingly, a company should consult with the company's legal counsel before allowing directors and executive officers to engage in a "same-day-sale" exercise of a stock option.

For accounting purposes, the implementation of a broker's "same-day-sale" exercise program does not result in the recognition of a compensation expense, because the company receives the full option exercise price for the option shares purchased, the company actually issues the shares, and no payment related to the exercise originates with the company.

Use of a Promissory Note   Some companies permit employees to deliver a promissory note to pay the total required option exercise price for the option shares being purchased. Generally, the promissory note will be a full recourse obligation secured by the option shares being purchased or other property acceptable to the company.

If the use of promissory notes is permitted, such arrangements must provide for the payment of at least the minimum amount of interest that is required under the Code. If the interest rate charged is less than the applicable federal rate, the Internal Revenue Service (IRS) will treat a portion of the amount repaid as imputed interest, which may have significant income tax consequences to the employee and the company. The applicable federal rates are published by the IRS monthly.

In addition, if the stock option is intended to be an incentive stock option, failure to provide for adequate interest for the promissory note may jeopardize the tax status of the option. Consequently, the promissory note must meet the interest requirements of Section 483 of the Code or interest will be imputed, thereby reducing the principal amount of the promissory note. To the extent that this occurs, the amount deemed paid for the option shares will be less than the fair market value of the company's stock on the date of grant. Because less than fair market value will be deemed paid for the shares, incentive stock option treatment will not be available.

Under current accounting standards, any failure to provide for adequate interest in a promissory note may be viewed as a reduction of the exercise price of the stock option, resulting in "variable" accounting treatment for the transaction (the compensation expense will be estimated at the time of grant and adjusted in each subsequent accounting period to reflect changes in the fair market value of the company's stock). Under "variable" accounting, the company ultimately recognizes a compensation expense for financial reporting purposes equal to the difference between the option exercise price and the fair market value of the company's stock on the date the option is ultimately exercised.

As previously noted, under the Securities Exchange Act of 1934, companies that are subject to the reporting requirements of the Exchange Act are prohibited from extending credit or arranging for the extension of credit in the form of a personal loan to their executive officers and directors. Because this prohibition applies to the delivery of a promissory note to purchase company stock, executive officers and directors may not exercise a stock option through the delivery of a promissory note.

Withholding Taxes

Upon the exercise of a nonqualified stock option, the company is obligated to withhold federal income tax from the optionee (if an employee) and, if the optionee is a resident of a state with an income tax, to withhold state income tax as well. In addition, withholding will be required for purposes of the Medicare insurance portion of the Federal Insurance Contributions Act (FICA) and may be required for purposes of the Social Security portion of FICA to the extent that the employee has not already satisfied his or her annual obligation.

Where the optionee is an employee of the company, arrangements must be made to satisfy any withholding tax obligations that arise in connection with the exercise. If the optionee is a local employee, generally any withholding tax payment due should accompany delivery of the stock option exercise notice. If the optionee is not a local employee, generally the date of exercise will be considered to be the date on which an executed stock option exercise notice is received by the company via facsimile transmission and/or funds representing the total required option exercise price for the number of option shares being purchased are wired to the company. The original exercise notice is then mailed to the company along with the necessary withholding tax payment, if applicable.

Where not addressed in the stock option plan or the grant agreement, the company may adopt a formal policy establishing the date on and price at which any applicable income and withholding taxes will be calculated. In accordance with Section 83 of the Code, the applicable taxes will be calculated based on the fair market value of the company's stock on the exercise date. If the amount of withholding taxes due cannot be calculated in advance, the policy usually states the time period within which the withholding tax payment must be received by the company. Frequently, a company will hold the certificate for the option shares purchased until full payment of all amounts due is received.

Trading Shares for Taxes

Some companies allow their employees to pay the withholding taxes due in connection with the exercise of a stock option by electing to have a portion of the option shares withheld from the exercise transaction. The number of option shares withheld is usually calculated based on the fair market value of the company's stock on the date of exercise. The employee receives only the net shares (after taking account of the withholding) from the exercise of the stock option.

Exercise Restrictions

To control administrative costs, the company may adopt a formal policy establishing a minimum number of option shares that must be exercised at any one time. This may be especially important if the company's vesting schedule contemplates frequent vesting dates (such as monthly vesting). For example, company policy may restrict the exercise of fewer than 100 option shares at a time unless the balance of the shares remaining in the grant are fewer than the minimum exercise amount.

Exercise of Unvested Shares

As previously described, some companies permit employees to exercise stock options before the date that the option shares vest. These unvested option shares will be subject to a right of repurchase in favor of the company in the event the employee terminates his or her employment before the vesting date. This right of repurchase expires either all at once or as to incremental portions of the option shares over the vesting period. When an exercise for unvested option shares occurs, typically the shares will be issued in the name of the employee and then held in escrow until they vest. The option shares cannot be sold while they are held in escrow, nor can they be used as collateral for loans. Consequently, the employee will usually execute and deliver to the company a form of joint escrow agreement or escrow instructions when exercising a stock option for unvested shares.

The unvested share repurchase right held by the company will be exercisable only upon the termination of employment of the employee and then only to the extent of any shares of stock previously acquired by the employee that remain unvested on the date of termination. Typically, the grant agreement will specify the rights and obligations of the company and the employee under this repurchase right.

Since a right of repurchase on unvested option shares renders the shares nontransferable and is considered to be a "substantial risk of forfeiture," the employee is normally not subject to taxation in connection with the purchase of the option shares until the shares vest. The employee may elect to close the compensatory element of the purchase and accelerate the time at which gain will be realized (and at which taxes, if any, will be paid) to the date of exercise by filing a Section 83(b) election with the IRS.

Confirmation of Exercise

After processing the exercise, generally the plan administrator will confirm the transaction by sending a written notice to the employee. In the case of an exercise of an incentive stock option, this notification is required by Section 6039 of the Code. The notification must include the following:

- The name, address, and identification number of the employer company.
- The name, address, and identification number of the employee purchasing the option shares.
- The date of grant.
- The date of exercise.
- The fair market value of the company's stock on the date of exercise.
- The number of option shares exercised.
- The type of stock option exercised.
- The total cost of the shares exercised.

In addition, this notification should be kept on file by the plan administrator, and one copy should be submitted to the accounting department along with the payment received for the total option exercise price. If the exercise of the stock option requires the withholding of income and/ or employment taxes, a copy of the notification should also be provided to the payroll department.

Issuance of Shares

The plan administrator must provide instructions to the company's transfer agent for the preparation and issuance of a certificate for the option
shares purchased. The instructions should include the number of shares
of stock to be issued, the number of certificates to be issued, the correct
name under which the shares are to be registered, and appropriate mail-
ing instructions. Generally, the transfer agent's instructions require the
signature of an authorized company representative.

In anticipation of the initial exercise of any stock options, the plan
administrator should provide the company's transfer agent with a list of
the relevant legends to be placed on the certificates for the option shares.
Transfer agents or the company's legal counsel are usually able to assist
with the drafting of these legends. Legends may be required by applicable federal and/or state securities laws in order to prevent transfers of
the option shares that are not in compliance with such laws. In addition,
if the option shares are subject to repurchase rights or transferability restrictions set forth in the stock option plan or imposed by the company,
the certificates should be appropriately legended to notify potential purchasers of these restrictions. Some companies legend certificates for incentive stock option shares in order to track disqualifying dispositions.

If the exercise is pursuant to a broker's "same-day-sale" program,
the plan administrator must also be in communication with the securities brokerage firm handling the transaction. Before the exercise, confirmation must be obtained that the option shares being purchased are
vested. Although actual practice will vary between companies, the employee will typically verify exercisability and then either the employee
or the plan administrator will contact the securities brokerage firm to
arrange for the option shares to be sold. The securities brokerage firm
will open an account for the employee if none currently exists. In addition to the stock option exercise notice, the employee must complete the
appropriate documents authorizing the securities brokerage firm to sell
all or a portion of the option shares.

Collateral Documents

In addition to the grant agreement, the company may provide several
other documents to an employee in connection with the grant and/or
exercise of a stock option. For purposes of compliance with applicable
federal and/or state securities laws, it is customary for the company to
provide each employee with a copy of the company's stock option plan

or with a document (often referred to as the plan "prospectus") that summarizes the principal terms and conditions of the plan, describes the tax consequences of participation in the plan, and advises the employee where to obtain additional information about the company and the plan.

Other relevant documents may include a form of stock option exercise notice, memoranda describing the company's exercise procedures, investment representation letters or statements (in the event the option shares have not been registered with the Securities and Exchange Commission), escrow instructions (in the event the option may be exercised for unvested shares of stock), a form of promissory note and security agreement, and the appropriate forms for conducting a broker's "same-day-sale" exercise.

Many companies also prepare and distribute fact sheets and/or question and answer memoranda that address many of the common questions asked by employees concerning their stock option grants.

Other Common Situations

Termination of Employment

A stock option plan usually addresses the treatment for stock options when an optionee terminates his or her employment or otherwise severs his or her relationship with the company. Typically, the optionee will have a specified period of time following termination in which to exercise his or her stock options to the extent of the option shares that have vested (and have not already been purchased) as of the date of termination. The optionee is not normally entitled to purchase option shares that vest after the termination date. This post-termination exercise period ranges in length from 30 to 90 days, depending upon the terms of the company's stock option plan. In the event that the termination of employment resulted from the death or disability of the optionee, the post-termination exercise period is typically extended to 6 or 12 months.

Repurchase of Unvested Shares

If the employee has exercised his or her stock option for unvested shares (which would be possible if the company allows its stock options to be exercised before the date that the option shares vest) and then terminates employment before these option shares have vested, the unvested shares will typically be subject to repurchase by the company.

Generally, the terms and conditions of the company's unvested share repurchase right will be set forth in the grant agreement. The company must notify the employee in writing within a specified period of time (usually 60 to 90 days following termination) of its decision to repurchase some or all of the unvested shares. The decision to repurchase the unvested shares is typically made by the board of directors. The repurchase price will be an amount equal to the original option price paid by the employee for the option shares. This payment will be made in cash or by cancellation of any outstanding indebtedness of the employee to the company. Typically, the company will hold the unvested shares pending vesting. Alternatively, if the option shares have been issued to the employee, payment of the repurchase amount will not take place unless and until the certificate for the unvested shares is delivered to the company.

Restrictions on Transfer

Occasionally, privately held companies impose restrictions on the ability of employees to transfer or dispose of vested option shares following the exercise of a stock option. Typically, the terms and conditions of these restrictions will be set forth in the grant agreement. The restrictions usually terminate when the company's securities become publicly traded.

Leaves of Absence

From time to time, an employee will be permitted to take a leave of absence from his or her position with the company. If the employee holds a stock option granted by the company, the plan administrator will face various questions concerning the status of the option during the leave of absence. For example, the company's stock option plan or the grant agreement may address how vesting will be calculated during the leave of absence. In the absence of an express provision, the company may want to establish a policy regarding whether the employee will receive vesting credit during all or any portion of the leave. Typically, companies will toll the vesting period (that is, suspend vesting) during an approved leave of absence unless vesting credit has been specifically authorized before the commencement of the leave or is required by law. Similarly, the company may want to establish a policy regarding whether the employee will be permitted to exercise his or her stock option while on leave.

For purposes of the "employment" requirement for incentive stock options, the income tax regulations provide that among other things, an employee must at all times during the period beginning with the date of grant of the stock option and ending on the date of exercise (or on the day three months before the date of such exercise) have been an employee of the company granting the option (or a related company). For these purposes, the employment relationship will be treated as continuing intact while the employee is on military, sick leave, or any other bona fide leave of absence if the period of such leave does not exceed 90 days. A leave of absence in excess of 90 days will not disrupt the employment relationship so long as the employee's right to reemployment with the company is guaranteed either by statute or by contract.

If the employee's leave of absence exceeds 90 days, or his or her right to reemployment is not guaranteed either by statute or by contract, the employment relationship will be deemed to have terminated on the 91st day of the leave. Thus, if the employment relationship is considered to have been terminated, the three-month period for preserving ISO status (and preferential tax treatment) will begin running, regardless of the company's determination of the status of the option for contractual purposes (that is, whether or not the post-termination exercise period will be deemed to have commenced). If the option is exercised within three months of the 91st day of the leave of absence, the option will be treated as an incentive stock option. If the option is exercised more than three months after the 91st day of the leave of absence, the option will be treated as a nonqualified stock option for tax purposes.

Although not relevant for income tax purposes, many companies apply the ISO standards regarding employment status to their nonqualified stock options as well. This enables them to determine when an employee's employment is to be considered terminated for purposes of calculating the commencement of the post-termination exercise period.

Capital Adjustments

From time to time, a company may engage in a transaction that changes or affects its capital structure, including its authorized capitalization and its outstanding securities. These transactions include but are not limited to stock splits, reverse stock splits, stock dividends, corporate combinations, recapitalizations or reclassifications of securities, and other changes that increase or decrease the number of outstanding securities that are effected without the receipt of consideration by the company.

Generally, a company's stock option plan will expressly provide for adjustments to be made in the number and class of shares of stock subject to the plan, and to the number of shares, option exercise price, and class of shares of stock subject to outstanding stock options, to ensure that there is no dilution or enlargement of either the number of shares of stock authorized for issuance under the plan or the individual equity interests of optionees as a result of the transaction. These provisions usually grant the board of directors of the company broad latitude to make the necessary adjustments on an equitable basis.

A stock split occurs on a designated "record date." On that date, all the outstanding shares of record will be adjusted according to the split ratio. Grants and exercises of stock options that occur between the record date and the "payable date" must be adjusted to reflect post-split conditions.

Tax Withholding

Federal and state withholding obligations for income and employment tax purposes will arise at the time of exercise (or at the time of vesting, as the case may be) if the optionee is an employee with regard to the compensation income, or "wages," recognized, if any. Relevant withholding taxes include:

- Federal income.
- Social Security.
- Medicare.
- State income (if applicable).
- State disability or unemployment (if applicable).

For federal income tax purposes, the compensation income recognized upon the exercise (or vesting) of a nonqualified stock option is treated as a supplemental wage payment. This payment is eligible for withholding one of two ways. First, the compensation income may be aggregated with the employee's regular salary payment for the period, with withholding computed on the total amount. Alternatively, the compensation income is eligible for withholding at the flat rate for supplemental wage payments.

In addition, employment taxes under FICA and the Federal Unemployment Tax Act (FUTA) may be due. FICA is made up of two separate taxes: (1) old age, survivor, and disability insurance (Social Security) and

(2) hospital insurance (Medicare). The Social Security component of FICA is collected up to an annual maximum. The Medicare component is collected against the employee's total income. The FICA rates and their applicable ceilings, if any, are subject to change annually. The company's payroll department should be contacted for notification as to when these rate changes occur. FICA taxes are imposed on both the employee and the company, while FUTA taxes are levied against the company.

The withholding taxes collected by the company are only an estimate of the employee's ultimate tax liability. It may be necessary for the employee to make additional quarterly tax deposits depending upon his or her personal tax situation (or to remit additional amounts owed when tax returns are filed). The company must furnish an employee (or former employee) exercising a nonqualified stock option with a Form W-2 for the year of exercise (or vesting) reporting the compensation income recognized as "wages." If the optionee is a non-employee, the compensation income is not subject to withholding but must be reported on a Form 1099-MISC for the year of exercise (or vesting).

Most states follow the federal treatment for income tax purposes and may require the withholding of state disability or unemployment taxes. Generally, state taxes are determined on the basis of the employee's state of residence.

Disposition of Option Stock

Income Tax Issues

Upon a sale or other disposition of nonqualified stock option shares, the optionee generally recognizes a capital gain or loss equal to the difference between the optionee's adjusted tax basis in the option shares and the sale price. However, upon a sale or other disposition of incentive stock option shares, preferential tax treatment is available if certain holding periods are satisfied. These holding periods require that the employee not dispose of the option shares within two years from the date the incentive stock option is granted nor within one year from the date the option shares acquired through the exercise are transferred to the employee. The exact time of transfer may be unclear, but it is generally believed that a transfer takes place no later than when the option shares are recorded in the employee's name in the company's stock records.

If an employee sells or otherwise disposes of the option shares within one year after the date of transfer or within two years after the date of grant, the employee is considered to have made a "disqualifying disposition" of the option shares. Consequently, for the year of the disposition, the employee recognizes compensation income equal to the difference, if any, between the option price and the lesser of the fair market value of the company's stock on the date of exercise and the amount realized from the disposition. Any additional gain recognized as a result of the disposition will be treated as capital gain.

When an employee engages in a disqualifying disposition of ISO shares that were acquired before vesting, the amount of compensation income recognized by the employee will be equal to the difference, if any, between the option price and the fair market value of the company's stock on the date of vesting.

Generally, a "disqualifying disposition" occurs when an employee no longer possesses the legal power to control or further dispose of the option shares. Thus, the transfer of option shares acquired upon the exercise of an incentive stock option into "street name" or into joint tenancy (with a right of survivorship) will not be considered to be a disqualifying disposition. Nor will a pledge of the option shares, a transfer from a decedent to an estate, or a transfer by bequest or inheritance. Finally, transfers of the option shares to certain types of trusts will not be considered disqualifying dispositions. In contrast, a sale or exchange of the option shares, a bona fide inter vivos gift of the option shares, or any other transfer of legal title to the option shares will constitute disqualifying dispositions. Similarly, a foreclosure on pledged option shares in the event of a default will constitute a disqualifying disposition.

Where an employee transfers the option shares to his or her non-employee spouse incident to a dissolution of marriage, the transfer is not considered to be a disqualifying disposition. And, under Section 424(c)(4) of the Code, the option shares will retain their ISO status in the hands of the non-employee spouse (including the original holding period). Where the non-employee spouse subsequently disposes of the option shares before the ISO holding periods have been satisfied, the transfer will then constitute a disqualifying disposition. The company should establish a procedure with its transfer agent to track all disqualifying dispositions.

Securities Law Restrictions

Requirements of the federal securities laws may limit the ability of an employee to resell shares of stock acquired upon the exercise of an employee stock option.

In the case of option shares that are acquired under an exemption from the registration requirements of the Securities Act of 1933, such shares are considered to be "restricted securities." Generally, restricted securities must be sold in reliance on the federal securities law resale exemption contained in Securities Act Rule 144.

In the case of option shares that have been registered for resale with the SEC, the shares may be resold by non-affiliates without regard to Securities Act Rule 144 and by affiliates in reliance on Rule 144 (but without regard to the holding period condition). The securities brokerage firm handling the sale may request company approval, generally of company legal counsel, before completing the transaction.

In addition, if the optionee is an officer or director of the company, he or she may be subject to a variety of so-called "insider trading" restrictions that may limit or prevent the sale. Accordingly, a company should always consult with the company's legal counsel before allowing an officer or director to engage in a sale or other disposition of shares, including option shares.

Conclusion

Administering an employee stock option plan in today's complex regulatory environment can be a challenging proposition. In addition to the tax, securities, and accounting rules that must be observed, a significant number of procedural matters must also be considered. A company adopting a stock option program for its employees will be well-advised to establish formal policies and procedures in order to ensure that all of the applicable legal requirements are satisfied, as well as the administrative aspects of the program. This includes guidelines for disseminating information and materials about awards granted to employees and for processing exercises when optionees elect to convert their awards to stock and, ultimately, to cash. Additional procedures can be implemented for addressing a variety of other common situations that may arise during the term of the plan. If these policies and procedures are implemented and consistently followed, the company can be assured that its employee stock option program will serve its primary objectives and that a high level of employee satisfaction can be achieved.

CHAPTER

2

Federal Securities Law Considerations for Incentive Stock Plans

William R. Pomierski and William J. Quinlan, Jr.

*F*OR A VARIETY OF REASONS, stock options continue to be one of the more popular forms of compensation. Most public companies maintain some form of stock option plan for their directors, officers, and/or key employees. In addition, many public companies are granting stock options at multiple levels within the organization, with some offering stock options to all full-time employees. Incentive stock plans are not, however, exclusive to public companies. In order to attract and/or retain talented individuals, many privately held entities and foreign issuers with operations in the United States are offering stock options to their key employees.

In recent years, the most common practice has been to adopt an omnibus-type incentive stock plan that covers not only stock options but also restricted stock, stock appreciation rights, performance shares, and performance units. This chapter will focus on the securities law aspects of the foregoing benefits payable in stock.

Although incentive stock plans are exempt from the burdensome requirements of the Employee Retirement Income Security Act of 1974 (ERISA), there are still a number of important rules and regulations that can apply. In particular, incentive stock plans maintained by "public companies" are subject to the Securities Exchange Act of 1934 (the "1934 Act"), which imposes various reporting requirements and restricts transactions in issuer securities by, among others, designated executive officers, directors, and persons with material non-public information. In addition, all incentive stock plans are potentially subject to the Securities Act of 1933 (the "1933 Act"), which requires registration of offers to sell securities unless a specific exemption from registration is available.

This chapter focuses on compliance with the federal securities laws rather than on enforcement. Suffice it to say that noncompliance can result in serious penalties and liabilities, including fines, forfeiture of profits, treble damages, and federal criminal prosecution, not to mention the adverse publicity and embarrassment to the corporation and the individuals involved. State securities laws must also be considered, but are beyond the scope of this chapter. In addition, appendix A to this chapter discusses the executive compensation impact of the corporate reform/governance law known as the Sarbanes-Oxley Act of 2002.

Impact of the 1934 Act on Incentive Stock Plans

In General

An incentive stock plan maintained by a "public company" must be administered in light of Section 16 of the 1934 Act and the rules promulgated thereunder (the "Section 16 Rules"). The Section 16 Rules essentially consist of two parts. The first part is Section 16(a) and its related rules, which require directors, certain officers, and principal stockholders of "public companies" to report to the Securities and Exchange Commission (SEC) all transactions in the issuer's securities.[1] The second part is Section 16(b) and its related rules, which require such persons to disgorge any "short-swing profits" received from transactions in the issuer's securities.[2]

Definition of "Public Company"

As indicated above, the Section 16 Rules apply only to "public companies."[3] For these purposes, a "public company" includes any corporation whose stock is *listed* on a national securities exchange or is traded on NASDAQ, excluding a "foreign private issuer" as described below. A "public company" can also include non-listed companies. Specifically, if a corporation has more than $10 million in assets *and* more than 500 shareholders, it will be considered a "public company" subject to the Section 16 Rules, regardless of whether its stock is listed on a national securities exchange or traded on NASDAQ.

Becoming a "public company" due to size and number of shareholders is an important consideration for non-listed companies that maintain incentive stock plans. If a corporation becomes a "public company" under the 500 shareholder/$10 million value rule, it must comply with the registration requirements under Section 12(g) of the 1934 Act, as well as the 1934 Act's proxy solicitation, periodic reporting, and short-swing trading provisions. Accordingly, non-listed corporations that grant stock options and other forms of equity compensation need to closely monitor the number of employees to whom shares are issued or sold in order to ensure that when and if outstanding awards are exercised or shares are otherwise delivered, the corporation will either stay below the 500 shareholder limit or will otherwise be in full compliance with the requirements of the 1934 Act.

In addition, the SEC now takes the position that an option (but not stock appreciation rights) is an equity security for purposes of the 500 shareholder test. This means that a private company can find itself subject to the 1934 Act if it grants options to more than 500 employees and/or consultants. To get around this problem, the Division of Corporation Finance issued a set of guidelines in its Current Issues and Rulemaking Projects Outline dated March 31, 2001. The guidelines are not self-executing, which means that a company with more than 500 holders of stock options should seek no-action letter relief. One of the most recent no-action letters is AMIS Holdings, Inc. (July 30, 2001). This no-action letter contains an analysis of each of the guidelines required by the Division of Corporation Finance.

Foreign Private Issuers

Publicly listed securities of a foreign private issuer, as defined in SEC Rule 3b-4(c), are exempt from Section 16 pursuant to Rule 3a12-3(b) under the 1934 Act.[4] The term "foreign private issuer" is defined in Rule 3b-4(c) to mean any foreign issuer *except* an issuer meeting the following conditions:

1. More than 50% of the outstanding voting securities of such issuer are held of record either directly or through voting trust certificates or depositary receipts by residents of the United States; and

2. Any of the following:

    (a) The majority of the executive officers or directors are United States citizens or residents,

    (b) More than 50% of the assets of the issuer are located in the United States, or

    (c) The business of the issuer is administered principally in the United States.

For these purposes, the term "resident," as applied to security hold-ers, means any person whose address appears on the records of the issuer, the voting trustee, or the depositary as being located in the United States. Note that there is no exemption for stockholders of foreign private issuers from the reporting obligations under Regulation 13D-G or for liability under Rule 10b-5, as described below.

Definition of "Reporting Persons"

The Section 16 reporting and short-swing profit rules do not apply to all transactions in issuer securities. Rather, only transactions by those indi-viduals who are either "designated executive officers" of the public com-pany[5] or members of its board of directors[6] (collectively "reporting persons") are subject to the information reporting requirements and short-swing trad-ing restrictions contained in Section 16 of the 1934 Act.[7]

"Designated executive officers" for these purposes includes only those officers of the issuing corporation with certain high level, policy-making re-sponsibilities who are designated as such by the corporation's board of di-rectors (or a committee thereunder) and are listed each year in the issuer's Form 10-K (Annual Report).[8] For purposes of the Section 16 Rules, an "of-ficer" is a corporate employee performing important executive duties of such character that he would be likely, in discharging these duties, to obtain con-fidential information that would aid him if he engaged in personal market transactions.[9] Merely having the title of an officer does not, by itself, cause an individual to become a "designated executive officer" for purposes of the Section 16 Rules. Instead, the determining factor is whether the individual's duties are commensurate with those of a policy-making position.

The term "officer" includes the following positions: president; principal financial officer; principal accounting officer (or if there is no such account-ing officer, the controller); any vice-president in charge of a principal busi-ness unit, division, or function; and any other officer or other person who performs a significant policy-making function. This can include officers of a parent or subsidiary corporation if they perform a policy-making function for the entity that issues the stock in question.[10] The issuing corporation should notify every director or designated officer who becomes subject to the Section 16 Rules of his or her status as a Section 16 reporting person.

Beneficial Ownership

It is important to note that in most circumstances, a reporting person is presumed to be the owner of all securities in which the reporting person has a "pecuniary interest"—that is, the opportunity to profit or share in any profit, either directly or indirectly.[11] This includes securities held by a spouse, children, grandchildren, parent, grandparent, sibling, and other relatives *sharing the same household,* including step-, in-law and adoptive relationships, and children living away from home while attending college ("household relatives").[12] For example:

> Officer "B" has a daughter who is in college, is financially dependent on "B," and owns Company stock. "B's" daughter sells her stock in September. "B" must report the daughter's sale to the SEC on "B's" Form 4 within two business days of the sale.

Even if the reporting person and a relative are not sharing the same household, the reporting person will be deemed the beneficial owner of securities if he or she actually controls the purchase and sale of securities owned by the relative or if the relative is a minor child.

A reporting person may also be deemed to be the beneficial owner of any stock held by a trust, corporation, partnership or other entity over which he or she has a controlling influence.[13] Special rules exist for trusts in which the reporting person acts as trustee and a member of his or her family has a pecuniary interest in the securities held by the trust.[14]

The potential application of the Section 16 Rules to shares held by household relatives and entities over which the reporting person has a controlling influence needs to be closely monitored to avoid inadvertent violation of the Section 16 Rules. If a question exists as to whether or not an individual is the beneficial owner of certain stock, a statement similar to the following can be included on the SEC stock ownership forms: "Reporting person expressly disclaims beneficial ownership of these shares. Reporting person cannot profit, directly or indirectly, from transactions in these securities."

Reporting Requirements Under Section 16(a) of the 1934 Act

The following discussion covers the Section 16 reporting requirements that are in effect on and after August 29, 2002 as mandated by the Sarbanes-Oxley Act of 2002. As of that date, all transactions with certain limited exceptions are required to be reported within two business days of the date of the transaction. (See appendix A to this chapter, which provides more information on the Sarbanes-Oxley Act of 2002.)

Section 16(a) of the 1934 Act and the rules promulgated thereunder require reporting persons to report to the SEC all transactions in the issuer's securities. As described below, reporting persons must file three kinds of SEC stock ownership forms:

- Initially, a statement of beneficial ownership of issuer stock when the person first becomes subject to Section 16 (Form 3);
- Periodic, as-needed, statements of changes in beneficial ownership (Form 4); and
- Annual statements of changes in beneficial ownership, if needed (Form 5).

Form 3

A reporting person must file a statement of beneficial ownership of issuer stock on Form 3 when the person first becomes a director or designated executive officer of the issuer.[15] If the issuer is already a "public company," Form 3 must be filed—meaning received by the SEC—within 10 days after appointment or designation of the individual as a director or designated executive officer. Otherwise, Form 3 must be filed on or before the date the issuer becomes a public company.

Forms 4 and 5

A reporting person is also required to file periodic statements of changes in beneficial ownership of issuer securities on Form 4 or Form 5, as applicable. Form 4 reports must be filed within two business days after the occurrence of the transaction resulting in a change in the reporting person's beneficial ownership (unless Form 4 is being used on a voluntary basis, as described below).[16] This would include changes in direct ownership of issuer securities, as well as changes in beneficial ownership by reason of transactions involving household relatives or entities over which the reporting person has a controlling interest.

Form 5 must be filed by a reporting person within 45 days after the end of the issuer's fiscal year and must report (1) transactions or changes in beneficial stock ownership not required to have been reported earlier on Form 4, and (2) transactions or changes that should have been reported earlier on Form 4 but were not ("delinquent filings").[17] A Form 5 would not be required from a reporting person who had no reportable transactions during the preceding year. (Rule 16a-3(f)(2)). Any transaction normally reportable on Form 5 at year-end may be voluntarily reported on an earlier Form 4 filed at any time before the due date of the Form 5.[18] To avoid confusion and the risk of late or non-filing, it is recommended that transactions which are reportable on the year-end Form 5 be nevertheless reported as soon as possible on a voluntary Form 4.

The SEC has emphasized the importance of timely filing stock ownership forms. A document will be deemed timely filed with the SEC for purposes of Section 16(a) only if it can be established that it was deposited with a delivery service in time for guaranteed delivery on or before the SEC deadline.[19] All Forms 3, 4, or 5 filed with the SEC must also be filed with the stock exchange on which the issuer's securities are listed, if any, but are not required to be filed with the NASDAQ. If the forms are filed by way of EDGAR, they will be deemed filed with the exchanges and NASDAQ without any additional filings with the exchanges or NASDAQ. This relief comes from SEC staff no-action letters to the exchanges dated July 22, 1998.

Transactions Required to Be Reported

Before the Sarbanes-Oxley Act, Forms 3, 4, and 5 were last revised in 1996, and the exemptions to such filings were broadened substantially. Certain stock transactions are now completely exempt from the reporting requirements of Section 16(a). The following will serve as a general guide for reporting transactions in issuer stock that may arise pursuant to a typical incentive stock plan:[20]

Transactions Required to Be Reported on Form 4 (within Two Business Days):

- Grant or exercise of a stock option or stock appreciation right.

- Delivery of stock to issuer to pay for exercise price of an option (i.e., pursuant to a stock-for-stock exercise) or to pay taxes.

- Amendment of a stock option (including the repricing of an outstanding option and the grant of replacement option upon exercise of predecessor option) or stock appreciation right.

- Grant of stock awards in the form of restricted stock or performance shares.

- Withholding of stock by the issuer to satisfy taxes required to be withheld on the exercise of an option or a stock appreciation right, or upon the vesting of a stock award or performance share award.

- Sale of stock acquired pursuant to the exercise of a stock option or stock appreciation right into the open market, including the sale of stock pursuant to a "cashless" option exercise arrangement.[21]

- Sale of stock received in connection with a stock award or a performance share award.

- Purchases and sales.

- Any of the foregoing transactions by a reporting person's spouse or other "household relatives," or by an entity over which the reporting person has a controlling interest.

Transactions Required to Be Reported on Year-End Form 5 (But It Is Recommended That These Transactions Be Reported Earlier on a Voluntary Form 4):

- Gifts or transfers of an option to family members, or to a family-controlled entity for estate planning purposes. (Rule 16b-5).

- Small acquisitions, but not from the issuer or an issuer sponsored stock benefit plan (Rule 16a-6).

Transactions That Are Not Required to Be Reported:

- Expiration or cancellation of stock options where no consideration is received by the reporting person (Rule 16a-4(d) and Rule 16b-6(d)).

- Vesting of an outstanding stock option, stock appreciation right, stock award, or performance shares.

- Change in beneficial ownership, i.e., from direct to indirect or vice versa (Rule 16a-13).

- Transfer of an option, SAR, stock award or performance shares pursuant to a domestic relations order, including any order entered pursuant to a divorce decree (Rule 16a-12).

Note that while the above-listed events do not have to be reported as transactions on the Section 16 stock ownership forms, the SEC does require that the net result of the transactions be reported in the total ownership column with a footnote explanation.

As a general rule, reporting persons should assume that any transaction in issuer stock must be reported to the SEC, even if the transaction is involuntary on the part of the reporting person or, when combined with another transaction, results in no net change in ownership. Because of the new two business day reporting requirement, reporting persons should be counseled to contact a designated representative of the issuer regarding any potential transaction involving the issuer's securities, no matter how minor it may seem, before consummating the transaction, to receive assistance in filing any needed SEC forms, as well as information regarding the potential Section 16(b) implications, which are described below. See the discussion in appendix A concerning a mandatory pre-clearance policy and appendix B for the suggested form of pre-clearance policy.

Also, a reporting person who has retired, terminated employment, or otherwise ceased to be a reporting person continues to have reporting obligations for a limited period following cessation of "insider" status.[22] Such a person is still required to report opposite-way non-exempt transactions on a Form 4 for six months after the last change in beneficial ownership while he or she was still a Section 16 reporting person. In addition, opposite-way non-exempt transactions made during the six months following cessation of insider status can be matched (for Section 16(b) purposes) with transactions made while an insider to find short-swing profits owed to the issuer. For example:

> "A" will cease to be a director of the Company on October 1. On September 20, "A" sells Company stock. "A" must not only report this sale on a Form 4 by September 22 (two business days), but must continue to file Form 4s to report any non-exempt purchases that occur before the next March 20, and any such purchases will be matched with the September 20 sale.

Issuer Reporting of Noncompliance

As indicated above, the SEC is serious about compliance with the Section 16(a) reporting requirements. Accordingly, public companies are required to report any noncompliance.[23] This report is set out in the issuer's proxy statement for its annual meeting under an appropriate and discrete caption that reads "Section 16(a) Beneficial Ownership Reporting Compliance." The Section 16 Rules also clarify that the issuer is entitled to rely on the Forms 3, 4, and 5 furnished to it, as well as written representations by a reporting person that no Form 5 is required.[24] Also, the SEC can impose fines for late filings or enjoin the late filer from serving as a director or officer of the issuer and/or other public companies, although the SEC typically employs this additional penalty only in egregious cases.

The Section 16 Rules make it clear that the issuer is obligated to consider the absence of certain forms. Specifically, the absence of a Form 3 filing by a Section 16 reporting person is an indication that disclosure is required. Similarly, the absence of a Form 5 is an indication that disclosure is required, unless the issuer has received a written representation that no Form 5 is required, or the issuer otherwise knows that no such filing is required.[25] A "safe harbor" from disclosure is available for an issuer who receives a written representation from the reporting person that no Form 5 was required.[26] This representation is usually set out in an officers and directors questionnaire which should be sent out annually by the issuer.

Proposed Amendments to Form 8-K Reporting Requirements

On April 11, 2002, the SEC proposed rules regarding insider transactions that, if adopted, would have required public companies to file current reports on Form 8-K that describe directors' and executive officers' transactions in company equity securities, directors' and executive officers' Rule 10b5-1 arrangements for the purchase and sale of company equity securities, and loans of money to a director or an executive officer made or guaranteed by the company or an affiliate of the company.[27] The SEC has not indicated what it will do with these proposals in light of the Sarbanes-Oxley Act of 2002, described in appendix A.

The new Section 16 rules adopted by the SEC on August 27, 2002 (effective August 29, 2002) also have a special up-to-five-business-day rule, but this rule has no application to stock benefit plans. See appendix A.

In light of the new Section 16 rules, the following recommendations will help in the administration of stock benefit plans (see appendix A for recommendation covering all types of benefit plans):

- Have a mandatory pre-clearance policy for all transactions as to which the timing is within the control of the Section 16 reporting person.

- Discontinue cashless exercise programs for Section 16 reporting persons for the time being (because of the loan prohibition in Section 402 of Sarbanes-Oxley Act) unless (1) the third party provider (usually a brokerage firm) of the program provides an opinion of qualified counsel that the particular program does not violate Section 402 and a representation of the provider that the program fully complies with the description of the program as to which the opinion relates or (2) the Section 16 reporting person arranges the transaction without involvement of the issuer and any credit extension to the Section 16 reporting person is from the broker or other third party and not the issuer.

- Educate all Section 16 reporting persons by a memorandum which they should read, sign and return.

- Obtain power of attorney with multiple attorneys-in-fact from all Section 16 reporting persons.

- Adopt electronic filing as soon as possible and apply immediately for EDGAR access codes for all Section 16 reporting persons.

Six-Month "Short-Swing" Trading Restrictions Under Section 16(b) of the 1934 Act

To deter insiders from profiting on short-term trading in the securities of their company, Section 16(b) of the 1934 Act requires a public company to recover from any such person the "statutory profit" realized by him or her in either a purchase and sale, or a sale and purchase (or any number of these transactions) which take place within a six-month period. It is important to note that the actual possession of inside information regarding the issuer is *not* a precondition to the recovery of short-swing profits under Section 16(b). This recoverable profit is not necessarily based on economic realities, and there have been situations where an individual actually lost money on a transaction but was held accountable for the return of "profits."

In determining whether there has been a purchase and sale within the meaning of Section 16(b), it is not necessary to establish that the same shares were purchased and sold, or sold and purchased, within the six-month period. Instead, all that needs to be established is that issuer stock (or warrants or similar rights to buy or sell issuer stock) was either purchased and sold, or sold and purchased, during a six-month period. The identity of the particular shares is irrelevant for determining Section 16(b) liability.

Like the reporting requirement under Section 16(a), Section 16(b) may apply to transactions made after an individual ceases having reporting-person status. That is, a purchase (or sale) after retirement or termination of employment from the issuer can be matched against any sale (or purchase) effected less than six months earlier at the time the individual was still a reporting person.

To compute statutory short-swing profits, the highest sale price and lowest purchase price during the six-month period are matched, regardless of whether the sale and purchase involved the same shares. For a series of transactions, the difference between the highest sale price and the lowest purchase price during the period is computed (regardless of the order in which they occur), then the difference between the next highest sale price and the next lowest purchase price, and so forth. These differences are then totaled to determine the "profit realized" in a series of transactions. For example:

Director "D" effects the following 100-share lot transactions of Company stock within a six-month period:

	Price per Share			
Purchases	$100	$80	$50	$30
Sales	90	70	40	40

Applying the method of calculation used under Section 16(b), the recoverable "profit realized" would be $8,000:

Transaction	Profit
Purchase at $30 and sale at $90 × 100 shares	$6,000
Purchase at $50 and sale at $70 × 100 shares	+2,000
	$8,000

For purposes of Section 16(b), it does not matter that Director "D" actually sustained an economic loss of $2,000 during the period:

Total of sale prices	$24,000
Total of purchase prices	– 26,000
Actual loss	($2,000)

As with Section 16(a), the director or officer is considered the beneficial owner of stock held by certain family members for short-swing profit purposes. For example:

Officer "E" purchased Company stock in September. His spouse, Mrs. "E," sold some shares of Company stock in December. Despite the fact that Mrs. "E's" accounts were separate from her husband's, her sale would be matched with his purchase; consequently, Officer "E" is liable for any short-swing profit on the matched transactions.

The recovery for short-swing profits belongs to the issuer and cannot be waived by it. If an issuer fails or refuses to collect or sue a reporting person for short-swing profits within 60 days of demand by a stockholder, the stockholder may bring suit in the issuer's name for recovery. Courts have often awarded attorney's fees to the plaintiff's counsel in these actions based upon the amount recovered. As a result, there are "strike lawyers" who carefully review SEC reports for violation of Section 16(b), with the intention of bringing lawsuits against the reporting person and/or the directors of the issuer if the issuer's directors fail to do so after demand. These lawyers receive a percentage of the recovery (up to 30%) as a reward for bringing the action and obtaining a recovery for the issuer. Any unpaid

Section 16(b) liability must be shown as an indebtedness of the reporting person to the issuer in the issuer's proxy statement.

Section 16(b) Exemptions

Not every transaction in issuer securities is considered a "purchase" or "sale" for purposes of the short-swing trading prohibition. There are several important exclusions and exemptions from Section 16(b) for certain kinds of stock transactions which are described next. The exclusions are set forth in Rule 16b-3, which is designed to facilitate the receipt of stock-based compensation by reporting persons without incurring liability under Section 16(b).[28]

Under Rule 16b-3, a transaction between the issuer and a reporting person that involves issuer equity securities will be exempt from the short-swing profit rules of Section 16(b) if it satisfies the appropriate conditions set forth in one of four categories: tax-conditioned plans; discretionary transactions; grants, awards and other acquisitions from the issuer; and dispositions to the issuer.[29] The exemptions for tax-conditioned plans and discretionary transactions (with respect to profit sharing and 401(k) plans) generally are not available for discretionary incentive stock plan transactions[30] and are not described herein. The third and fourth exemptions are the ones that provide the relevant exemptions for incentive stock plan transactions and therefore are discussed below in greater detail.

Grants, Awards, and Other Acquisitions from the Issuer   Any grant or award of issuer stock from the issuer to a reporting person is an exempt transaction under Section 16(b) if it satisfies any one of the three conditions described below. Grant and award transactions are those that provide issuer stock to participants on a basis that does not require either the contribution of assets or the exercise of investment discretion by participants. Examples of grant and award transactions that are not participant-directed include grants of stock options, stock appreciation rights, restricted stock, or performance share awards. A participant-directed transaction, on the other hand, requires the participant to exercise investment discretion as to either the timing of the transaction or the assets into which the investment is made. Examples of participant-directed transactions include the exercise of an option or stock appreciation right or the sale of shares acquired thereunder. Participant-directed dispositions to the issuer are potentially eligible for the "Dispositions" exemption described below.

Any transaction involving a grant, award, or other acquisition by a reporting person from the issuer (other than a transaction not meeting the definition of a discretionary transaction) will be exempt from Section 16(b) if any one or more of the following conditions are met:

- The issuer's board of directors or a committee of the board comprised of two or more "Non-Employee Directors"[31] approves the acquisition in advance;[32]

- The issuer's shareholders approve the acquisition in advance or ratify it not later than the date of the next annual meeting of shareholders;[33] *or*

- The insider holds the securities acquired for six months following the date of acquisition.[34]

Thus, exercises of stock options or stock appreciation rights will be exempt from Section 16(b) if approved by the issuer's board of directors, by a committee consisting of two or more Non-Employee Directors, or by the issuer's shareholders.

The SEC has made clear that this approval requirement relates to each specific transaction and is not satisfied by approval of a plan in its entirety, except for plans where the terms and conditions of each transaction are fixed in advance, such as a formula plan.[35] Where the terms of a subsequent transaction are provided at the time a transaction is initially approved, the subsequent transaction does not require further specific approval. For example, the acquisition of common stock that occurs upon the exercise of a stock option or stock appreciation rights is exempt as long as the exercise is pursuant to the terms provided for in the option as originally approved.[36] Similarly, if an option as originally approved specifically provides for the automatic grant of "reload" options, reload grants pursuant to those terms would not require subsequent approval. Conversely, if a reload option was not specifically contemplated at the time of approval of the initial option grant, the replacement grant would require subsequent approval.

Note that if an option, SAR, or stock award does not satisfy one of the approval requirements, it may in any event qualify for an exemption from Section 16(b) under the six-month holding period rule. This rule provides that the acquisition of a security will be exempt from Section 16b-3 if the security is held by the recipient for six months following the acquisition or, in the case of a derivative security, if the underlying security is held for six months after the acquisition of the derivative security.[37] In the case of a stock option, this means that the grant will be an exempt *purchase* of issuer securities if the option (or the underlying issuer stock) is held for at least six months from the date of grant. For example, if an option is granted on May 1, 2002, and the option is exercised on or after November 1, 2002, the exercise of that option will be an exempt purchase that cannot be matched up with any other nonexempt sales. However, if the option is exercised earlier and the underlying stock is sold before November 1 (in this example), the option grant itself can be treated as a nonexempt purchase of issuer stock matchable against the subsequent sale.

Dispositions to the Issuer   In addition to the potential Section 16(b) impact of the grant or exercise of an option, the disposition of shares in connection with an option also must be considered. The issue here is whether or not a disposition of issuer securities in connection with or following the exercise of a stock option will be an exempt or nonexempt sale.

In this regard, all dispositions of issuer securities by a reporting person pursuant to open market transactions will be treated as *nonexempt* sales that can potentially be matched against any nonexempt purchases occurring within six months of the sale. As a result, sales of issuer securities into the open market pursuant to a "cashless exercise" arrangement with a broker or other third party will result in nonexempt sales of issuer securities by a reporting person.

However, dispositions of issuer securities *back to the issuer* will be exempt if approved in advance by the issuer's board of directors, by a committee of the board comprised of two or more Non-Employee Directors, or by the shareholders.[38] Note that these are the same approval requirements described above in connection with grants, awards, and other acquisitions. Unlike the exemptions for "acquisitions," however, the six-month holding period rule does *not* apply to "dispositions" of issuer securities.

Thus, as long as the approval requirements are met, the Section 16(b) Rules will exempt a disposition of issuer stock by a reporting person *back to the issuer* pursuant to (1) the right to have securities withheld, or to deliver securities already owned, either in payment of the exercise price of an option or to satisfy the tax withholding consequences of an option exercise, (2) the expiration, cancellation, or surrender to the issuer of a stock option or stock appreciation right (SAR) in connection with the grant of a replacement or reload option,[39] or (3) the election to receive, and the receipt of, cash in complete or partial settlement of an SAR.[40] Additionally, the Section 16 Rules will give the issuer the flexibility to redeem its equity securities from reporting persons in connection with nonexempt replacement grants and in discrete compensatory situations such as individual buy-backs.

For issuers that intend to provide reporting persons with the ability to engage in share-for-share exercises or the delivery of issuer securities to satisfy tax withholding, it is recommended that these features be included in the original option grant so as to avoid the need for additional approval of the disposition of securities at the time of option exercise. Also, it is important to note that the sale of shares to pay the exercise price of an option under a cashless exercise program will be exempt from Section 16(b) *only* if the issuer is the purchaser, and not if the shares are sold on the open market by a broker or other third party.

Merger No-Action Letter   In 1999, the SEC issued a no-action letter setting forth how shares acquired by officers and directors of a public company within six months of that company being acquired for cash or stock in a merger can be protected from the short-swing profit recapture under Section 16(b) pursuant to the exemption in Rule 16b-3.[41] This no-action letter has become the standard under which these transactions are being conducted. It relies on the exemption for dispositions to the issuer in Rule 16b-3(e). Language should be put in merger documents to protect the directors and executives of public target companies referencing the procedures in this no-action letter.

Drafting and Other Considerations   Under the Section 16 Rules, it is no longer necessary that an employee benefit plan be in writing or that the plan receive shareholder approval in order to qualify for the Section 16b-3 exemptions. The shareholder approval element of the Section 16 Rules relates to each individual option grant rather than the plan in its entirety and therefore is not needed. As a result, most issuers will rely on the board of directors' or the committee's approval to satisfy an exemption under Section 16(b). However, most issuers have continued to seek shareholder approval of their incentive stock plans to satisfy other requirements, such as requirements of the stock exchanges, NASDAQ, state corporate law, Internal Revenue Code Section 162(m) (which requires shareholder approval of an option plan to qualify for one of the exemptions to the $1 million deduction limitation for compensation paid by public corporations), or Code Section 422 (which requires shareholder approval of an incentive stock option plan).

Under Rule 16b-3 before the 1996 amendments, amending a stock option plan required shareholder approval if the amendment would (1) materially increase the benefits accruing to participants under the plan, (2) materially increase the number of securities that could be issued under the plan, or (3) materially modify the requirements for participation in the plan. Following the 1996 amendments, shareholder approval of plan amendments is not required, except for increases in shares to satisfy stock exchange rules, etc., as described above.

Employers with incentive stock plans adopted before the 1996 amendments to the Section 16 Rules may wish to amend their plans to remove some of the restrictions imposed by Rule 16b-3 before the 1996 amendments. For example, provisions requiring disinterested administration, restrictions on transferability of options, or shareholder approval of plan amendments (unless required by other rules or regulations) may be removed. Likewise, to the extent that the plan mandates a six-month holding period, this restriction may be removed, unless the issuer otherwise desires to retain the holding period in order to ensure the availability of an exemption under the Section 16 Rules without the need for shareholder, director, or committee approval.

Transaction Review and Assistance   Because of the complexities involved in reporting under Section 16(a) and the danger of short-swing recapture under Section 16(b), most companies have developed programs to assist directors and officers in complying with these federal statutes. The compliance program usually consists of the following:

- All directors and designated officers must contact the issuer's designated compliance officer before they, a family member, or a trust or other entity which they control engage in any transactions in company stock, including gifts, purchases, sales, etc.

- The designated compliance officer usually prepares the Section 16 reports and files them with the SEC.

- All directors and designated officers are requested to execute a power of attorney enabling the designated compliance officer to sign and file the necessary forms with the SEC.

- Brokers representing directors and designated officers are informed of the company's policies concerning insider trading and Section 16 reporting.

- See the model pre-clearance policy included in appendix B to this chapter.

Trading While in Possession of Inside Information

As a general rule, any person with material non-public information about the issuer is obligated under Rule 10b-5 under the 1934 Act to refrain from purchasing or selling common stock until such information has been released into the marketplace.[42] Although stock options or stock appreciation rights may be exercised at any time even if the holder has material non-public information about the issuer, such person is obligated under Rule 10b-5 to refrain from selling common stock acquired upon exercise of an option or stock appreciation right until the material non-public information has been released into the marketplace.

This concept generally prohibits cashless exercises of stock options (involving open market sales through a broker or other third party) while in possession of material non-public information, but it does not prohibit stock-for-stock exercises or share withholding to pay taxes where the issuer is the purchaser. These transactions are with the issuer, who is the ultimate insider and presumed to have full knowledge. If the issuer is holding back on "good news," these transactions will be at a bargain price to the issuer and will not create insider trading liability as long as the person exercising the option has full knowledge of the "good news." If the issuer is holding back on "bad news," the person exercising the option is receiving too high a price, but once again this does not create insider trading liability. At worst, it creates a claim of corporate waste by the shareholders if they become aware of the transaction. This claim can be defended against on the basis that it was in the best interest of the company to permit the transaction.

To be found liable for insider trading, the reporting person must have misused material, non-public information. Information is considered "material" for these purposes if there is a substantial likelihood that a reasonable investor would consider it important in arriving at a decision to buy, sell, or hold stock of the issuer. Examples of inside information that might be deemed material include:

- Actual or projected sales or earnings (including changes of previously announced estimates).
- Actual or projected significant capital expenditures.
- Actual or projected significant borrowings.
- Public or private sale of a significant amount of additional securities of the company, or major financings or refinancings.

- Non-business matters affecting the market for company securities (such as upcoming research, brokerage firm recommendations, or the intention of parties to buy or sell an abnormal amount of securities).

- A proposed merger, acquisition, joint venture, or disposition of stocks or assets, or a tender offer for another company's securities.

- Any action or event that could have a significant effect on annual sales or earnings.

- Any action or event that may result in a special or extraordinary charge against earnings or capital, or significant changes in asset values or lines of business.

- A significant change in capital investment plans.

- Major new products, discoveries, or services.

- A call of securities for redemption or a program to repurchase company shares.

- A change in control or significant management changes.

- Significant litigation and changes in pending litigation.

- Significant changes in operating or financial circumstances.

- Significant labor disputes or other pay-related issues.

- Significant actions by regulatory bodies.

- Prohibited information on other companies learned through special business relationships with them.

- Dividend increases or decreases.

- Rating agency upgrades or downgrades.

The foregoing list is for illustration only and is not exhaustive; other types of information may be material at particular times, depending upon all the circumstances.

The most dangerous time to engage in a purchase or sale of issuer stock is shortly in advance of the public release by the issuer of important financial information, such as quarterly or year-end results, or other important news. Many companies impose blackouts on their officers and directors beginning 15 days before the end of the quarter or fiscal year and ending 2 or 3 days after the releases of earnings. The safest time to engage in purchases or sales is the period—commonly referred to as a window period—shortly following the release and publication of such information. However, engaging in transactions during a window period presumes that the person is not aware of any other material information which has not been made public. Even after such information has been released, it is important to be sure that sufficient time has elapsed to enable the information to be disseminated to and considered by investors.

1933 Act Registration Requirements; Resales by Plan Participants

The 1933 Act makes it unlawful for any person to sell or to offer to sell any security unless an effective registration statement has been filed with respect to such security or the offer is pursuant to an available exemption from registration.[43] There are a number of exemptions from the registration rules listed below that may be available for stock issued pursuant to an employer sponsored incentive stock plan. Failure to comply with the registration requirements may give the purchaser of securities a rescission right.[44] In order to allow for marketability of shares acquired in connection with an incentive stock plan, it is important to make sure the shares have been properly registered or an exemption from registration is available.

Registration Requirements

Section 5 of the 1933 Act provides that it is unlawful for any person, directly or indirectly, to use any form of interstate transportation or communication or the mails to offer a security for sale unless a registration statement has been filed with respect to such security or to sell, carry, or deliver for sale any security unless a registration statement is in effect for such security.[45] Thus, in implementing an equity-based compensation arrangement, an employer must consider whether the arrangement involves the issuance of a security and, if so, whether the security to be issued under such plan should be registered pursuant to the provisions of the 1933 Act, or whether one or more exemptions from registration may be available.

Even if an exemption from registration is applicable, the employer should also consider whether participants in the plan are, without violation of federal securities laws, free to sell securities received under such a plan. The latter consideration, of course, relates to the value of the plan benefits to employees as an incentive compensation device.

Registration on Form S-8 If an issuer is subject to the reporting requirements of the 1934 Act—that is, the issuer is a "public company" (including, in this instance, a foreign private issuer)—registration of stock to be issued to officers, directors, and employees under any employee benefit plan of the employer can be accomplished very simply by filing Form S-8 with the SEC.[46] The Form S-8 consists of a prospectus and a registration statement. This registration statement incorporates by reference the employer's current and future 1934 Act reports, including certain information incorporated into such reports to satisfy certain Form S-8 updating requirements. The prospectus is not filed with the SEC. Thus the registration statement can remain "alive" for a number of years without any need to rewrite and redistribute the prospectus. Most changes to the information in the prospectus can be made by means of a prospectus supplement or appendix. Not only does registering the stock on Form S-8 satisfy the employer's requirements under Section 5 of the 1933 Act, but it also permits all plan participants, except "affiliates," to sell stock received under the registered plan freely and immediately.

• *Sales by Affiliates.* As a result of their control relationship with the employer, affiliates[47] may be deemed to be acting as the corporate issuer when they sell the issuer's stock. Thus, even though stock issued pursuant to an incentive stock plan may be registered on Form S-8, an affiliate may not freely sell such stock unless an exemption applies or unless the affiliate's sale itself is registered.[48] In most cases, resales by affiliates are made pursuant to the exemption from registration provided by SEC Rule 144.[49] If the shares being sold by the affiliate have been registered under the 1933 Act (on Form S-8, for example), the one-year holding period requirement of Rule 144 does not apply. However, the other conditions of Rule 144 continue to apply.

As an alternative to Rule 144, an affiliate's shares can be registered for resale, either by means of a separate registration statement or by means of a resale prospectus filed together with the plan's registration statement on Form S-8. A resale prospectus filed with Form S-8 may under certain circumstances be prepared in accordance with the requirements of Form S-3, even though the issuer is not otherwise eligible to use that abbreviated form. Most companies do not use this resale prospectus because of the negative impact it has on the trading market for the stock.

Finally, an affiliate may be able to sell stock received under a stock plan in a privately negotiated transaction. However, the various considerations that apply to such sales under the securities laws are complex, and careful consultation with counsel is recommended before any such transaction is undertaken.

Issuance of Stock Without Registration   In certain instances, stock can be issued pursuant to an incentive stock plan without registration of the stock or the plan. However, under most of the available exemptions from registration, the participant will receive stock that is not freely tradable. Some of the exemptions from registration do not require the employer to provide specified information; nevertheless, sales under any of these exemptions will remain subject to the antifraud provisions of the 1933 and 1934 Acts. Several of the commonly used exemptions from registration for incentive stock plans are briefly described below.

- *Non-public Offering.* Section 4(2) of the 1933 Act provides an exemption for a "private placement" of securities, which is an offering of stock to a limited number of investors who have access to the same information normally provided in a public offering *and* who are sophisticated enough both to assess and bear the risks of investing in the issuer's securities. No specific information is required to be disclosed to purchasers, but their access to information about the employer is generally considered to be an element of the exemption. This exemption may be available for the issuance of stock to the employer's top executives, but it is less likely to be available for a broad-based stock compensation program.

- *Regulation D Offerings.* Regulation D contains three alternative exemptions from registration under Section 3(b) of the 1933 Act, set forth as Rules 504, 505, and 506.[50] All of the Regulation D exemptions require the filing of a relatively simple form with the SEC. Rule 505 provides an exemption to offerings of up to $5 million in any 12-month period to as many as 35 nonaccredited investors. Note that the $5 million limit during any such 12-month period is reduced by the amount of any other offerings exempt under Section 3(b) of the 1933 Act.

  Rule 504 exempts an offering of up to $500,000 of stock in any 12-month period, again reduced by the amount of any other offerings exempt under Section 3(b) of the 1933 Act. The Rule 504 exemption does *not* require that offerees be sophisticated or knowledgeable about the issuer or that specific information about the issuer be disclosed. However, the dollar limitation of Rule 504 can be a significant problem in the case of a stock option plan because the offering is deemed to be continuing for the entire period during which the options are exercisable.

  The final Regulation D exemption from registration is found in Rule 506. Rule 506 does not limit the size of the offering but instead limits the number of purchasers and requires that purchasers, either alone or with a financial advisor, be capable of evaluating the investment. Under both Rule 505 and Rule 506, specific disclosures are required unless the offering is made exclusively to "accredited investors" (which term includes executive officers, directors, and as well as individuals meeting specified income or net worth tests).

- *Rule 701.* Rule 701 (as described in greater detail below) can also exempt sales under compensatory benefit plans if certain conditions are met.[51] This exemption is non-exclusive and can be used in conjunction with Regulation D and other exemptions. In the authors' view, an exemption under Rule 701 is preferable to Regulation D, and in many cases an exemption under Regulation D is a fallback to qualifying under Rule 701.

Rule 701

For certain compensatory issuances of stock or stock options to employees and other service providers, Rule 701 provides an exemption from the registration requirements of the 1933 Act for offers and sales of securities. The primary features of Rule 701 are as follows:

- The purpose of the issuance must be compensation. If the purpose of the plan is to circumvent registration requirements and is not for compensation purposes, then the exemption is not available.

- Rule 701 is an exemption from federal securities laws and does not provide an exemption from applicable state securities laws. Many states, however, have adopted equivalent exemptions that either specifically provide for issuances made pursuant to Rule 701 or generally exempt issuances that are made for compensatory purposes.

- The issuer cannot be a reporting company under Section 13 or 15(d) of the 1934 Act nor an investment company required to be registered under the Investment Company Act of 1940.[52]

- The participants may be employees, directors, general partners, trustees (if the issuer is a business trust), officers, or consultants and advisors, and their family members who acquire such securities through gifts or domestic relations orders.[53] Further limitations on the participants are detailed below.

- Limitations are imposed on the sales price or amount of securities that can be issued pursuant to Rule 701. Basically, the limitation is that during any 12-month period the aggregate sales price or amount of securities sold in reliance on Rule 701 cannot exceed the greatest of (1) $1 million, (2) 15% of the total assets of the issuer, or (3) 15% of the outstanding amount of the class of securities being offered and sold in reliance on Rule 701. Further details are provided below.

- Although this is an issuer-only exemption, Rule 701 also provides special rules for resale after the company has gone public. Further resale details are provided below.

- No SEC notice is necessary for an issuance pursuant to Rule 701. Notice requirements, however, exist under some state securities regulations.

- The issuance must be made pursuant to a written compensation contract or written compensatory plan.[54]

- Disclosures must be provided. The issuer must deliver to investors a copy of the benefit plan or contract. If the aggregate sales price or amount of securities sold exceeds $5 million in a consecutive 12-month period then certain other disclosures must be made a reasonable period before the date of sale, as detailed below.

- Rule 701 transactions are not integrated with other exempt transactions.[55]

- Rule 701 is not exclusive, so that other exemptions may be claimed.

Participants   As noted above, the participants may be employees, directors, general partners, trustees (if the issuer is a business trust), officers, or consultants and advisors, and their family members who acquire such securities through gifts or domestic relations orders. In a recent amendment of Rule 701, the SEC has significantly restricted the definition of "consultants and advisors" who may participate in a Rule 701 issuance and has harmonized the Rule 701 interpretation of the phrase with the Form S-8 interpretation.[56] Consultants and advisors must be natural persons and provide bona fide services to the issuer, its parents, or their majority-owned subsidiaries.

In addition to the above basic requirements to be a consultant or advisor, securities promoters may not participate under the exemption because they do not qualify as consultants or advisors. This exclusion covers people whose services are inherently capital-raising or promotional, such as brokers, dealers, those who find investors, those who provide shareholder communications services, and those who arrange for mergers or take the company private. Business advisors whose activities are not inherently capital-raising or not promotional would be allowed to participate in an offering under Rule 701.

Independent agents, franchisees and salespersons that do not have an employment relationship with the issuer are also not within the scope of "consultant or advisor." A person in a *de facto* employment relationship with the issuer, however, such as a non-employee providing services that traditionally are performed by an employee, with compensation paid for those services being the primary source of the person's earned income, would qualify as an eligible person under the exemption. Other persons displaying significant characteristics of "employment," such as the professional advisor providing bookkeeping services, computer programming advice, or other valuable professional services may qualify as eligible consultants or advisors, depending upon the particular facts and circumstances.

The term "employee" specifically includes insurance agents who are exclusive agents of the issuer, its subsidiaries or parents, or derive more than 50% of their annual income from those entities.

Limitations on Issuances   During any 12-month period the aggregate sales price or amount of securities sold in reliance on Rule 701 cannot exceed the greatest of (1) $1 million, (2) 15% of the total assets of the issuer (or of the issuer's parent if the issuer is a wholly-owned subsidiary and the parent fully and unconditionally guarantees the obligations of the issuer), or (3) 15% of the outstanding amount of the class of securities being offered and sold in reliance on Rule 701. Both the total assets and outstanding amount of securities are measured at the issuer's most recent annual balance sheet date, if it is no older than its last fiscal year end.

The aggregate sales price means the sum of all cash, property, notes, cancellation of debt, or other consideration received or to be received by the issuer for the sale of the securities. Non-cash consideration must be valued by reference to bona fide sales of the consideration made within a reasonable time or, in the absence of such sales, on the fair value as determined by an accepted standard. The value of services exchanged for securities issued must be measured by reference to the value of the securities issued. Thus, compensatory arrangements for consultant and employee services must be valued, and they cannot be valued at "zero" or as a gift. Options must be valued based on the exercise price of the option, and if options are subsequently repriced, then a recalculation of the aggregate sales price under Rule 701 must be made. The aggregate sales price of options is determined upon the grant of the options, regardless of when the options become exercisable or are exercised. Deferred compensation and similar plans are measured as of the date an irrevocable election to defer compensation is made. The aggregate sale price of other securities not mentioned above is determined on the date of sale.

The total assets of the issuer for the 15%-of-total-assets test are determined by using the calculation of assets on the balance sheet of the issuer. While not specifically mandated by the SEC, in applying for an exemption under Rule 701, companies use the assets total from their balance sheets.

The amount of outstanding securities for the 15% of the outstanding class of securities test is calculated by including all currently exercisable or convertible options, warrants, rights, or other securities. This amount does not include options, warrants, or rights that are not presently exercisable, and it also does not include presently non-convertible securities.[57] "When these securities become exercisable or convertible, subsequent calculations may consider such securities." The amount of outstanding securities does not include securities issuable pursuant to Rule 701. That is, the amount of outstanding securities does not include exercisable options, warrants or rights issued pursuant to Rule 701 that have not yet been exercised.

In relation to the 15%-of-outstanding-class-of-securities test, for the purposes of determining the number of outstanding shares of a class, separate classes of common stock may be considered as a single class if the rights of such separate classes are nearly identical.[58]

Resale Limitations   Securities issued under Rule 701 are "restricted securities" as defined in Rule 144. Resales of securities issued pursuant to Rule 701 must be in compliance with the registration requirements of the 1933 Act or an exemption from those requirements. Ninety days after the issuer becomes subject to the reporting requirements of Section 13 or 15(d) of the 1934 Act, securities issued under Rule 701 may be resold by persons other than affiliates of the issuer, subject to certain limitations, and by affiliates subject to further limitations.[59]

Disclosures   If the aggregate sales price or amount of securities sold exceeds $5 million in a consecutive 12-month period, then certain other disclosures must be made a reasonable period before the date of sale, which are in addition to the disclosure of the written benefit plan or contract. These additional disclosures include (1) if the plan is subject to ERISA, a copy of the summary plan description required by ERISA, or, if the plan is not subject to ERISA, a summary of the material terms of the plan; (2) information about the risks associated with investment in the securities sold pursuant to the compensatory benefit plan or compensation contract; and (3) financial statements as of a date no more than 180 days before the sale of securities in reliance on Rule 701. If the issuer relies on its parent's total assets to determine the amount of securities that may be sold, the parent's financial statements, which must meet certain standards if the parent is a reporting company under Section 13 or 15(d) of the 1934 Act, must be delivered. If the sale involves a stock option or other derivative security, the issuer must deliver disclosures a reasonable period of time before the date of exercise or conversion.

Sales Under Rule 144

U.S. securities laws are based on the premise that every person who wants to sell a security must establish an exemption from applicable federal and state securities law registration requirements or must comply with such registration requirements. When a normal investor wishes to sell IBM or General Motors securities he or she can rely on the exemption in Section 4(1) of the 1933 Act, but what if the selling stockholder is an affiliate of the issuer or has acquired the securities from the issuer or an affiliate of the issuer in a transaction not registered under the 1933 Act? To answer this question, one must understand Rule 144 promulgated under the 1933 Act. It covers sales of unregistered securities ("restricted stock") by nonaffiliates and sales of all securities by affiliates of the issuer.

Under the 1933 Act, an "affiliate" of the issuer (which includes all directors and certain executive officers) may not sell issuer securities unless the sale is covered by a registration statement or falls within an exemption from the registration requirements of the 1933 Act. The exemption most frequently used by directors and officers is SEC Rule 144.[60] Rule 144 serves as a safe harbor, allowing directors and officers to sell securities without complying with the SEC's registration requirements, provided that certain specific conditions are met.

For purposes of Rule 144, "restricted stock" is stock acquired from the issuer or an affiliate of the issuer in a transaction *not* involving a public offering. Unless shares of common stock issued upon exercise of stock options have been registered under the 1933 Act on a Form S-8, such stock will be considered restricted stock. No shares of restricted stock may be sold unless either the sale of such stock is registered with the SEC or the sale is exempt from the registration requirements, as in the case of a sale that falls within the provisions of Rule 144. Rule 144 is not the only exemption available. Private sales in particular may be eligible for other exemptions. Also, sales to large institutional buyers may be permitted under Rule 144A. However, Rule 144 provides essentially the only way to sell restricted shares in the public market.

In general, "affiliates" are persons in control of the issuer. The term "affiliate" includes *all* directors and certain key executive officers of the issuer. In 1997 the SEC proposed a bright-line test for the definition of affiliate that would indicate that a person would not be deemed to be an affiliate if the person is not (1) a 10% owner, (2) a Section 16 reporting person, or (3) a director of the issuer. While this proposal has not yet been enacted, it is indicative of what the SEC is thinking.[61]

Affiliates usually sell issuer securities under SEC Rule 144. Generally speaking, a Rule 144 transaction is an unsolicited broker's transaction on a stock exchange or NASDAQ. It requires that the issuer be current in its filings with the SEC, and it limits the amount to be sold in any three-month period. A Rule 144 transaction also requires the advance filing of SEC Form 144.

As indicated above, a designated executive officer or director of the issuer is considered an "affiliate" of the issuer. All issuer stock held by such affiliates is "control stock," which generally can be sold only (1) pursuant to a 1933 Act registration statement (as a "selling stockholder"), (2) pursuant to the private placement exemption, or (3) pursuant to Rule 144. If an affiliate received the stock from the issuer or another affiliate in a nonregistered transaction, it is also "restricted stock." Stock received through the exercise of a registered stock option is not restricted stock. Such shares are, however, considered "control" stock.

Control stock includes all issuer stock owned by an affiliate, regardless of how the stock was acquired. This includes stock purchased in the open market or received under a registered or unregistered employee stock option plan. Under Rule 144, stock held by any household relative of an affiliate, as well as any stock held by a corporation or trust in which an affiliate has a 10% ownership or beneficial interest, is attributable to the affiliate, and the holder of such stock must also comply with Rule 144 in connection with its sale. Stock received by others by gift or pledge from an affiliate or a household relative retains its restrictions and must be sold under Rule 144 by the donee or pledgee, except that all Rule 144 restrictions lapse in the hands of the donee or pledgee once two years have passed since the date of acquisition of the stock by the donor.

Rule 144 essentially does two things. First, it sets forth the circumstances under which restricted stock may be sold, and second, it sets forth the circumstances under which affiliates may sell *any* shares of common stock (restricted or unrestricted). Persons who own restricted stock but are not affiliates of the issuer and who have not been affiliates during the three months preceding a sale may freely sell restricted stock under Rule 144 so long as they have held the stock for at least two years before the sale. (The holding period is determined using the rules described below.) Unlike sales by affiliates and sales of restricted stock held for less than two years, these sales may be made *without* complying with the other requirements of Rule 144 described below, and the shares need not bear a restrictive legend.

Restricted stock held for less than two years, and any stock held by affiliates, may be sold under Rule 144 pursuant to the following requirements:

Availability of Current Public Information The issuer must have been subject to the reporting requirements of Section 13 of the 1934 Act for a period of at least 90 days and must have filed the SEC reports required of it for at least 12 months before the sale of securities (or for such shorter period as the issuer was required to file such reports).[62] Potential sellers are entitled to rely on a statement made on the facing sheet of the most recent Form 10-Q or Form 10-K to the effect that required reports have been filed, or upon a written statement from the issuer that all reporting requirements have been met, unless they know or have reason to know that the issuer has not complied with such requirements.

Holding Period for Restricted Securities Restricted stock must have been "beneficially owned" for at least one year.[63] (Affiliates selling unrestricted shares are not subject to this requirement.) To be beneficially owned, restricted stock that was purchased (rather than obtained, e.g., by gift) must have been fully paid for. Securities received in certain stock splits, stock dividends, recapitalizations, and conversions are deemed to have been acquired when the underlying securities were acquired, but securities received upon exercise of warrants are generally deemed to be acquired when the warrants were exercised and the exercise price paid. Securities being sold by a pledgee, donee, trust, or estate will in certain circumstances be deemed to have been held from the dates of acquisition by the pledgor, donor, settlor, or decedent, as the case may be. Each stockholder's shares must be analyzed separately in order to determine when they become eligible for sale under Rule 144.

Quantity Rule 144 also places an upper limit on the amount of securities that may be sold by a single stockholder in any three-month period.[64] The maximum number of shares that may be sold is limited to the greater of (1) 1% of the total number of shares outstanding as last reported or (2) the average weekly reported volume of trading in the issuer's common stock during the four calendar weeks preceding notice of the sale. Sales of this amount may be made in successive three-month periods. For an affiliate these limitations apply to total sales of *both* restricted securities and unrestricted securities. For non-affiliates, the volume limitations apply only to sales of restricted securities made during the first two years after such securities were acquired.

In determining amounts that may be sold by a stockholder (affiliate or non-affiliate), sales by the following are deemed made by the stockholder:[65] (1) relatives living in the same home, (2) trusts or estates in which the stockholder or such relatives collectively have 10% or more of the beneficial interest or act as trustee or executor, and (3) corporations and other organizations in which the stockholder or such relatives collectively own 10% or more of any class of equity securities. In addition, in determining amounts that may be sold by a pledgee, donee, estate, or trust, sales by the pledgor, donor, decedent, or settlor during the same three-month period must be included if the securities being sold were acquired by the pledgee, donee, estate, or trust within two years before the date of the intended sale. Persons agreeing to act in concert for the purpose of selling stock in the issuer must aggregate their sales in determining whether or not the quantity limitations are met. Stock sold pursuant to a registration statement or another exemption is not aggregated.

Manner of Sale Sales can be made only in "brokers' transactions," i.e., transactions in which the broker merely executes an order to sell without compensation exceeding normal brokers' commissions.[66] The seller may not solicit orders for the stock or make payments to any person other than the broker. The broker may not solicit or arrange for the solicitation of orders to buy in connection with the transaction. In addition, the broker must satisfy himself or herself after reasonable inquiry that the sale is being made pursuant to the provisions of Rule 144.

Notice Notices of intended sales must be filed with the SEC, except for transactions that do not exceed 500 shares or $10,000 in proceeds during any three-month period.[67] Three copies of a notice on Form 144 must be transmitted to the SEC concurrently with the placing of an order with a broker to execute a sale under the Rule.

Conclusion

As reflected by the above discussion, the federal securities laws issues attributable to an incentive stock plan are numerous and complex. Many times, compliance problems are attributable to a failure by the issuing corporation to either (1) adequately communicate the various securities law reporting and trading restrictions governing the purchase and sale of employer securities by its directors and officers or (2) provide sufficient support to enable such persons to comply with these rules. Companies offering stock options and other equity compensation, particularly public companies, are well advised to provide directors and officers with a summary description of the relevant securities laws and to establish a program for assisting directors and officers in complying with these laws. Along these lines, many companies establish a "code of business conduct" prohibiting insider trading by its employees and establishing "blackout" periods during which company stock may not be traded by officers, directors, and other reporting persons possessing material information about the company. As much assistance as can be provided to directors and officers to make sure that they understand and comply with the trading and reporting restrictions will go a long way towards avoiding noncompliance problems that might otherwise be easily avoided.

APPENDIX A

The Sarbanes-Oxley Act of 2002:
Its Impact on Executive Compensation Plans

On July 30, 2002, President Bush signed into law the Sarbanes-Oxley Act of 2002 (the "2002 Act"), which makes far-reaching changes in federal regulation applicable to corporate America and its executives, auditors and advisers. In addition to corporate governance and accounting reforms, the 2002 Act makes several changes that immediately impact many executive compensation arrangements (including stock benefit plans) and their administration. Directors, executives, Section 16 compliance officers and human resources administrators will want to consider closely the following provisions under the 2002 Act:

- Prohibition on personal loans to directors and executive officers
- Accelerated Section 16 filing deadlines
- Restrictions on stock transactions during retirement plan blackout periods
- Forfeiture of executive pay due to accounting restatements
- Freeze on extraordinary payments to directors and officers

Prohibition on Personal Loans to Directors and Executive Officers

Section 402 of the 2002 Act amends Section 13 of the 1934 Act to prohibit publicly held U.S. and non-U.S. companies from making or extending personal loans to directors and executive officers. Section 402 became effective on July 30, 2002, subject to grandfathering provisions and certain limited exceptions.

General Loan Prohibition Under Section 402   Section 402 states that "[i]t shall be unlawful for any issuer (as defined in Section 2 of the Sarbanes-Oxley Act of 2002), directly or indirectly, including through any subsidiary, to extend or maintain credit, to arrange for the extension of credit, or to renew an extension of credit, in the form of a personal loan to or for any director or executive officer (or equivalent thereof) of that issuer." Unless grandfathering treatment or an exception applies, effective July 30, 2002, issuers are prohibited from extending a personal loan in any manner to a director or executive officer.

Directors and Executive Officers　The term "director" is defined in Section 3(a)(7) of the 1934 Act as "any director of a corporation or any person performing similar functions with respect to any organization, whether incorporated or unincorporated." There are real questions about advisory, emeritus, or honorary directors, and the SEC interpretations under Section 16 of the 1934 Act may be relevant to this issue. The SEC has indicated in various releases that it believes that advisory and emeritus directors generally should be treated as directors for Section 16 purposes, but that honorary directors should not be so treated.

As noted above, the provisions of Section 402 of the 2002 Act are implemented as an amendment to the 1934 Act. Accordingly, unless and until the SEC adopts a different definition, the term "executive officer" under Section 402 should be interpreted in a manner consistent with existing SEC rules. 1934 Act Rule 3b-7 defines an "executive officer" (for purpose of, among others, proxy, 10-K and other 1934 Act disclosure) as the "president, any vice president of the registrant in charge of a principal business unit, division or function (such as sales, administration or finance), any other officer who performs a policy making function or any other person who performs similar policy making functions for the registrant." Executive officers of subsidiaries may be deemed executive officers of a publicly held company if they perform policy-making functions for the publicly held company.

Grandfather Protection　A limited grandfather provision provides some relief but raises many questions. Section 402 exempts loans maintained before July 30, 2002, "provided that there is no material modification to any term of any such extension of credit or any renewal of any such extension of credit" on or after July 30, 2002. A material modification of any term results in loss of grandfather treatment. Any action that might be considered to be a change to the terms of a loan should be carefully considered, given that Section 402 may be violated even if the change is minor and does not affect the overall financing arrangement.

Identifying Transactions Potentially Subject to Section 402　The ambiguity as to what is a "personal loan" and the breadth of what may be considered an arrangement for "extension of credit" suggest that publicly held companies should immediately identify all transactions potentially subject to Section 402. Common arrangements that may be viewed to involve an extension of credit are split-dollar life insurance and cashless stock option exercises. The following is a partial list of other transactions with directors and executives officers that may be treated as an extension of credit:

- Loans to purchase stock, a personal residence or other property
- Loans to meet margin calls upon a decline in the price of the company's stock
- Loans for relocation to a different geographic area
- Routine advances for business purposes (such as reimbursement accounts and travel expense allowances), particularly if repaid over long period of time
- Personal use of company credit cards
- Indemnification payments made under company by-laws or an employment agreement before a determination of entitlement to such payment
- Use of company funds to meet an executive's payroll tax obligations for non-qualified deferred compensation benefits
- Signing bonuses subject to repayment on early termination of employment

Cashless Stock Option Exercises Under Section 402   A common executive compensation practice that may be affected by Section 402 is the cashless exercise of stock options facilitated through a broker. In a cashless exercise, the option holder instructs a brokerage firm to sell a sufficient number of the shares being acquired by the option exercise to satisfy the option price and any applicable withholding taxes. The broker sells the shares and remits the exercise price and any taxes required to be withheld to the company with any balance remitted to the option holder. The company delivers the requisite number of shares to the broker and the balance to the option holder.

There are two common methods to execute a cashless exercise of a stock option. A broker may sell the shares on the date of receipt of exercise instructions and remit the exercise price and withholding taxes to the company a few days later, on the date of the settlement of the sale of those shares. Alternatively, a broker may sell the shares on the date of receipt of the instructions and remit the exercise price and withholding taxes immediately to the company, treating the amount as a margin loan to the option holder. Other variations on this practice also exist.

Any of these cashless exercise methods may be viewed as resulting in an "extension of credit" under Section 402. A broker-assisted direct sale involves the company making stock or cash available to the option holder for the exercise, albeit only for a very short period of time. While a margin loan from a broker does not involve the use of the company funds, it may also be subject to Section 402 to the extent that the company is viewed as having "arranged" this financing by establishing the cashless exercise program with the brokerage firm. None of these methods would seem to be the type of loan targeted by the Congress under the 2002 Act. It is considered likely that the SEC will issue guidance to clarify the impact of Section 402 on cashless exercise programs, but not in the foreseeable future.

Accelerated Section 16 Filing Deadlines

Section 403 of the 2002 Act amended Section 16(a) of the 1934 Act to require Section 16 reporting persons (directors, 10% or more stockholders, and certain executive officers) to report changes in beneficial ownership of issuer securities within two business days. The two-day filing requirement became effective August 29, 2002, under amended Section 16 rules adopted by the SEC on August 27, 2002 (SEC Release No. 34-46421).

The 2002 Act also requires the SEC to adopt rules requiring that Section 16(a) reports be filed electronically (rather than in paper form) no later than July 30, 2003. The SEC has indicated that they intend to promulgate such rules much sooner than July 2003. To file electronically, SEC rules require each Section 16 reporting person to apply for and obtain his or her own access codes to the SEC's Electronic Data Gathering, Analysis and Retrieval System (EDGAR).

Foreign Private Issuers

Currently, foreign private issuers with securities registered under the Exchange Act are not subject to any aspect of Section 16. The SEC has indicated that it does not intend to change the exemption for foreign private issuers.

SEC Rulemaking

Highlights of the revised Section 16 reporting rules are follows:

- All transactions that occurred before August 29, 2002, remain reportable under prior Section 16 reporting rules. This means, for example, that a stock option exercise on August 28 would still be reportable on a Form 4 by September 10, and that a "discretionary transaction" (such as a transfer in or out of a company stock fund) under a 401(k) plan on

August 28 can be deferred until 45 days after the end of the issuer's fiscal year and reported on a Form 5.

- All transactions occurring on or after August 29, 2002, must be reported on a Form 4 received by the SEC no later than 5:30 p.m. (Eastern Time) on the second business day following the transaction date except as set forth in Sections 4, 5 and 6 below. These include:
  — Option grants and exercises
  — Stock awards, performance share awards, and SARs
  — Option repricings, cancellations, regrants, and amendments
  — Dispositions to the issuer, including stock swaps and share withholding to pay taxes
  — Open market purchases and sales

- All of the reporting deferrals for transactions between the issuer and Section 16 reporting persons set forth in Rule 16b-3 will be subject to two-business day reporting on Form 4 except for the following:
  — Routine purchases under the payroll deduction provisions of a 401(k) plan (including an excess benefit plan), employee stock purchase plan, or employee stock ownership plan (ESOP), which transactions remain exempt from reporting (but must be included in the shares beneficially owned column).
  — "Discretionary transactions" under 401(k) and other employee benefit plans and certain transactions made pursuant to so-called Rule 10b5-1 plans, which transactions must be reported on a Form 4 under a special "deemed execution" rule discussed below, which can allow up to five-business day reporting.

- All of the exemptions contained in the Section 16(a) rules remain in effect and may either be voluntarily reported on a Form 4 at any time up to the due date of the Form 5 or reported on a Form 5 within 45 days of the end of the issuer's fiscal year. These include:
  — Gifts
  — Expiration of options without consideration
  — Small acquisitions but not from the issuer or an employee benefit plan sponsored by the issuer
  — Stock splits and stock dividends
  — Pro-rata distributions

- — Transfers under domestic relations orders
- — Changes in form of beneficial ownership
- — Regular dividend reinvestment plan contributions
- The SEC has adopted special limited deferred reporting rules (up to five business days depending upon circumstances) for the following transactions:
  - — Transactions pursuant to a contract, instruction, or written plan for the purchase or sale of issuer equity securities that satisfies the affirmative defense conditions of Rule 10b5-1(c) where the Section 16 reporting person does not select the date(s) of execution (such as the first date of each month).
  - — Discretionary transactions where the Section 16 reporting person does not select the date(s) of execution.
  - — Deferred compensation plan investments in a company stock fund, but only if they fall within the scope of a Rule 10b5-1 plan.
  - — Transactions that occur over more than one day, but only if they fall within the scope of a Rule 10b5-1 plan.

  These transactions are subject to reporting on Form 4 within two business days of the "deemed execution" date of the transaction. The deemed execution date of the transaction will be the earlier of (1) the date on which the executing broker, dealer, or plan administrator notifies the Section 16 reporting person of the execution of the transaction, and (2) the third business day following the trade date. (The SEC noted in its Release adopting the new rules that a trade confirmation sent through the mail could take several days to arrive and the SEC would, therefore, usually expect brokers, dealers and plan administrators to provide the information needed for Section 16(a) reporting purposes to the Section 16 reporting person either electronically or by telephone.)
- The rules with respect to the timing of the filing of Form 3 (initial statement of beneficial ownership) have not changed. For a company that is already public, the Form 3 must be filed within 10 days of the person becoming a Section 16 reporting person. For companies going public, the Form 3 must be filed before the company goes public. The SEC noted that a transaction might be required to be filed on Form 4 before the due date of Form 3. In this situation, the SEC encouraged the filing of both the Form 3 and the Form 4 by the due date of the Form 4.
- Electronic filings made on EDGAR need not be presented in the standard box format and may omit the horizontal and vertical lines separat-

ing information items, so long as all required information is presented in the proper order. Specific information is required when a deemed execution date is applicable.

Recommendations

The following recommendations should be considered in order to comply with the revised Section 16 rules:

- Have a mandatory pre-clearance policy for all transactions as to which the timing is within the control of the Section 16 reporting person. Appendix B provides a suggested form of such pre-clearance policy.

- For transactions as to which timing is outside the control of the Section 16 reporting person, require brokerage firms conducting transactions for Section 16 reporting person to provide promptly upon trade execution, and certainly by the third business day, the information needed for Section 16(a) reporting purposes to the Section 16 reporting person either electronically or by telephone.

- Review and update the procedures for discretionary transactions under benefit plans to ensure that the Section 16 reporting person receives timely notification (no later than three business days) of execution of the transaction from the plan administrator.

- Educate all Section 16 reporting persons by a memorandum that they should read, sign and return.

- Discontinue cashless exercise programs for Section 16 reporting persons for the time being (because of the loan prohibition in Section 402 of Sarbanes-Oxley Act) unless (1) the third party provider (usually a brokerage firm) of the program provides an opinion of qualified counsel that the particular program does not violate Section 402 and a representation of the provider that the program fully complies with the description of the program as to which the opinion relates or (2) the Section 16 reporting person arranges the transaction without involvement of the issuer and any credit extension to the Section 16 reporting person is from the broker or other third party and not the issuer.

- Obtain power of attorney with multiple attorneys-in-fact from all Section 16 reporting persons.

- Adopt electronic filing as soon as possible and apply immediately for EDGAR access codes for all Section 16 reporting persons. Section 16 reporting persons can obtain a Form ID for obtaining EDGAR access codes from the SEC at *http://www.sec.gov/about/forms/formid.pdf.*

Forfeiture of Compensation and Stock Sale Profits by CEOs and CFOs Upon Restatements Due to Misconduct

Section 304 of the 2002 Act requires forfeiture of certain bonuses and profits realized by the CEO and CFO of a company that is required to prepare an accounting restatement due to the company's "material noncompliance, as a result of misconduct, with any financial reporting requirement under the securities laws." Specifically, the CEO and CFO must reimburse to the company any bonus or other incentive- or equity-based compensation received and any profit realized from the sale of the company's stock sold, during a specified recapture period. Reimbursement is required whether or not the CEO or CFO engaged in or knew of the misconduct. The "recapture period" is the 12-month period following "the first public issuance or filing with the SEC (whichever first occurs) of the financial document embodying such financial reporting requirement."

It is unclear how one determines when targeted compensation is "received" for purposes of Section 304. The application of Section 304 of the 2002 Act to common executive compensation arrangements will be difficult to apply in practice. For example, is equity-based compensation "received" upon the grant or exercise of a stock option, or both? Is restricted stock "received" upon grant or vesting? Are performance-based non-qualified deferred compensation benefits "received" in the year earned or in the year of actual receipt? Do constructive principles similar to those under the tax laws apply? These and other types of interpretative questions will require regulatory guidance or legislative clarification.

This provision applies to both U.S. and non-U.S. companies. The SEC may exercise its authority to exempt non-U.S. companies.

Freeze on Extraordinary Payments to Directors and Officers

Section 1103 of the 2002 Act allows the SEC, during an investigation of an issuer or its directors, officers, partners, controlling persons, or other employees, to seek a temporary order in federal court requiring the issuer to escrow "extraordinary payments" to such person for 45 to 90 days (or, if such person is charged with a violation of the securities laws, until conclusion of the proceedings). There is no definition of "extraordinary payments" other than to indicate that it includes compensation. "Extraordinary payments" might include bonuses, stock option exercises, payments under a non-qualified deferred compensation plan and severance pay.

This provision applies to both U.S. and non-U.S. companies. The SEC may exercise its authority to exempt non-U.S. companies.

APPENDIX B
Section 16 Mandatory Pre-clearance Policy

(As Authorized by the Board of Directors of the Company)

To: Section 16 Insiders (all directors and executive officers)

The Sarbanes-Oxley Act of 2002 amended Section 16(a) of the Securities Exchange Act of 1934 to accelerate the reporting by Section 16 Insiders of all transactions involving the Company's stock. Effective August 29, 2002, Section 16 Insiders will be required to report changes in beneficial ownership involving the Company's stock within two business days of the transaction. Failure to file on a timely basis will result in the person being named as a delinquent filer in the Company's proxy statement. Repeated failure to file on a timely basis can result in civil actions against the individual by the SEC which has the power to seek fines for delinquent filings and bring injunctive actions against delinquent filers. Under the Securities Enforcement Remedies and Penny Stock Reform Act of 1990, the SEC is also empowered to seek removal of an officer or director from office and to ban such persons from future service as an officer or director of a public company. The SEC has used these remedies in extreme situations.

The Board of Directors believes that the only way to assure timely compliance is to impose a mandatory pre-clearance policy for all transactions by Section 16 Insiders and members of their immediate family involving the Company's stock. Transactions covered by this policy include, without limitation, stock option grants and option exercises, stock awards and stock equivalent awards, purchases and sales publicly or privately, gifts, and transfers in or out of trusts or limited partnerships or any other estate planning devices.

Accordingly, all Section 16 Insiders and members of their immediate family may not engage in any transactions involving the Company's stock without first notifying the Vice President-Chief Financial Officer *and* the [Vice President-General Counsel and Secretary]. This notice must be given in writing to the designated persons at least three business days before the proposed transaction. Failure to comply with this Policy will result at a minimum in embarrassment to the Company and the Section 16 Insider. It also can expose the Section 16 Insider to the civil actions and penalties discussed above.

If you have any questions about the pre-clearance policy, please contact the [Vice President-General Counsel and Secretary.]

Notes

1. 1934 Act, § 16(a) and Rules 16a-1 to 16a-13.
2. 1934 Act, § 16(b) and Rules 16b-1 to 16b-8.
3. 1934 Act, §§ 12(a) and 12(g)(1).
4. The exemption in Rule 3a12-3(b) under the 1934 Act reads as follows:

    Securities registered by a foreign private issuer, as defined in Rule 3b-4, shall be exempt from sections 14(a), 14(b), 14(c), 14(f) and 16 of the Act.
5. 1934 Act, § 16(a), Rule 16a-1(f).
6. 1934 Act, § 3(a)(7).
7. The application of the Section 16 Rules to "principal shareholders" who are neither designated executive officers nor directors is beyond the scope of this chapter.
8. Rule 16a-1(f).
9. SEC Release No. 34-37260 (May 31, 1996).
10. Rule 16a-1(f).
11. Rule 16a-1(a)(2).
12. Rule 16a-1(a)(2)(ii)(A), Rule 16a-1(e).
13. Rule 16a-1(a)(2)(ii)(B), (E), and (F).
14. See Rule 16a-8.
15. 1934 Act, § 16(a), Rule 16a-3.
16. Rule 16a-3(a).
17. Rule 16a-3(f)(1)(ii).
18. Rule 16a-3(g)(5).
19. Rule 16a-3(h).
20. Rule 16a-4.
21. A "cashless exercise" is an arrangement under which a stock brokerage firm agrees to pay the issuer the funds required for the exercise of a stock option. The broker provides the funds either in the form of a loan to the option holder from a margin account in which the shares acquired are held as collateral or as an advance on the proceeds from the sale of some or all of the shares acquired on the exercise. Most brokers offer this service. See the discussion on cashless exercise in appendix A.
22. Rule 16a-2(b).
23. Item 405(a)(1), Regulation S-K.
24. Item 405(a)(2), Regulation S-K.
25. SEC Release No. 34-37260.
26. Item 405(b)(2), Regulation S-K.

27. SEC Release No. 33-8090 (April 12, 2002).

28. 1934 Act, Rule 16b-3.

29. The Section 16 Rules exempt only transactions between a reporting person and the issuer and not between the issuer and persons who are subject to § 16 solely because they beneficially own greater than 10% of the issuer's equity securities.

30. This assumes the option plan is not an employee stock purchase plan that satisfies the relevant provisions of § 423 of the Internal Revenue Code. Under the tax-conditioned plan exemption, certain transactions in issuer securities in connection with an employee stock purchase plan governed by Code § 423 are exempt without further condition from § 16(b).

31. Under Rule 16b-3(b)(3), a "Non-Employee Director" is defined as a director who (1) is not currently an officer or otherwise employed by the issuer, or a parent or subsidiary of the issuer; (2) does not receive compensation directly or indirectly from the issuer, its parent, or subsidiary for services rendered as a consultant or in any capacity other than as a director, except for an amount for which disclosure would not be required pursuant to Item 404(a) of Regulation S-K (i.e., "Certain Relationships and Related Transactions—Transactions with Management and Others"); (3) does not possess an interest in any other transaction for which disclosure would be required pursuant to Item 404(a) of Regulation S-K; and (4) is not engaged in a business relationship for which disclosure would be required pursuant to Item 404(b) of Regulation S-K (i.e., "Certain Relationships and Related Transactions—Certain Business Relationships").

32. 1934 Act, Rule 16b-3(d)(1).

33. 1934 Act, Rule 16b-3(d)(2).

34. 1934 Act, Rule 16b-3(d)(3).

35. SEC Release No. 34-37260, Part II, D.

36. The disposition of the option that occurs upon exercise would be exempt pursuant to the rule relating to dispositions described below. In the same manner, if the terms of an award of stock options, as approved, provide for a stock-for-stock exercise (a "stock swap"), the disposition of company stock in connection with the subsequent stock swap would be exempt without further condition if effected pursuant to those terms. Conversely, if a stock swap was not approved at the time of the initial grant, it would require subsequent approval.

37. Rule 16b-3(d)(3), Note (3).

38. SEC Release No. 34-37260, Part II, E.

39. A "reload option" generally means an option that is granted in replacement of shares purchased upon the exercise of a prior granted option. Reload option programs generally work in tandem with a stock-for-stock exercise feature. If the optionee exercises his or her option by delivering previously

owned issuer shares, the issuer may grant a new option replacing the number of shares delivered to exercise the prior option.

40. SEC Release No. 34-37260, Part II, E.

41. See *Skadden, Arps, Slate, Meagher & Flom,* SEC No–Action Letter (April 28, 1999).

42. Also, the Insider Trading and Securities Fraud Enforcement Act provides civil penalties for insider trading in the amount of the greater of $1 million or three times the profit gained or loss avoided. It also prescribes criminal penalties of a maximum 10-year jail term and a maximum fine of $1 million for individuals.

43. 1933 Act, § 5.

44. 1933 Act, § 12.

45. 1933 Act, § 5(a)(1).

46. SEC Release No. 33-6188, Part VI, A.

47. An "affiliate" is defined as any person in control or sharing control of the issuer. All directors, the CEO, CFO, and general counsel are presumed to be affiliates. Other vice presidents are presumed *not* to be affiliates. This is a question of fact to be determined by each company.

48. SEC Release No. 33-6188, Part VI, A.

49. For a more detailed discussion of Rule 144, see "1933 Act Registration Requirements; Resales by Plan Participants—Sales Under Rule 144" below.

50. 1933 Act, Rules 504-506.

51. 1933 Act, Rule 701.

52. A privately held subsidiary of publicly held parent may rely on Rule 701, and may issue securities to its publicly held parent or other majority-owned subsidiaries of its parent. *American Bar Association,* SEC No-Action Letter [1999–2000 Transfer Binder] Fed. Sec. L. Rep. (CCH) ¶ 77,604 at 76,132 (Aug. 3, 1999).

53. Former employees, directors, general partners, trustees, officers, or consultants and advisors can participate only if they were employed by or provided services to the issuer at the time the securities were offered.

54. A compensatory benefit plan is defined as any purchase, savings, option, bonus, stock appreciation, profit sharing, thrift, incentive, deferred compensation, pension or similar plan.

55. A general solicitation in connection with a Rule 701 transaction, however, may cause an integration problem with respect to exemptions that do not permit general solicitation.

56. SEC Release No. 33-7646 (April 7, 1999).

57. *American Bar Association Subcommittee on Employee Benefits and Executive Compensation,* SEC No-Action Letter, LivEDGAR (September 6, 1988).

58. *Osler Health, Inc.,* SEC No-Action Letter (February 11, 1998).

59. See Rule 701(g).

60. 1933 Act, Rule 144.

61. SEC Release No. 33-7391 (February 20, 1997).

62. 1933 Act, Rule 144(c)(1).

63. 1933 Act, Rule 144(d)(1).

64. 1933 Act, Rule 144(e).

65. 1933 Act, Rule 144(a)(2).

66. 1933 Act, Rule 144(f).

67. 1933 Act, Rule 144(h).

3

State Securities Law Considerations for Incentive Stock Plans

Matthew Topham

HE TERM "BLUE SKY LAWS" refers to state statutes that prescribe the methods by which stock and other securities may be sold or offered for sale within the state. They are known as "blue sky" laws because many of the business deals that these laws were intended to address were so questionable they had no more substance to them than "air" or "blue sky."[1] As with the federal securities laws, these statutes generally prohibit companies and shareholders from selling (or offering to sell) stocks and securities unless the sale is registered with the state's securities commission or fits into one of the exemptions from registration provided by the state's blue sky laws. In most states, these exemptions parallel or complement many of the federal exemptions.[2] However, this chapter does not discuss exemptions from federal securities laws, which must also be considered before offering or selling securities.

In many cases, in order to qualify for an exemption under state blue sky laws, the issuer must take certain steps before issuing the security. In the case of securities granted or sold pursuant to employee stock option, stock purchase, or other benefit plans, these steps may include filing the relevant plan with the state securities administrator or including specific provisions in the plan. Failure to comply with these steps could render an exemption unavailable and leave the issuer with no alternative but to register the security before it is either offered or sold. Therefore, it is critical for issuers to plan ahead and evaluate possible exemptions from registration, preferably at the time the plan is being drafted and certainly before any securities are issued. To demonstrate how this process might work, this chapter uses a fictitious company, Sample Corporation, to show how blue sky laws apply in both the states of Washington and California.

Identifying the Relevant Blue Sky Laws and Related Regulations

Determining the Relevant Jurisdiction

The first step in the process of seeking a valid exemption from registration for the grant of a stock option, the issuance of stock upon the exercise of the option, or the sale of stock pursuant to an employee stock purchase plan is identifying which blue sky laws apply. Most states require registration of securities that are offered for sale or sold in their jurisdictions. In addition, some blue sky laws treat an offer to sell as occurring in both the place from which the offer originates as well as the place where the employee receives the offer. If the issuer (the company that is issuing the securities) and employee are located in the same state, then the issuer only needs to be concerned with the blue sky laws of that one state. If, however, the issuer is located in one jurisdiction and the employee is located in another, then the issuer may be required to comply with the blue sky laws in both jurisdictions.

As a hypothetical example, take Sample Corporation, a Washington corporation that has its headquarters in Seattle. Sample adopted an equity incentive plan that allows for the grant of incentive stock options, nonqualified stock options, and restricted stock grants to employees, consultants, and directors. The plan is administered by a committee of Sample's board of directors, which includes Sample's president, and all options are granted out of Sample's headquarters. Sample's president would like to hire a software engineer who lives in Palo Alto, California. Sample's president calls the California engineer at home and offers her a job with Sample with a compensation package consisting of a salary of $10,000 per month and a stock option to purchase 100,000 shares of Sample common stock at a price of $1 per share vesting over a four-year period. The California employee accepts this offer. Under these circumstances, Sample should expect to comply with the blue sky laws of both Washington and California with respect to the option grant for the reasons explained below.

The Washington blue sky law provides that it is unlawful for any person to offer or sell any security in Washington unless the security is registered by coordination or qualification, the security or transaction is exempted, or the security is a federal covered security.[3] An "offer to sell" under the Washington blue sky law includes every attempt or offer to dispose of, or solicitation of an offer to buy, a security or interest in a security for value.[4] In this example, an offer to sell occurred in Washington because the issuer is based in Washington, the offer originated in Washington, and the securities offered will be issued in Washington. There may be some debate as to whether the offer of the stock option in exchange for employment was "for value" for purposes of the Washington blue sky law. Although there is no Washington case law directly on point, there is authority in other jurisdictions that supports the position that when an employee bargains for compensation that includes stock or stock options, the employee has provided value for the securities.[5] Even if the stock options were not considered to have been offered for value, under Washington law, the offer of the stock option also included the offer to sell the underlying stock at $1 per share, which is probably sufficient to satisfy the requirement that the offer be for value for purposes of Washington blue sky law.[6]

California blue sky law treats an offer to sell as occurring in both the location where the offer originates and the location where the offeree receives the offer.[7] The definition of an "offer to sell" under California blue sky law is similar to the definition under Washington blue sky law.[8] In addition, under California blue sky law, every sale or offer of a right to purchase another security includes an offer and sale of the other security at the time of the offer of the right to purchase such other security.[9] This means that the offer of the stock option included the offer and sale of the underlying stock. And because this offer was directed to and received by the employee in California, Sample should comply with the California blue sky law in addition to the Washington blue sky law with respect to the stock option grant.

Reviewing the Relevant Blue Sky Laws

Once the issuer has determined the relevant jurisdictions, the next step is to review the blue sky laws for those jurisdictions. The blue sky laws for a particular state are typically contained in the state's securities act (the exact title of the securities act will vary from state to state). Each state's securities act contains a section dealing with exemptions. In some states, all of the exemptions are contained in a single section, while in other states there are separate sections for exempt securities and exempt transactions. It is not sufficient to review only the exemptions listed in the state securities act. In many cases, the legislature delegates the authority to the state securities administrator[10] to create additional exemptions beyond or to further qualify those listed in the securities act. Therefore, the issuer must also review the regulations, if any, promulgated under the securities act as well as any decisions, comments, no-action letters, or other interpretive guidance published by the state securities administrator.

Continuing with the example of Sample Corporation, Sample should start by reviewing the Washington State Securities Act, which is contained in Title 21 of the Revised Code of Washington. However, Sample should also review Title 460 of the Washington Administrative Code, which contains rules and regulations governing the offer and sale of securities that have been adopted by the Washington Department of Financial Institutions pursuant to statutory authority. Sample should also review the California Corporate Securities Law of 1968, which is contained in Sections 25000 through 25707 of the California Corporations Code. In addition, California has blue sky regulations contained in Title 10 of the California Code of Regulations.

Identifying Applicable Exemptions

A stock option and the stock underlying the option are separate securities. Therefore, in the case of stock option plans, the issuer must have an exemption for both the grant of the stock option and the issuance of the underlying stock. In many cases, the exemption that covers the grant of a stock option will also cover the issuance of stock upon the exercise of that option. However, an issuer should not presume this will be the case and should confirm the existence of a valid exemption for both the grant of the option and the issuance of the stock upon exercise ahead of time.[11] Several states have broad exemptions either for securities or transactions relating to employee benefit plans, which are referred to in this chapter generally as "blanket exemptions." These blanket exemptions, as well as other exemptions and the requirements to qualify for those exemptions are outlined below.

Stock Option Grants and Sales Under Stock Purchase Plans

Exempt Securities   A number of state blue sky laws specifically exempt from registration securities issued in connection with certain employee benefit plans, specifically including stock option plans.[12] Other blue sky laws exempt investment contracts or securities issued in connection with an employee's stock purchase, savings, pension, profit-sharing, or similar benefit plan, without specifically mentioning stock option plans.[13] The state securities administrators in many of the states with an exemption of the latter type (i.e., exemptions that do not specifically mention stock option plans), treat stock option plans as a "similar benefit plan" for purposes of the exemption. However, the issuer should confirm that this is the case with the state securities administrator before issuing stock options.[14]

Even if exemptions related to employee benefit plans apply, most attach additional requirements or conditions to that exemption. For example, some blue sky laws require that the issuer submit a plan to the state securities administrator within a set number of days before or after issuing securities under that plan or that the content of the plan include certain substantive provisions. What follows are just some of the most common requirements contained in blanket exemptions for exempt securities issued in connection with employee benefit plans.

1. *Securities must be issued in connection with a plan that meets the requirements for qualification under the Internal Revenue Code.* One common requirement contained in exemptions for securities issued in connection with benefit plans is that the applicable benefit plan must qualify under certain sections of the Internal Revenue Code. For example, Washington blue sky law provides an exemption for:

    > Any security issued in connection with an employee's stock purchase, savings, pension, profit-sharing, or similar benefit plan if: (a) The plan meets the requirements for qualification as a pension, profit sharing, or stock bonus plan under section 401 of the internal revenue code, as an incentive stock option plan under section 422 of the internal revenue code, as a nonqualified incentive stock option plan adopted with or as a supplement to an incentive stock option plan under section 422 of the internal revenue code, or as an employee stock purchase plan under section 423 of the internal revenue code; or (b) the director is notified in writing with a copy of the plan thirty days before offering the plan to employees in this state. In the event of late filing of notification the director may upon application, for good cause excuse such late filing if he or she finds it in the public interest to grant such relief.[15]

The referenced sections of the Internal Revenue Code contain requirements that must be satisfied in order for the plan to be qualified under those sections. For example, Section 422, which governs incentive stock options, includes requirements, among others, relating to exercise price, expiration, and transferability. In order for a plan to qualify under Section 422, it must include these provisions. Section 423 imposes requirements on employee stock purchase plans relating to eligibility, shareholder approval, purchase price and duration of the right to purchase. If an issuer intends to rely on an exemption such as Wash. Rev. Code Section 21.20.310(10)(a), it must satisfy the applicable requirements from the Internal Revenue Code. In the example above, Sample's equity incentive plan provides for the issuance of incentive stock options, nonqualified stock options and restricted stock grants. Although it is possible that the Washington state securities administrator might conclude that this plan would qualify as a "nonqualified incentive stock option plan adopted with or as a supplement to an incentive stock option plan under section 422 of the [I]nternal [R]evenue [C]ode" for purposes of Wash. Rev. Code Section 21.20.310(a), there is no interpretive guidance that supports this conclusion. Therefore, Sample should not rely on Wash. Rev. Code Section 21.20.310(a) and should instead submit the plan to the director of the Washington Department of Financial Institutions in accordance with Wash. Rev. Code Section 21.20.310(b) at least 30 days before offering securities under the plan to employees in Washington.[16]

2. *Securities must be issued in connection with a plan that has been submitted to the state securities law administrator.* Several jurisdictions require the issuer to submit any plan to the state securities law administrator before any securities are issued pursuant to such plan.[17] Other jurisdictions have exemptions, such as the Washington statute cited above, that require the issuer to submit the plan only if it does not qualify under certain sections of the Internal Revenue Code.[18] The state securities administrator typically has a certain number of days after receipt of the plan to disallow or deny the exemption.

3. *Securities must be issued pursuant to a plan that only applies to employees and directors.* Most exemptions for securities issued pursuant to benefit plans refer specifically to plans for employees. However, issuers frequently adopt stock option plans that provide for grants to directors and consultants as well as employees. The question is whether securities issued to directors and consultants under such plans qualify for the blanket exemption for employee benefit plans. Some state blue sky laws specifically provide that the exemption applies to directors and consultants as well as employees. In other states, the state securities administrator takes the position that the exemption only applies to consultants to the same extent Rule 701 of the Securities Act of 1933 (the "Securities Act") applies to consultants. Rule 701 is the federal

law exemption covering offers and sales of securities under a written compensatory benefit plan. Rule 701 specifically allows for grants to officers, directors, consultants and advisors, but it imposes certain requirements on consultants and advisors. For example, consultants and advisors must be natural persons (i.e., individual human beings as opposed to corporations, limited liability companies, trusts, etc.) and must provide bona fide services that are not in connection with the offer or sale of securities in a capital-raising transaction and do not directly or indirectly promote or maintain a market for the issuer's securities. The issuer should research any interpretive guidance provided by the state securities administrator on whether the blanket exemption for employee benefit plans applies to securities issued to consultants and directors under such plans and, if so, whether there are any restrictions with respect to such persons, such as those contained in Rule 701. If the issuer cannot find any written guidance on this issue, the issuer should contact the state securities administrator directly.

Exempt Transactions Unlike the state blue sky laws described above that treat securities granted in connection with certain employee benefit plans as exempt *securities,* some state blue sky laws treat the issuance of securities in connection with an employee benefit plan as an exempt *transaction.*[19] Several of these blue sky laws require that in order for the transaction to be exempt, either the plan must be qualified under certain provisions of the Internal Revenue Code or the sale of securities under the plan must meet the exemption contained in Rule 701. An example of this requirement is contained in the Ohio blue sky laws, which provide the following:

(5) The sale of any security pursuant to a pension plan, stock plan, profit-sharing plan, compensatory benefit plan or similar plan is exempt pursuant to division (V) of section 1707.03 of the Revised Code if:

   (a) The security is sold pursuant to a plan qualified under sections 401 to 425 of the Internal Revenue Code of 1986;

   (b) The sale of the security is exempt from the provisions of section 5 of the Securities Act of 1933 because it meets the exemption set forth in rule 701 of the Securities Act of 1933 and any commission, discount or other remuneration paid or given for the sale of the security in this state is paid or given only to dealers or salespersons licensed by the division; or

   (c) The security is effectively registered under sections 6 to 8 of the Securities Act of 1933 and is offered and sold in compliance with the provisions of section 5 of the Securities Act of 1933.[20]

In jurisdictions such as Ohio that have a blanket exemption based on Rule 701, the issuer must comply with the requirements of Rule 701 (unless the plan qualifies under an appropriate section of the Internal Revenue Code), discussed above, in order to qualify for the state blue sky law exemption.

For example, California blue sky law contains a transaction-based blanket exemption for an offer or sale of any security issued by a corporation pursuant to an option plan or agreement where the security at the time of issuance is exempt from registration under the Securities Act pursuant to Rule 701, provided that the terms of the option plan or agreement comply with Sections 260.140.41, 260.140.45, and 260.140.46 of Title 10 of the California Code of Regulations and the issuer files a notice of transaction with the state securities administrator no later than 30 days after the initial issuance of any security under that plan.[21] Section 260.140.41 requires the plan to contain specific provisions, including, among other things, restrictions on the minimum exercise price, the maximum exercise period and term of the plan or agreement, the vesting period, and the issuer's ability to repurchase securities issued under the plan. Section 260.140.45 provides that the total number of securities issuable upon exercise of all outstanding options, and the total number of securities called for under any bonus or similar plan or agreement shall not exceed 30% of the then-outstanding securities of the issuer unless a higher percentage is approved by at least two-thirds of the outstanding securities entitled to vote. Section 260.140.46 provides that the plan or agreement must provide that the security holders will receive financial statements at least annually. This California exemption highlights the importance of planning ahead to make sure that the necessary provisions are included in the option plan or agreement. A company such as Sample, which is based in Washington but may periodically grant options to employees in California, should consider adding a separate section to its option plan that contains the language required by Sections 260.140.41, .45 and .46 and only applies to options granted to California employees, directors, or consultants. Alternatively, Sample could leave these provisions out of the plan and handle grants to California employees, directors, and consultants through separate agreements that contain the required language.

Limited Offering Exemptions   In the event the issuer does not qualify for a blanket exemption of the type described above, another alternative is to issue the stock options under a private offering exemption. Because these exemptions typically limit the number of purchasers to somewhere between five and thirty-five persons, they are not a practical alternative for an issuer seeking an exemption for the issuance of stock options to a large number of employees. However, these exemptions are useful in situations where the issuer only plans to issue options to a few key executives or wants to grant options without a written plan or agreement that qualifies for the blanket exemption. These exemptions may require providing advance notice to the state securities administrator and generally have specific restrictions that may include limitations on the number of offerees, the number of purchasers, the aggregate value of securities sold, the number of shareholders after the offering, and written material that must be provided to offerees. Therefore, as is the case with the blanket exemptions, it is imperative that the issuer research the exemption before the offering.

One limited offering exemption that is important to mention in this context is Rule 506 of Regulation D, which was adopted pursuant to the Securities Act. Although Rule 506 is a federal law exemption, it is relevant in the context of a chapter on state blue sky laws because, pursuant to the National Securities Markets Improvement Act of 1996, offers and sales under Rule 506 are exempt from state blue sky laws with the exception of notice requirements in certain jurisdictions. Some of the advantages of Rule 506 over state law limited offering exemptions are (1) Rule 506 does not limit the dollar amount of securities that can be offered; (2) if the offering is only made to "accredited investors" as defined in Rule 501 of Regulation D, then the issuer is not required to provide the participants with any specific disclosure materials; and (3) the number of purchasers is limited to 35, but accredited investors do not count against this number (i.e., there can be an unlimited number of accredited investors). The definition of "accredited investor" includes, among others, (1) any corporation, partnership or limited liability company not formed for the specific purpose of acquiring the securities offered, with total assets in excess of $5,000,000; (2) any director, executive officer, or general partner of the issuer of the securities being offered or sold, or any director, executive officer, or general partner of a general partner of that issuer; (3) any natural person whose individual net worth, or joint net worth with that person's spouse, at the time of his purchase exceeds $1,000,000; and (4) any natural person who had an individual income in excess of $200,000 in each of the two most recent years or joint income with that person's spouse in excess of $300,000 in each of those years and has a reasonable expectation of reaching the same income level in the current year.

Including nonaccredited investors in a Rule 506 offering destroys much of the benefit the rule provides because issuers must provide nonaccredited investors who participate in a Rule 506 offering with extensive disclosure. In some cases, this disclosure is comparable to what would be required in a registration statement. Rule 506 offerings are frequently used for sales to institutional investors or high net worth individuals. However, because the definition of accredited investor includes executive officers and directors, Rule 506 can be an effective tool for issuing stock options or selling stock to officers and directors before a benefit plan has been established or outside of a plan that does not have enough shares available. Note that it is impermissible to elect a person to be an officer or director solely for the purpose of making that person an accredited investor.

Issuance of Stock Upon Exercise of Options

As discussed above, the stock issued upon exercise of a stock option is a security distinct from the option itself and must either be registered or exempt from registration. In general, if a stock option was granted pursuant to a valid exemption, then there will be a valid exemption for the issuance of stock upon the exercise of that stock option. This chapter presumes that, as is typically the case, employee stock purchase plans only involve the sale of common stock and do not involve the sale of any derivative or convertible security that can subsequently be exercised for or converted into common stock. Accordingly, this section does not address employee stock purchase plans.

Blanket Exemptions   Although some of the blanket exemptions referenced above specifically cover the issuance of stock upon the exercise of stock options that were granted pursuant to the exemption,[22] most of the blanket exemptions refer broadly to any securities issued in connection with particular types of benefit plans. The question is whether this language is broad enough to cover stock issued upon the exercise of a stock option that was granted pursuant to an employee benefit plan. In order to answer this question in a particular jurisdiction, the issuer should review any regulations or interpretive guidance created by the applicable state securities administrator. If these sources do not provide an answer, the issuer should contact the state securities administrator directly and confirm that the exemption covers both the grant of the stock option and the issuance of stock upon the exercise of the option. In all likelihood the state securities administrator will confirm such is the case, but it is best to clarify this in advance.

For example, as discussed above, Wash. Rev. Code Section 21.20.310(10) exempts "[a]ny security issued in connection with an employee's stock purchase, savings, pension, profit-sharing, or similar benefit plan." The Washington state securities administrator has issued interpretive guidance clarifying that this language covers both the stock option and the stock issued upon exercise of the option. Therefore, the issuance of stock upon the exercise of Sample's stock options granted pursuant to the plan should be exempt pursuant to Wash. Rev. Code Section 21.20.310(10).

California's blue sky law treats the grant of a stock option as a sale of the underlying stock at the time the option is granted.[23] Therefore, assuming the grant of the options was exempt pursuant to Cal. Corp. Code Section 25102(o), Sample does not need to find a separate exemption for the issuance of the stock upon exercise because the issuance of that stock does not constitute an offer or sale for purposes of California blue sky law.

Exemption for Transactions Pursuant to an Offer to Existing Security Holders   In the event that a blanket exemption is not available to cover the issuance of stock upon the exercise of a stock option, the issuer should research whether the applicable blue sky laws provide an exemption for transactions with existing security holders. This is a common exemption that is generally appropriate for the issuance of a security upon the exercise or conversion of an already outstanding security, such as a warrant or a convertible security (for example, preferred stock). In most states, this exemption requires that either no commission or other remuneration is paid or given directly or indirectly for soliciting any security holder in the state or the issuer first files a notice specifying the terms of the offer and the state securities administrator does not disallow the exemption within a set number of days, which ranges from thirty days to five business days, depending on the jurisdiction.[24]

Limited Offering Exemption   If a blanket exemption or an exemption for transactions with existing security holders is not available, the issuer should research whether a limited offering exemption is available. As discussed above, limited offering exemptions are subject to a variety of qualifications, which the issuer must carefully research before relying upon the exemption. If the issuer is unable to find a valid exemption, then the issuer must consider registration, which is discussed below.

Additional Exemptions Available for Public Companies   In addition to the exemptions above, which are available for both public and private companies, the blue sky laws of most states contain an exemption that may cover the issuance of stock of public companies upon the exercise of stock options. This exemption is for securities that are listed, or authorized for listing, on the New York Stock Exchange, the American Stock Exchange, the national market system of the Nasdaq stock market, or any successor to such entities. This exemption does not apply to the grant of the stock options themselves because the stock options are not listed on any exchange or the national market system. However, this exemption would apply to listed stock issued upon the exercise of stock options.

Registration

If an issuer is unable to find an applicable exemption for granting stock options, issuing stock upon the exercise of stock options, or selling stock pursuant to an employee stock purchase plan, then the issuer must register the securities that the issuer intends to offer (i.e., stock options or stock). Registration is typically done through coordination or qualification and involves the filing of a registration statement with the state securities administrator. The registration statement generally includes information about the issuer, its subsidiaries, officers and directors, capitalization, kind and amount of securities to be offered, anticipated proceeds from the offering and use of the proceeds, a copy of any prospectus or offering circular to be used in connection with the offering, an opinion of counsel as to the legality of the security being registered, and financial statements meeting specified requirements. In many states, registration by coordination is available only if the issuer has already filed a registration statement with respect to such securities under the Securities Act. Registration by coordination generally requires filing with the state securities administrator a copy of the documents filed pursuant to the Securities Act and an abbreviated registration statement as compared to what is required for registration by qualification.

Conclusion

While blue sky laws vary from state to state and can cause confusion about whether or not an issuer needs to register securities, in most cases companies can qualify for an exemption when it comes to the offering and sale of stock options or stock under employee benefit plans. Working with an experienced attorney who thoroughly understands and can carefully review blue sky laws in the state in which the issuer is based (as well as in those states in which the issuer's employees participating in the plan might reside), companies should be able to avoid the time and expense of registration.

Notes

1. Paul G. Mahoney, "The Origins of the Blue Sky Laws: A Test of Competing Hypotheses," University of Virginia Law School. December 2001. See, e.g., Hall v. Geiger-Jones Co., 242 U.S. 539, 550, 37 S. Ct. 217, 220, 61 L. Ed. 480, 489 (1917) ("The name that is given to the law indicates the evil at which it is aimed; that is, to use the language of a cited case, 'speculative schemes which have no more basis than so many feet of blue sky;' or, as stated by counsel in another case, 'to stop the sale of stock in fly-by-night concerns, visionary oil wells, distant gold mines, and other like fraudulent exploitations.'").

2. It is important to note that certain employee benefit plan securities, which are exempted from federal registration requirements by § 3(a)(2) of the Securities Act of 1933, are also preempted from state regulation (except for enforcement actions with respect to fraud), under the National Securities Improvements Act, Pub. L. No. 104-290, 110 Stat. 3416 (1996). Section 3(a)(2) exempts, among other things:

    > any interest or participation in a single trust fund, or in a collective trust fund maintained by a bank, or any security arising out of a contract issued by an insurance company, which interest, participation, or security is issued in connection with (A) a stock bonus, pension, or profit-sharing plan which meets the requirements for qualification under section 401 of the Internal Revenue Code of 1954, (B) an annuity plan which meets the requirements for the deduction of the employer's contributions under section 404(a)(2) of such Code, or (C) a governmental plan as defined in section 414(d) of such Code which has been established by an employer for the exclusive benefit of its employees or their beneficiaries for the purpose of distributing to such employees or their beneficiaries the corpus and income of the funds accumulated under such plan, if under such plan it is impossible, prior to the satisfaction of all liabilities with respect to such employees and their beneficiaries, for any part of the corpus or income to be used for, or diverted to, purposes other than the exclusive benefit of such employees or their beneficiaries, other than any plan described in clause (A), (B), or (C) of this paragraph (i) the contributions under which are held in a single trust fund or in a separate account maintained by an insurance company for a single employer and under which an amount in excess of the employer's contribution is allocated to the purchase of securities (other than interests or participations in the trust or separate account itself) issued by the employer or any company directly or indirectly controlling, controlled by, or under common control with the employer, (ii) which covers employees some or all of whom are employees within the meaning of section 401(c)(1) of such Code, or (iii) which is a plan funded by an annuity contract described in section 403(b) of such Code.

This chapter presumes that the securities in question do not fall within the exemption set forth in § 3(a)(2) and are not preempted from state regulation.

3.   Wash Rev. Code § 21.20.140.

4.   Wash. Rev. Code § 21.20.005(10).

5.   "When an individual 'commits herself to employment by a corporation in return for stock or the promise of stock,' she will be considered an investor worthy of protection under the federal securities laws. See *Yoder v. Orthomolecular Nutrition Inst., Inc.*, 751 F.2d 555, 560 (2d Cir. 1985). Where a plaintiff accepted employment with the issuer in return for an annual salary of $40,000 plus options to purchase up to 30,000 shares of the issuer's stock, the court held that plaintiff 'purchased' the options. *Yoder*, 751 F.2d at 560. Similarly, in *Rudinger v. Insurance Data Processing, Inc.*, the plaintiff bargained for and received an employment contract wherein he was to receive a certain number of stock options in addition to an annual salary of $100,000. 778 F. Supp. 1334, 1338-39 (E.D. Pa. 1991). The court declared '[a]n agreement exchanging a plaintiff's services for a defendant corporation's stock constitutes a 'sale' under the terms of the Securities Exchange Act.' Id.; see also, e.g., *Campbell v. National Media Corp.*, No. 94-4590, 1994 WL 612807 (E.D. Pa. Nov. 3, 1994) (finding that grant of options to purchase 50,000 shares in executive's employment agreement was a purchase of securities); *Collins v. Rukin*, 342 F. Supp. 1282, 1289 (D. Mass. 1972) (finding that stock options were a 'quid pro quo offered to induce plaintiff to enter into the employ of [the issuer]'). These cases indicate that where a potential employee acquires the right to options as part of his or her bargained-for compensation, courts will infer that the employees made an intentional decision to 'purchase' the options." *In re Cendant Corp. Securities Litigation*, 76 F. Supp. 2d 539, 544 (D.N.J. 1999).

The cases cited above were decided by federal courts and considered issues based on federal securities laws. Therefore, these decisions do not create binding authority in most states. But these cases do indicate that at least some courts treat an agreement to work in exchange for securities as a purchase of such securities for value. Note, however, that under some circumstances courts have held that interests in stock-related benefit plans do not constitute a "security." See, e.g., *Childers v. Northwest Airlines, Inc.*, 688 F. Supp. 1357, 1363 (D. Minn. 1988) (holding that employees' participation in employee stock ownership plan cannot be characterized as a "purchase" of a security since participating employees did not furnish value). Therefore, the question of whether securities issued in connection with employment have been acquired for value should be considered carefully on a case-by-case basis.

6.   Wash. Rev. Code § 21.20.005(10).

7.   Cal. Corp. Code § 25008(b) ("An offer to sell or to buy is made in this state when the offer either originates from or is directed by the offeror to this state and received at the place to which it is directed.").

8.   Cal. Corp. Code § 25017(b).

9.   Cal. Corp. Code § 25008(b).

10. The responsibility for administering the state securities laws varies from state to state and may rest on the department of financial institutions, a securities commission or some other department or agency. This chapter refers to the applicable agency or department generally as the "state securities administrator."

11. This issue does not arise in connection with employee stock purchase plans, because issuers typically sell shares of common stock and not derivative or convertible securities under such plans.

12. See, e.g., Ariz. Rev. Stat. § 44-1844A.14; Ark. Code § 23-42-503(a)(8); Cal. Corporations Code § 25102 (o); 815 Ill. Comp. Stat. 5/3 [N]; Iowa Code § 502.202 [11]; Ky. Rev. Stat. Ann. § 292.400(11); Me. Rev. Stat. Ann. tit. 32, § 10502[1]L; Mich. Stat. Ann. § 451.802(a)(10); N.C. Gen. Stat. § 78A-16(11); Nev. Rev. Stat. § 90.520[2](l); N.M. Stat. Ann. § 58-13B-26[K]; 71 Okla. Stat. § 401(a)(8); 70 Pa. Stat. § 1-202(g); R.I. Gen. Laws § 7-11-401(12); Utah Code Ann. § 61-1-14(1)(j).

13. See, e.g., Ala. Code § 8-6-10(10); Alaska Stat. § 45.55.900(a)(5); Colo. Rev. Stat. § 11-51-307(1)(i); Conn. Gen. Stat. § 36b-21(a)(11); Del. Code Ann. tit. 6, § 7309(a)(11); Haw. Rev. Stat. § 485-4(11); Idaho Code § 30-1434(1)(k); Ind. Code § 23-2-1-2(a)(7); Kan. Stat. Ann. § 17-1261(j); Md. Code Ann., Corporations and Associations § 11-601(11); Mass. Gen. Laws ch. 110A, § 402(a)(11); Minn. Stat. § 80A(15) Subdivision 1(h); Miss. Code § 75-71-201(11); Mo. Rev. Stat. § 409.402(a)(11); Mont. Code Ann. § 30-10-104(10); N.J. Stat 49:3-50(a)(11); N.Y. Gen. Bus. Law § 359-f.[2](e); Or. Rev. Stat. § 59.025(12); Va. Code Ann. § 13.1-514[A][10]; Wash. Rev. Code § 21.20.310(10).

14. Essentially every state's blanket exemption for securities issued in connection with employee benefit plans specifically lists stock purchase plans.

15. Wash Rev. Code § 21.20.310(10).

16. A problem may arise if the issuer issues the securities before sending the director notice and a copy of the plan. In that situation, the issuer must apply to the director, which can grant relief from the failure to meet the 30 day pre-filing requirement for good cause upon finding that it is in the public interest to grant such relief.

17. See, e.g., Del. Code Ann. tit. 6, § 7309(a)(11); Idaho Code § 30-1434(1)(k); Mass. Gen. Laws ch. 110A, § 402(a)(11).

18. See, e.g., Ark. Code § 23-42-503(a)(8); Ky. Rev. Stat. Ann. § 292.400(11); Md. Code Ann., Corporations and Associations § 11-601(11); Mo. Rev. Stat. § 409.402(a)(11); Wash. Rev. Code § 21.20.310(10).

19. See, e.g., Fla. Stat. § 517.061(15); Ga. Code Ann. § 10-5-9(9)(C); La. Rev. Stat. Ann. § 51:709(9)(c); Ohio Admin. Code § 1301:6-3-03(E)(5); N.D. Cent. Code § 10-04-06[11]; Tex. Rev. Civ. Stat., Art. 581-5[I](b).

20. Ohio Admin. Code Section 1301:6-3-03(E)(5).

21. Cal. Corp. Code § 25102(o).

22. See La. Rev. Stat. Ann. § 51:709(9)(d).

23. See Cal. Corp. Code § 25017(e). "Every sale or offer of a warrant or right to purchase or subscribe to another security of the same or another issuer, as well as every sale or offer of a security which gives the holder a present or future right or privilege to convert the security into another security of the same or another issuer, includes an offer and sale of the other security only at the time of the offer or sale of the warrant or right or convertible security; but neither the exercise of the right to purchase or subscribe or to convert nor the issuance of securities thereto is an offer or sale."

24. See, e.g., Alaska Stat. § 45.55.900(b)(7); Col. Rev. Stat. § 11-51-308(1)(l); Conn. Gen. Stat. § 36b-21(b)(12); Del. Code Ann. tit. 6 § 7309(b)(11); Fla Stat. § 517.061(6); Haw. Rev. Stat. § 485-6(11); Idaho Code § 30-1435(1)(k); 815 Ill. Comp. Stat., 5/4[B]; Ind. Code § 23-2-1-2(b)(11); La. Rev. Stat. Ann. § 51:709(8); Mass. Gen. Laws, ch. 110 A, § 402(b)(11); N.M. Stat. § 58-13B-27[N]; 70 Pa. Stat. § 1-203(n); Tex. Rev. Civ. Stat., Art. 581-5[E]; Utah Code Ann. § 61-1-14(2)(j); Va. Code Ann. § 13.1-514[B][8]; Wash. Rev. Code § 21.20.320(11).

Preparing for an Initial Public Offering

Mark A. Borges

℘OR MANY COMPANIES, an initial public offering (IPO) of securities is a significant measure of the success of the enterprise. There are several reasons for conducting an IPO. The most frequently cited motive is to raise additional capital for the business. Other reasons include enhancing the image of the company, spreading the risk of future development activities, and providing an avenue to liquidity for the company's founders and other shareholders.

The IPO process can be quite complex and involves the combined efforts of many parties: the company's management; the underwriters for the transaction; and the company's attorneys, accountants, and other professional advisors. If the company maintains a stock option plan for its employees, several issues related to the IPO must be addressed. Identifying and preparing for these issues will greatly ease the transition from a closely held business to a public reporting corporation.

In addition, administering the stock option plan in an environment where there is a public market for the company's securities is significantly more complex than when the company was closely held. Exercises of outstanding stock options are much more common and more complex. Officers and directors are subject to a multitude of restrictions in connec-

The Securities and Exchange Commission, as a matter of policy, disclaims responsibility for any private publication or statement by any of its employees. The views expressed herein are those of the author and do not necessarily reflect the views of the Commission or of the author's colleagues upon the staff of the Commission.

tion with their participation in the stock option plan. Regulatory compliance increases, particularly as it relates to the public disclosure of plan activity. It becomes imperative to have a stock plan administrator to manage these increased responsibilities.

This chapter summarizes some of the key issues involving a company's stock option plan both before and immediately after an IPO. While it is intended to provide a checklist of matters that the company should consider in connection with its IPO, it is not exhaustive. Because the requirements for conducting an IPO are revised from time to time and the regulatory considerations affecting stock option plans are constantly changing, a company should consult its professional advisors to ensure the appropriate application of the rules discussed here to its particular situation.

Overview of the IPO Process

While a comprehensive discussion of the IPO process is beyond the scope of this chapter, it is helpful for the stock plan administrator to have a basic understanding of the regulatory framework in which the offering takes place.

An IPO represents a company's first sale of securities to the general public. Typically, the company engages one or more investment banks to "underwrite" the offering; that is, to act as intermediaries for the distribution of the securities to the ultimate purchasers.

Any offering of securities is subject to compliance with the Securities Act of 1933 (the "Securities Act"), the basic purposes of which is to ensure that complete and accurate information about the securities being offered to the public is available. To meet this objective, the Securities Act requires that the offering either be registered with the Securities and Exchange Commission (SEC) or satisfy the conditions of an appropriate exemption from the registration requirement. Because of the general nature of an IPO, it is always conducted as a registered transaction with the SEC.

One common misconception regarding an IPO is that it registers all of the company's securities. In fact, registration under the Securities Act covers only the specific securities actually being offered and only for the specific purposes of the offering described in the registration statement. Typically, the securities sold in the IPO are previously authorized but unissued shares of the common stock of the company. Frequently, the founders and other shareholders of the company also sell some of their shares in the offering.

In addition to complying with the Securities Act, the company must satisfy the securities laws in each state in which the shares of stock will be offered. For most IPOs, this means compliance with the securities laws of virtually all 50 states. Fortunately, most states have available exemptions that can be used to avoid the registration process within those states. Most state securities laws provide exemptions for securities that are listed or approved for listing on a national securities exchange. Other states exempt sales of securities to registered broker-dealers or financial institutions.

The securities offered in the IPO must also be designated for trading on a stock market—either an "exchange" market such as the New York Stock Exchange, or the "over-the-counter" (OTC) market. Unless and until a company can meet the stringent listing requirements of an exchange, its securities will be traded on the OTC market. The National Association of Securities Dealers, Inc. (NASD), the self-regulatory organization that oversees the OTC market, maintains an electronic automated quotations system to facilitate the trading of many OTC stocks (the NASDAQ). Today, it is common for a company that is about to conduct its IPO to apply for inclusion on the National Market System (NMS) of the NASDAQ. Listing on the NASDAQ/NMS requires, among other things, agreement by the company to observe the market's corporate governance requirements, which reflect minimum standards for conducting its internal corporate affairs.

Planning Considerations Before an IPO

A number of matters involving the company's stock option plan will require the attention of the company's management before an IPO.

Amending the Stock Option Plan

While a stock option plan will, in most material respects, operate similarly whether a company is closely held or publicly traded, there will be some features of the plan that company management should consider changing before the company's IPO. Some of these changes may require shareholder approval, either for regulatory purposes or as required by the plan itself. Preplanning is desirable because it is generally easier to obtain shareholder approval while the company's securities are still closely held. Typical amendments to consider include the following:

Increase Plan Share Reserve Company management should review the plan share reserve to ensure that there is a sufficiently large pool of shares available to cover projected future stock option grants for a predetermined period of time (generally, at least one to two years).

Revise Plan Eligibility Criteria The stock plan administrator should review the plan eligibility provision to determine whether the plan permits grants to the appropriate categories of individuals. For example, if the company has not provided for grants to non-employee consultants and advisors in the past, it may be desirable to expand the category of eligible participants to include such individuals. Conversely, if the company has granted stock options to consultants and advisors in the past but now plans a shift in philosophy as a public reporting company, the plan can be amended to restrict future grants to such individuals. Finally, the company should determine how non-employee director stock option grants will be handled after the IPO, either under the general stock option plan or through a separate directors' stock option plan.

Individual Grant Limitations Section 162(m) of the Internal Revenue Code (the "Code") limits the ability of public reporting companies to deduct from their corporate income taxes compensation in excess of $1 million paid to certain executive officers. An exception to this deduction limit is available for "performance-based" compensation. In order for stock options granted to these executive officers to qualify for this exception, among other things, the stock option plan must contain a maximum per-employee share limitation.

This per-employee share limitation will be deemed to have been satisfied if the stock option plan states the maximum number of shares of stock for which stock options may be granted during a specified period to any employee. Accordingly, company management, in consultation with the company's professional advisors, should select an appropriate limitation that will act as the maximum number of shares subject to a stock option that can be granted under the plan during a specified period to any employee.

Eliminate Contractual Restrictions The stock option plans of most closely held companies impose certain contractual restrictions on the ability of an optionee to sell or otherwise transfer his or her option shares following the exercise of a stock option. Typically, these restrictions take the form of a right of first refusal (on third-party transactions), a vested share repurchase option, or a similar arrangement. To the extent that such provisions do not automatically terminate upon the IPO, they should be deleted from the plan.

Enhance Exercise Payment Methods In anticipation of the establishment of a public market for the company's securities, company management should consider expanding the range of permissible payment methods under the stock option plan. To the extent that the stock option plan does not expressly permit broker-assisted same-day exercise and sale transactions, such a provision should be added to the stock option plan.

As permitted under Regulation T, a securities brokerage firm may advance funds to an optionee to cover the exercise price and any associated withholding taxes as if the firm had the certificate for the shares of stock underlying the stock option in its possession, provided the optionee has delivered to the firm an executed notice of exercise and a copy of irrevocable instructions from the optionee directing the company to deliver the option shares to the firm. The instructions must designate the account into which the option shares are to be deposited (either a margin account or a cash account). Where the option shares are to be immediately sold by the securities brokerage firm, a cash account will be designated from which the sale proceeds would fund the exercise.

While it is not required, the company may find that it is more expedient to amend its stock option plan to permit this type of exercise. This will provide the company with more flexibility in structuring its same-day exercise and sale arrangements with one or more securities brokerage firms. The company will also want to consider any applicable tax, securities law, and accounting issues that may be associated with amending the stock option plan to add this provision.

Company management should consider whether it is appropriate to amend outstanding stock options to add a brokers' same-day exercise and sale provision for those instruments. Once again, applicable legal and accounting implications should first be considered before taking such action.

Composition of Plan Administration Committee Typically, a stock option plan will identify the body authorized to administer the plan and will also set forth certain guidelines for the committee's composition and operation. Most stock option plans provide that the company's board of directors or a committee of the board, such as the compensation committee, is responsible for administering the plan. While it may not require

a formal plan amendment, company management should seek to coor-
dinate the composition of the plan administration committee to comply
with the conditions of the Rule 16b-3 exemption and the "performance-
based" compensation exception to Section 162(m) of the Code.

For purposes of Rule 16b-3, stock option grants may be approved by
a committee of two or more "non-employee" directors. For purposes of
the "performance-based" compensation exception of Section 162(m), the
compensation committee must be composed solely of two or more "outside" directors. The definition of a "non-employee" director differs in
several respects from the definition of an "outside" director. The definition of a "non-employee" director tends to be less restrictive than the
definition of an "outside director" because it focuses only on a director's
current, rather than past, status.

Under Rule 16b-3, a "non-employee director" is an individual who
is not currently an officer or otherwise employed by the company or a
parent or subsidiary corporation; does not receive compensation, directly
or indirectly, from the company or its parent or subsidiary corporations
for services rendered as a consultant or in any capacity other than as a
director (except for an amount for which disclosure would not be required under the "related-party transaction" rules of Regulation S-K);
does not possess an interest in any other transaction for which disclosure would be required under the "related-party transaction" rules of
Regulation S-K; and is not engaged in a business relationship with the
company for which disclosure would be required under the "related-
party transaction" rules of Regulation S-K.

For purposes of the "performance-based" compensation exception
of Section 162(m), a director is considered to be an "outside" director if
the director (1) is not a current employee of the publicly held corporation, (2) is not a former employee of the publicly held corporation who
is receiving compensation for prior services (other than benefits under a
tax-qualified retirement plan) during the taxable year, (3) has not been
an officer of the publicly held corporation either currently or at any time
in the past, or (4) does not currently receive remuneration, either directly
or indirectly, in any capacity other than as a director (including any payment in exchange for goods or services).

"Current remuneration" includes remuneration paid by the company, directly or indirectly, to the director personally; remuneration paid
by the company to an entity in which the director has a beneficial ownership interest of more than 50%; remuneration paid by the corporation
in its preceding taxable year to an entity for which the director is em-

ployed or self-employed other than as a director (unless it is a de minimis amount that is less than the lesser of $60,000 or 5% of the entity's
gross revenue for the entity's taxable year ending within the publicly held
corporation's taxable year); or remuneration paid by the corporation in
its preceding taxable year to an entity in which the director beneficially
owns a 5% to 50% interest (unless it is a de minimis amount that is less
than the lesser of $60,000 or 5% of the entity's gross revenue for the
entity's preceding taxable year ending within the publicly held
corporation's taxable year).

For purposes of Section 162(m), whether a director is a current employee or a former officer is determined on the basis of the facts at the
time that the individual serves as a director on the compensation committee. For purposes of these rules, an officer is an administrative executive who is or was in regular and continued service. The determination
of whether an individual is or was an officer is based on all of the facts
and circumstances in the particular case, including, without limitation,
the source of the individual's authority, the term for which the individual
is elected or appointed, and the nature and extent of the individual's
duties.

Once the company has determined its strategy for complying with
Section 162(m), it should identify the appropriate directors to comprise
the compensation committee of the board of directors. It may be necessary to add individuals to the board of directors to ensure that one or
both of the exemptions will be available for future transactions and periods. Company management should review the stock option plan to
determine if any coordinating amendments need to be made to the stock
option plan.

Other Amendments Because of limitations on the ability of the
company's officers and directors to obtain liquidity for their option shares
due to federal and state insider trading restrictions, company management may want to consider amending the stock option plan to permit
optionees subject to Section 16 of the Securities Exchange Act of 1934 (the
"Exchange Act") to tender shares of stock to satisfy any income tax withholding obligations that arise in connection with the exercise of their stock
options.

Company management should also review the "change of control"
provisions in the stock option plan and outstanding stock option agreements and employment agreements, if any, for consistency and to ensure that future stock option grants will contain the desired features. In

addition, the company's accountants should be consulted to consider the effect that the change of control provisions and any contemplated changes may have on the accounting treatment of a future acquisition of the company.

Finally, the company may want to consider changing the standard form of employee stock option grant from an incentive stock option to a nonqualified stock option. Generally, this change does not require a formal amendment to the stock option plan; instead, it requires a change to the company's philosophy for stock options. If the company anticipates that most employees will use a broker-assisted same-day exercise and sale procedure to exercise their stock options, it may find that, for practical purposes, nonqualified stock options are preferable because they are simpler to administer and ensure that the company will receive a corporate income tax deduction upon exercise of the options.

Adoption of Employee Stock Purchase Plan

Concurrent with an IPO, many companies implement a broad-based employee stock purchase plan. Often, this plan will supplement the company's stock option plan. Occasionally, the plan will substitute for a stock option plan where the company believes that it may no longer be possible to grant meaningful stock options to all employees.

Generally, an employee stock purchase plan provides eligible employees with the opportunity to purchase shares of the company's stock at certain predetermined intervals (generally once or twice each year). Shares are usually purchased at a discount from the fair market value of the company's stock. Typically, the purchase price is 85% of the lesser of the fair market value of the company's stock at the beginning or end of a specified period of time. The purchase price for the shares is paid in the form of payroll deductions authorized by the employee. Unless an employee withdraws from the plan before the date of purchase, shares are automatically purchased on that date by dividing the applicable purchase price into the accumulated payroll deductions for the employee.

In addition to the economic benefits provided by these plans, a company can, by satisfying the conditions of Code Section 423, ensure that employees participating in the plan receive preferential tax treatment for federal income tax purposes in connection with their acquisition and disposition of shares.

By satisfying several statutorily enumerated requirements, a Section 423 employee stock purchase plan can offer several distinct tax advantages to participants. First, a Section 423 plan offers employees the opportunity for tax deferral. Participants in a Section 423 plan are not required to recognize income in connection with the purchase of shares of stock under the plan until the shares are sold. In addition, a Section 423 plan offers the opportunity for the recharacterization of most of the income ultimately recognized upon a disposition of the shares into capital gain. Specifically, if certain holding period requirements are met, a portion of the discount from current fair market value that results on the purchase of the shares will be subject to tax as capital gain income rather than as compensation income taxable at ordinary income rates.

To qualify for preferential tax treatment under Section 423, an employee stock purchase plan must meet the following requirements:

- Participation in the plan must be limited to employees.

- The plan must be approved by shareholders of the company within 12 months before or after its adoption by the board of directors.

- The purchase price for the shares of stock may not be less than 85% of the lesser of the fair market value of the company's stock at the time an employee enrolls in the plan or the fair market value of the company's stock on the date of purchase.

- The term of an option granted pursuant to the plan may not exceed 27 months (or five years if the purchase price is determined only on the date of purchase).

- All employees must be allowed to participate in the plan (with certain exclusions).

- All participants in the plan must have the same rights and privileges.

- Employees owning stock possessing 5% or more of the total combined voting power or value of all classes of the stock of the company or its parent or subsidiary corporations may not participate in the plan.

- An employee may not purchase more than $25,000 worth of stock on a cumulative basis (based on the fair market value of the company's stock at the time of enrollment in the plan) for each calendar year in which an option is outstanding at any time.

By offering shares of stock at a discount from fair market value, an employee stock purchase plan virtually ensures that employees will obtain a favorable return on their investment. An employee stock purchase plan enables employees to acquire an equity interest in their company, an objective beneficial to the company because it provides both incentive and motivation for employees to work harder in the common interest, thereby aligning the interests of the employees with those of its shareholders. From the company's perspective, an employee stock purchase plan can be a convenient means by which the company can raise capital on a continuing basis. It also can be used to promote widespread stock ownership among employees and to recruit and retain talented employees. For a company that may be unable or unwilling to grant stock options to all employees, an employee stock purchase plan allows the company to offer a company-wide equity participation program while limiting stock option grants. In recognition of the tendency of employees participating in an employee stock purchase plan to regularly liquidate their stock holdings, some companies will offer stock options as an investment program and an employee stock purchase plan as a liquidity mechanism.

To an employee, an employee stock purchase plan provides an easy way to purchase company stock at a discount. And, if the plan is qualified under Section 423, the employee incurs no federal income tax liability at the time of purchase. The plan may provide a strong motivational tool for an employee, since the employee recognizes that his or her individual performance can directly affect the company's prospects and, therefore, the value of the company's stock.

Adoption of Directors' Stock Option Plan

The company may also want to consider adopting a separate stock option plan for the members of its board of directors. While it is quite common to grant stock options to non-employee directors out of the company's primary stock option plan while the company is closely held, separate arrangements are often implemented after an IPO.

Traditionally, such plans were "formula" plans under which eligibility was limited to non-employee directors; the plan, by its terms, specified the amount, price, and timing of option grants; and the company's ability to amend these plan provisions more than once every six months was limited. These "formula" plans played an important role in ensuring that a company could provide stock options to its non-employee directors without jeopardizing their "disinterested" status for purposes of administering the company's discretionary employee stock plans. Under current SEC rules, "disinterested" status is no longer needed to ensure that grants or awards to officers and employee-directors under a company's discretionary stock plans are exempt from the "short-swing profits" recovery provisions of Section 16(b). Still, many companies continue to use "formula" plans as a way of minimizing conflict-of-interest issues that might arise where non-employee directors are both administrators and beneficiaries of the companies' stock option programs.

Exchange Act Rule 16b-3 does not prohibit non-employee directors (or the full board, for that matter) from awarding themselves grants of the company's securities or stock options on those securities. Nor does it automatically subject these transactions to shareholder scrutiny. Instead, such transactions will be subject to state laws governing corporate self-dealing. As a result, companies must decide whether to use a separate "formula" plan or to simply include them as participants in their general employee stock option plan. For shareholder relations purposes, as well as to maintain the impartiality of the directors, a company may find that it is still prudent to implement a non-employee director "formula" plan.

Assisting Employees in the Disposition of Their Stock Options

Tax Considerations Once the company's employees are informed of the impending IPO, most individuals will have questions concerning the impact of the transaction on their stock options. Some employees will seek counseling concerning their stock options and may look to the stock plan administrator to advise them on how to proceed. While the stock plan administrator should avoid giving individual tax and financial advice, it may be prudent to schedule one or more informational meetings for employees to provide them with basic information about their stock options and outline the key planning considerations they should address with financial advisors.

Securities Law Restrictions In addition, it will be helpful to educate the employees on the resale limitations imposed contractually and under the federal securities laws that will affect their ability to sell their option shares following the IPO.

Generally, an employee who has acquired shares of stock under the company's stock option plan will hold "restricted securities." For purposes of the federal securities laws, "restricted securities" are securities acquired from a company in a transaction or series of transactions that has not been registered under the Securities Act. Under the Securities Act, any proposed sale of the option shares must either be registered or exempt from registration.

Securities Act Rule 144 provides an exemption from the registration requirement of the Securities Act for a person seeking to resell "restricted securities." To sell "restricted securities" in reliance on Rule 144, several conditions must be satisfied. First, the company must be subject to the reporting requirements of the Exchange Act and must be current in meeting its reporting obligations. Next, the securities to be sold must have been fully paid for and held for a period of at least one year. Third, the amount of securities that can be resold during any three-month period must not exceed the greater of (1) 1% of the outstanding stock of the company or (2) the average weekly trading volume of the company's stock during the four calendar weeks preceding the date of the proposed sale. Fourth, all sales must be made in unsolicited brokers' transactions or directly to market makers. Finally, a notice of the proposed sale, on Form 144, must be filed with the SEC (and any national securities exchange on which the securities are admitted for trading) before or concurrently with the sale if the proposed sale involves more than 500 shares or has an aggregate sale price over $10,000.

For purposes of Securities Act Rule 144, the one-year holding period is measured from the date that the securities are paid for in full. Payment with a promissory note that is essentially financed by the company does not constitute full payment unless the note is a full-recourse obligation and is collateralized by property other than the shares of stock being purchased, which property has a fair market value at least equal to the total purchase price of the shares. In addition, the promissory note must be repaid in full before the sale of the restricted securities.

In addition to transactions in "restricted securities," Securities Act Rule 144 is the primary exemption from the registration requirements of the Securities Act for resales of securities by "affiliates" of the company. For purposes of the federal securities laws, an "affiliate" includes any person directly controlling or controlled by the company or any person under direct or indirect common control with the company. While the determination of "affiliate" status ultimately depends on the facts and circumstances of each individual case, the officers, directors, and principal shareholders of a company generally are considered "affiliates" of the company.

Securities Act Rule 144 applies to any sale of securities by an affiliate (whether of registered securities or "restricted securities"). The conditions of the rule to be satisfied in the case of an affiliate transaction depend on the nature of the securities to be resold. If the securities are "restricted securities," all of the conditions of Rule 144 described above must be met.

If the securities have previously been registered, then all of the conditions of Rule 144, other than the holding period condition, must be met.

Typically, a company will place a restrictive legend on the certificate for shares of stock that are either "restricted securities" or held by an affiliate. This legend is intended to alert the company's transfer agent and/or a stock brokerage firm assisting with the proposed sale to the fact that the shares are subject to the conditions of Securities Act Rule 144. In addition, the company may issue "stop transfer" instructions to its transfer agent as a precaution against inadvertent sales that do not comply with Rule 144. Rule 144 is applicable to resales of "restricted securities" and securities held by affiliates, however, whether or not a legend appears on the certificate or stop transfer instructions have been issued.

Following the IPO, unless an employee's option shares acquired before the offering are first registered with the SEC, such shares must be sold in reliance on Securities Act Rule 144. One significant exception to this requirement exists. If the stock option was granted under the exemption provided by Securities Act Rule 701, a special resale provision in the rule will be triggered following the IPO. While option shares acquired pursuant to Rule 701 are deemed to be "restricted securities" for resale purposes, 90 days after the company becomes subject to the reporting requirements of the Exchange Act, non-affiliates may sell their Rule 701 option shares without regard to Rule 144 (other than the manner-of-sale condition) and affiliates may sell their Rule 701 option shares pursuant to Rule 144 (but without regard to the holding period condition).

Contractual Restrictions Notwithstanding compliance with applicable securities laws, employees may still be restricted contractually from selling their option shares immediately following an IPO. Frequently, the underwriter for the offering will require the officers, directors, and principal shareholders of the company to agree not to sell any shares of stock in the public market for a period of up to 180 days following the IPO. This is done primarily to ensure stabilization of the market price for the company's stock during the post-IPO period. This restriction is often called the "underwriters' lockup" or "market standoff" requirement.

Where there are a large number of stock options outstanding at the time of the IPO, it is not uncommon for the underwriters to request that each optionee agreement be bound by the lockup provision. This may require the stock plan administrator to obtain written agreements from each optionee, agreeing to the applicable restrictions. Many companies include a lockup provision in their standard stock option agreements to avoid having to obtain lockup agreements individually in connection with the offering. An explanation of these provisions and their applicability should be included in the information provided to the employees about the IPO.

Regulatory Considerations Before an IPO

Section 16

The officers, directors, and principal shareholders of any company that has a class of equity securities registered under Section 12 of the Exchange Act are subject to the provisions of Section 16 of the Exchange Act. Generally, registration of a class of securities is required under Section 12(b) of the Exchange Act where a company elects to have equity securities listed for trading on a national securities exchange or under Section 12(g) of the Exchange Act where the company has more than 500 shareholders of record and total assets exceeding $10 million as of the end of the company's fiscal year. In addition, a company may voluntarily register a class of its equity securities under Section 12(g).

Where a company intends to have its securities listed for trading on a national securities exchange in connection with its IPO, compliance with Section 16 is required. While such a situation arises from time to time, it is far more common today for a company to seek to have its securities quoted on the NASDAQ National Market System or the OTC Bulletin Board. Under NASDAQ rules, a company must comply with the NASDAQ corporate governance requirements, which among other things require registration under Section 12 of the Exchange Act on a voluntary basis. Consequently, today many companies file under Section 12 concurrently with their IPOs, thereby subjecting their officers, directors, and principal shareholders to compliance with Section 16 at the effective date of the IPO.

Under Section 16, officers and directors and beneficial owners of more than 10% of the class of equity securities registered under the Exchange Act must disclose their holdings of, and transactions involving, the equity securities of their company and further must return to the company any profits that they realize in the event of any "short-swing" trading in such securities.

Determination of Corporate Insiders   Initially, the stock plan administrator must assist in the determination of who will be subject to Section 16 as a result of the Section 12 registration. Section 16 applies to any officer or director of a Section 12 company, as well as any beneficial owner of more than 10% of the company's registered equity securities. The determination of directors subject to Section 16 is generally straightforward: it includes each member of the company's board of directors. The determination of officer status for purposes of Section 16 can be more challenging.

The rules under Section 16 contain a specific definition of who is to be considered an "officer" for purposes of Section 16. A Section 16 "officer" includes a company's (1) president; (2) principal financial officer; (3) principal accounting officer (or, if there is none, the controller); (4) any vice president in charge of a principal business unit, division, or function (such as sales, administration, or finance); (5) any other officer performing a significant policy-making function; (6) any other person performing a significant policy-making function; and (7) officers of parent or subsidiary companies who are performing policy-making functions for the company.

The rules under Section 16 make it clear that function, rather than title, will be determinative of "officer" status. In establishing whether an individual is to be treated as a Section 16 officer, the policy-making responsibilities of the individual will be a key factor. The rules further provide that if a company identifies an individual as an "executive officer" (in its proxy statement or annual report on Form 10-K), a presumption will arise that the board of directors made this judgment and that the individual is a Section 16 officer. Consequently, once the initial group of Section 16 officers has been identified, the company's board of directors should formally confirm this status. Thereafter, the board of directors should consider taking action annually to review and confirm the identities and titles of its officers subject to Section 16.

Section 16 Reporting A corporate insider must prepare and file an initial report concerning the insider's holdings of equity securities of the Section 12 company on Form 3, the initial statement of beneficial ownership of securities. Generally, a Form 3 must be filed with the SEC within 10 days after the corporate insider first becomes subject to Section 16, listing the insider's holdings of equity securities as of that date. In the case of a company registering a class of equity securities under Section 12 of the Exchange Act for the first time, however, a Form 3 must be filed with the SEC for each corporate insider by the effective date of the Section 12 registration. Where Section 12 registration is being made concurrent with the IPO, such filings must take place by the effective date of the IPO. The Form 3 must list and describe all of the equity securities of the company beneficially owned by the corporate insider before the effective date of the Section 12 registration. A Form 3 must be filed whether or not the corporate insider owns any equity securities of the company.

A corporate insider must prepare and file subsequent reports concerning changes to the insider's holdings of equity securities on either Form 4 or Form 5.

"Cheap" Stock

Before an IPO, company management should closely monitor the prices at which the company grants stock options to its employees. The SEC will scrutinize the methodology used to set the exercise price for these stock option grants to ensure that the company has not issued "cheap" stock, that is, stock issued at prices below the stock's true market value. The SEC often presumes that stock options granted during the period immediately before an IPO involve "cheap" stock unless the options were granted at the offering price, and will require the company to record a compensation expense for these stock options to the extent that the exercise price is less than the offering price. Disputes are common in which a company and the SEC will disagree about whether the stock options were properly valued and accounted for in the company's financial statements.

Where the SEC presumes that the stock options were not priced at fair market value at the time of grant, it will require the company to record a compensation expense for the "discount" reflected in the stock options. Such a result can both delay the offering (as the parties wrangle over the proper valuation for the stock options) and change the financial statements, altering investors' views of the company and the proposed offering.

To minimize potential problems, the company should begin documenting the methodology employed to price its stock option grants during the 12- to 18-month period before the IPO. Important factors in responding to an SEC inquiry include the number of months between the stock option grant and the IPO, the difference between the exercise price and the offering price, and whether significant changes in the company's business prospects have taken place since the grant date. The most persuasive factor is whether the company used the services of an independent professional appraiser in setting the stock option exercise price. Many companies retain an independent appraiser to assist in the stock option valuation process during the months before the offering.

Preparing the Registration Statement

The purpose of a formal registration statement is to ensure that complete and accurate information is available about the company and the securities to be offered. The registration statement contains certain detailed information as required by the Securities Act and the SEC rules and forms.

Generally, a registration statement contains two parts: (1) the "prospectus," which must be furnished to each prospective and ultimate purchaser of the securities, and (2) "Part 2," which is filed with the SEC and is available to the public. The basic registration form is Form S-1, which must be used in any offering of securities for which no other form is authorized or prescribed.

Under the SEC's "integrated disclosure system," the basic disclosure requirements for all of the Securities Act and Exchange Act documents are set forth in a series of SEC regulations. The required disclosures with respect to the company's financial statements are set forth in Regulation S-X. The textual disclosures for the registration statement itself are contained in Regulation S-K (or, in the case of certain small entities, Regulation S-B). The requirements under the SEC's Electronic Data Gathering and Retrieval (EDGAR) system, which prescribes electronic filing of all required disclosure documents, are set forth in Regulation S-T.

Compliance with these requirements results in a disclosure document that is both comprehensive and complex. While most of the registration statement will be prepared by the company's corporate securities attorneys, there are certain portions of the document that require detailed disclosure of the company's equity compensation plans and arrangements and other related information.

Executive Compensation Disclosure   Under Item 402 of Regulation S-K, the company must disclose information concerning the various forms of compensation paid to senior executives and directors, the criteria used in reaching compensation decisions, and the degree of the relationship between a company's compensation practices and corporate performance. The requirements consist of approximately 10 separate disclosure items, which are sometimes grouped into "soft" and "hard" disclosures. The "soft" (subjective) disclosures include the Board Compensation Committee Report, the Performance Graph, the Compensation Committee Interlocks and Insider Participation Report, and the Option/SAR (stock appreciation rights) Repricing Report. In addition to this subjective disclosure, extensive tabular disclosure is required covering the actual compensation packages of a company's senior executive officers. The compensation of each of these executives is highlighted in up to six separate tables or charts. The stock plan administrator will frequently be called upon to assist with the preparation of the specific tabular disclosure.

The executives subject to this heightened disclosure include (1) all individuals who have served as the chief executive officer of the company (or acted in a similar capacity) during the last completed fiscal year (regardless of the level of compensation paid to the individual during that year), (2) each of the company's four most highly compensated executive officers (other than the CEO) who were serving as executive officers at the end of the last completed fiscal year whose combined base salary and bonus exceed $100,000 for the fiscal year, and (3) up to two additional individuals who would have been among the four most highly compensated executive officers but for the fact that the individual was not serving as an executive officer of the company at the end of the last completed fiscal year. These individuals are referred to as the "named executive officers."

- *Summary Compensation Table.* The linchpin of the tabular disclosure requirements, the Summary Compensation Table, is designed to provide a comprehensive overview of a company's executive pay practices in a single location within the registration statement. This information is intended to enable prospective investors to understand clearly the compensation paid for the prior fiscal year, to evaluate the company's pay policies in light of its overall performance, and to compare trends in compensation practices between companies.

  The Summary Compensation Table covers the actual compensation paid to each of the named executive officers during the last three completed fiscal years. If the company has not been a reporting company under the Exchange Act for the prior three years (as will typically be the case in an IPO), the table need only cover the shorter period that the company has been a reporting company, but must cover at least the last completed fiscal year.

  The Summary Compensation Table divides the compensation of the named executive officers between its annual and long-term components. The annual compensation to be disclosed consists of the executive's base salary and bonus (which must be identified and disclosed separately) and five other designated items (which are to be aggregated and reported as a single amount). Cash or unrestricted shares of stock earned for services performed in a covered year are to be included in the table as salary or bonus. Restricted stock awards, stock options, or other long-term incentive compensation that is received in lieu of salary or bonus need not be reported here but should be included in determining whether a person is a named executive officer.

The other annual compensation items include (1) perquisites and other personal benefits; (2) earnings paid or payable, but deferred at the election of the executive, on deferred compensation, restricted stock, options, and SARs at above-market interest or preferential dividend rates; (3) earnings paid or payable, but deferred at the election of the executive, on long-term incentive plan compensation; (4) amounts reimbursed to the executive during the prior fiscal year for the payment of taxes (or "gross-ups"); and (5) preferential discounted stock purchases. Perquisites are reportable where the aggregate amount exceeds the lesser of either $50,000 or 10% of the executive's annual base salary and bonus. Additional disclosure is required of the type and amount of any perquisite or other personal benefit that has a value in excess of 25% of the total amount of perquisites and benefits reported.

The long-term compensation to be disclosed consists of restricted stock awards, stock option and free-standing SAR grants, long-term incentive plan payouts, and any other compensation not properly reportable in any other category.

- *Stock Option/SAR Grants Table.* The Stock Option/SAR Grants Table requires disclosure of stock option and free-standing SAR grants made during the last fiscal year to each of the named executive officers. Unlike the Summary Compensation Table, this disclosure covers only the last completed fiscal year, and each stock option and/or SAR grant must be identified and discussed separately (unless the grants have the same exercise price and expiration date and are not subject to different performance thresholds).

  Among other things, this table must include for each grant (1) the number of securities underlying the options and/or SARs granted; (2) the percentage the grant represents of the total number of options and/or SARs granted to all employees during the prior fiscal year; (3) the per-share exercise price of the option and/or SAR grant; (4) where the option or SAR has been granted at a discount, the fair market value of the company's stock on the date of grant; and (5) the expiration date of the option and/or SAR grants.

To aid shareholders in understanding the potential realizable value of each stock option and/or SAR grant, this table must also include disclosure of either the potential realizable value of the grant at assumed annual rates of appreciation in the company's stock of 5% and 10%, compounded over the term of the option and/or SAR (which translates into potential appreciation of 63% and 159% for 10-year options or SARs), or the value of the options and/or SARs as of the grant date computed under a valuation method selected by the company (such as the Black-Scholes option-pricing model). Where a company elects to disclose the potential realizable value, it is permissible to show the appreciation at other assumed rates of return (such as the company's historic rate of return) in addition to the mandated rates of return. If the option or SAR has been granted at a discount, disclosure is required showing the value of the grant at the grant date market price of the underlying securities. Where the company elects to disclose the grant date value, it must also describe the valuation method used as well as any material assumptions. Where a variation of the Black-Scholes or binomial option-pricing model is used, the description must cover the assumptions used relating to the expected volatility, risk-free rate of return, dividend yield, and time of exercise. Any adjustments for nontransferability or risk of forfeiture also must be disclosed.

Information must be also be provided in a footnote to this table covering the material terms of each option and/or SAR grant, any standard or formula that may cause the exercise price of an option and/or SAR to be adjusted (including indexing or premium pricing provisions), any provision of the grant that could cause the exercise price to be lowered, and the potential consequences of such a provision.

- *Stock Option/SAR Exercises Table.* The Stock Option/SAR Exercises Table requires disclosure of stock option exercises, as well as exercises of free-standing SARs, that occurred during the last fiscal year for each of the named executive officers. While this disclosure covers only the last completed fiscal year, unlike the Stock Option/SAR Grants Table, all exercises may be aggregated and reported as a single amount.

  Among other things, this table must include the number of shares received upon exercise (or, if no shares were received, the number of securities with respect to which the option and/or SAR was exercised) and the aggregate dollar value realized upon exercise. If any of the named executive officers holds unexercised stock options, the table must also include the total number of unexercised options and/ or SARs held at the end of the last completed fiscal year (separately identifying the exercisable and unexercisable options and SARs) and the aggregate dollar value of the "in-the-money," unexercised options and SARs held at the end of the last completed fiscal year (separately identifying the exercisable and unexercisable options and SARs).

- *Long-Term Incentive Plan Awards Table.* The disclosure rules require a separate table disclosing awards made to any of the named executive officers during the last fiscal year under any long-term incentive plans. This table covers only the last completed fiscal year. The disclosure consists of the number of shares of stock or units awarded and the material terms of each award, including a general description of the formula or criteria to be used in determining the amounts payable and the range of performance needed to achieve the payout amounts. As with the Board Compensation Committee Report, it is permissible to use generalized disclosure to safeguard any confidential business information related to the performance goals.

  Among other things, the Long-Term Incentive Plan Awards Table must include (1) the number of shares, units, or other rights awarded under any long-term incentive plan, and, if applicable, the number of shares underlying any such unit or right; (2) the performance or other time period until payout or maturation of the award (that is, the "earn-out" period); and (3) the dollar value of the estimated payout, the number of shares to be awarded as the payout, or a range of estimated payouts denominated in dollars or number of shares under the award (threshold, target, and maximum amount). This last item is not required for plans where the payout is based on stock price.

  For purposes of the disclosure requirements, a "long-term incentive plan" includes any plan providing for compensation intended to serve as an incentive for performance to occur over a period of longer than one year, but does not include restricted stock, options, or SARs.

Director Compensation Under the disclosure rules, the company must describe, stating amounts, any standard arrangements under which directors are compensated for their services provided as directors, including additional amounts payable for committee or special assignments. Other arrangements under which directors were compensated during the last completed fiscal year for any service provided as a director must also be disclosed, stating the amount paid and the name of the director. This latter requirement is intended to pick up consulting arrangements that a director may have with the company.

Employment Contracts and Other Arrangements   Under the disclosure rules, the company must report on the terms and conditions of any employment contract between the company and any of the named executive officers. The company must also disclose any compensatory plan or arrangement with any of the named executive officers if (1) the amount involved, including all periodic payments and installments, exceeds $100,000, and (2) the plan or arrangement is triggered by a termination of employment (as a result of resignation, retirement, or otherwise), a change in control of the company, or a change in the executive's responsibilities following a change in control of the company. Actual payments made under these arrangements are reportable in the "All Other Compensation" column of the Summary Compensation Table regardless of the amount.

Securities Ownership   The registration statement must disclose the identities and certain related information concerning beneficial ownership of the company's securities, including stock options, by certain principal shareholders (primarily 5%-or-more shareholders), members of management and the board of directors, and any selling shareholders.

Shares Eligible for Future Sale   The registration statement must disclose, with specificity, the number of shares of stock of the company that are eligible for future sale following the IPO. This discussion typically sets forth the source of these shares of stock, the basis for such future sales, and any contractual or securities law restrictions on such sales. To the extent that the company intends to register its stock option plan and other employee stock plans following the IPO, disclosure of these plans is required. This information provides prospective investors with a complete description of the potential dilutive effect that sales of these shares of stock could have once any restrictions on resale have lapsed.

Establishing a Same-Day Exercise and Sale Program

As noted above, the company will probably elect to establish a broker-assisted same-day exercise and sale program to provide optionees with an efficient means to finance the exercise of their stock options. A broker-assisted same-day exercise and sale is a means by which an employee can finance the exercise of a stock option by immediately selling through a securities brokerage firm that number of option shares from the stock option being exercised necessary to satisfy the payment of the total required option price for the option shares being purchased plus any withholding taxes due to the company.

The company may elect to make formal arrangements with one or more securities brokerage firms to facilitate these transactions. Not only do such arrangements, sometimes referred to as "captive broker" programs, simplify the administration of these programs, they also enable the transactions to be completed more expeditiously. The company will keep the securities brokerage firm or firms updated on outstanding stock options and vested shares, thereby enabling optionees to contact the brokerage firm directly when they want to exercise their stock options. To further simplify the administration of these transactions, some companies will establish an "omnibus" account with one or more securities brokerage firms and transfer a block of shares to the account for the purpose of ensuring that sufficient shares are available to deliver upon the settlement of the sale.

Under the recently enacted Sarbanes-Oxley Act of 2002, reporting companies are prohibited from making personal loans to their directors and executive officers. Presently, there is a question as to whether stock option exercises by a director or executive officer using a broker-assisted same-day exercise and sale program constitute prohibited loans under this statute. Consequently, a company should consult its professional legal advisors when establishing a broker-assisted same-day exercise and sale program to determine whether the program may be extended to its directors and executive officers.

Financial Statement Disclosures

Stock Option Valuation   While the company probably has accounted for its stock options using the "intrinsic value" method of accounting under APB Opinion No. 25, if it has been preparing audited financial statements while it has been a closely held entity, it has also been complying with the footnote disclosure requirements of Statement of Financial Accounting Standards (SFAS) No. 123. This accounting standard requires companies that continue to rely on APB Opinion No. 25 for purposes of measuring and recognizing compensation expense for employee stock plans to disclose in a footnote to their financial statements the pro forma effect that stock option grants and other awards would have had on net income and, for publicly traded companies, earnings per share if the company had adopted the new "fair value" method.

In the case of employee stock options granted by a publicly traded company, "fair value" is to be determined using an option-pricing model, such as the Black-Scholes or a binomial model, that takes into account, as of the grant date, the option price and the expected life of the option, the current price of the underlying shares of stock and its expected volatility, expected dividends on the stock, and the risk-free interest rate for the expected option term.

A closely held company must calculate the "minimum value," rather then the "fair value," for its employee stock option grants. This exception to the "fair value" requirement is provided because the lack of a trading history precludes a closely held company from being able to establish a volatility assumption for its stock, which is an integral component of the "fair value" calculation. The "minimum value" approach is a valuation method that reflects a present value calculation that ignores stock price volatility. The minimum value of a closely held company's employee stock options can be determined two ways. First, it can be determined using a simple present value calculation. In essence, the company can compute minimum value by taking the difference between its current stock price and the present value of the option exercise price plus the present value of the expected dividends on the stock, if any. Alternatively, minimum value can be computed using an acceptable option-pricing model with a stock price volatility assumption of zero.

Once the company becomes a publicly traded company, however, the "fair value" method of accounting must be used. For these purposes, the company is considered to be a "publicly traded" company upon the filing of a registration statement for its IPO, rather than the effective date of the registration. Consequently, company management should be aware that any stock option grants made after the filing of the registration statement will need to be valued using "fair value" rather than "minimum value." This means that the company must establish a stock price volatility assumption for use in the fair value calculation.

Regulatory Considerations After an IPO

After an IPO, the company's compliance obligations will increase substantially, primarily as a result of the application of the Exchange Act to the company. The Exchange Act regulates the trading of securities following their initial issuance by a company. Among other things, the Exchange Act imposes certain disclosure and reporting requirements on public reporting companies, prohibits the use of fraudulent and deceptive or manipulative practices in connection with trading in securities, restricts the trading activities of certain corporate insiders, and regulates the use of credit in connection with the purchase of securities. Recently, these compliance obligations were significantly enhanced as a result of the enactment of the Sarbanes-Oxley Act of 2002.

Section 12 of the Exchange Act requires companies to register a class of equity securities with the SEC if the class is listed for trading on a national securities exchange or if the company has more than 500 shareholders of record and total assets exceeding $10 million as of the end of the company's fiscal year. In addition, a company may voluntarily register a class of its equity securities under Section 12.

Under Section 13(a) of the Exchange Act, any company that has registered a class of equity securities under Section 12 must file periodic reports with the SEC. These reports include the quarterly report on Form 10-Q, the annual report on Form 10-K, and the current report on Form 8-K, which is used to disclose certain major nonrecurring events (such as a change in control of the company or a significant acquisition or other corporate transaction).

In addition, the company is subject to the proxy rules of Section 14 of the Exchange Act, and the officers, directors, and principal shareholders of the company must file reports and conduct their trading activities in conformity with the requirements of Section 16 of the Exchange Act.

Even where a company has not registered a class of equity securities under Section 12 of the Exchange Act, Section 15(d) of the Exchange Act requires companies with an effective registration statement under the Securities Act that are not otherwise subject to the registration requirements of Section 12 of the Exchange Act to comply with the reporting requirement of Section 13(a) of the Exchange Act until such time as they have less than 300 shareholders of record at the beginning of any subsequent fiscal year.

Some of the primary compliance requirements that affect administration of the company's stock option plan include the following:

Section 16

Assuming the company has registered a class of its equity securities with the SEC under Section 12 of the Exchange Act in connection with its IPO, the officers and directors of the company will be subject to Section 16 following the offering. Section 16 governs the reporting obligations and regulates the trading activities of the directors, officers, and principal shareholders of public reporting companies in the equity securities of their own companies. Specifically, directors and officers of a company that has a class of equity securities registered under the Exchange Act and beneficial owners of more than 10% of the class of equity securities so registered (often called "corporate insiders") must disclose their holdings of, and transactions involving, the equity securities of their company, and further must return to the company any profits that they realize in the event of any "short-swing" trading in such securities.

Section 16 Reporting   Under Section 16(a), a corporate insider must file reports with the SEC (which reports are available to the public) disclosing their holdings of, and transactions involving, the equity securities of the insider's company. This reporting is required for any equity securities that the corporate insider beneficially owns. Typically, the stock plan administrator, or other designated individual, will be responsible for assisting the company's officers and directors in complying with their filing obligations. Under the Sarbanes-Oxley Act of 2002, all Section 16(a) reports will need to be filed with the SEC electronically by the summer of 2003.

The filing of Form 3 is discussed above. Following a company's registration of a class of equity securities under Section 12 of the Exchange Act, each time an individual joins the company as an officer or director, or is promoted to officer or director status, a Form 3 must be filed with the SEC by the new corporate insider.

With limited exceptions, a Form 4, the current statement of changes in beneficial ownership, must be filed with the SEC within two business days after the date of execution of a transaction that results in a change in the corporate insider's beneficial ownership of the company's equity securities that is not otherwise eligible for deferred reporting under a specific SEC rule. In other words, a Form 4 must be filed within two business days whenever there is an acquisition or disposition of equity securities by a corporate insider (such as an open-market purchase or sale), including any exercise or conversion of a derivative security, such as an employee stock option. Under the Section 16 rules, any transaction that may be reported on a deferred basis on Form 5 may be reported on an earlier filed Form 4.

Generally, a Form 5, the annual statement of changes in beneficial ownership, must be filed with the SEC within 45 days after the end of the company's fiscal year to report any change in the corporate insider's beneficial ownership of the company's equity securities that is otherwise eligible for deferred reporting. In other words, a Form 5 must be filed whenever there is an acquisition or disposition of equity securities by a corporate insider (such as a bona fide gift) that is eligible for deferred reporting and that has not been previously reported on Form 4.

Special "Look-Back" Rule   Before an IPO, a closely held company may grant stock options and otherwise issue shares of stock to its officers and directors. In addition, such individuals may have other transactions involving the company's equity securities during the pre-IPO period.

To discourage officers and directors of pre-public reporting companies from using their knowledge of the impending offering for their own economic advantage, Exchange Act Rule 16a-2 provides that purchase and sales of the company's equity securities during the six-month period preceding the IPO are subject to Section 16 if carried out by officers or directors who become subject to Section 16 solely as a result of the IPO.

This means that any pre-IPO purchase or sale must be disclosed if it occurs within six months of any Form 4 reportable transaction taking place after the IPO. Likewise, such pre-IPO transactions can be matched for purposes of the Section 16(b) "short-swing profits" recovery provision with any IPO sale of securities or any post-IPO transaction that takes place within a six-month period. Consequently, it is important for the stock plan administrator to ensure that any pre-IPO stock option grants or other awards of stock under an employee stock plan comply with the applicable conditions of the Exchange Act Rule 16b-3 exemption (as discussed below).

Section 16 "Short-Swing Profits" Liability   Under Section 16(b), a company that has registered a class of equity securities under Section 12 of the Exchange Act may recover from a corporate insider any profits that are realized as a result of the purchase and sale, or sale and purchase, of the company's equity securities within a period of less than six months. Section 16(b) imposes strict liability on a corporate insider who meets the required elements of the provision. In other words, disgorgement of any profits realized from the "short-swing" transactions is required whether or not the corporate insider actually used material, nonpublic information to conduct the trades. Moreover, Section 16(b) may operate to require that the corporate insider forfeit "short-swing profits" to the company even where the insider has, in fact, realized no economic gain from the transactions.

For purposes of Section 16(b), the terms "purchase" and "sale" are interpreted broadly and may include acquisitions and dispositions involving derivative securities as well as acquisitions and dispositions arising in connection with a merger or other corporate transaction. Certain types of transactions, however, such as a bona fide gift, are exempt from "purchase" or "sale" status by virtue of a specific SEC rule and thus are outside the scope of Section 16(b). In addition, under the broad definition of "beneficial ownership," transactions by other persons can be attributed to a corporate insider for purposes of Section 16(b). For example, in certain situations, the equity securities of a Section 12 company held by relatives of a corporate insider will be deemed to be beneficially owned by the insider. Thus, a purchase or sale of the securities by a member of an insider's immediate family may be matched with a sale or purchase by the insider that occurs within the same six-month period to trigger "short-swing profits" recovery.

Where "short-swing" trading has occurred, the amount of "profits" recoverable by the Section 12 company is to be determined by pairing the corporate insider's transactions within the six-month period so as to match the transaction with the highest sale price and the transaction with the lowest purchase price. It does not matter whether the purchase or the sale occurred first, and it is not necessary for the same securities to have been involved in each of the matched transactions. The sum of the "profits" from these matched purchases and sales is the amount that the corporate insider must turn over to the company. As previously noted, because gains are not offset by losses, it is possible for a corporate insider to realize "profits" for purposes of Section 16(b) even though the insider actually lost money from the trading activities.

Typically, the stock plan administrator will assist the company's officers and directors in avoiding the operation of Section 16(b) when planning and executing their transactions involving the company's equity securities. In addition, the stock plan administrator should ensure that transactions involving the company's employee stock plans satisfy an appropriate exemptive condition of Exchange Act Rule 16b-3 so as to ensure that such transactions are not considered to involve either a "purchase" or a "sale" for purposes of Section 16(b). Under Rule 16b-3, a transaction between a company (including an employee benefit plan sponsored by the company) and its officers and directors is exempt from the "short-swing profits" recovery provisions of Section 16(b) if it satisfies the applicable conditions of the exemption.

Typically, routine, non-volitional transactions pursuant to a "tax-conditioned plan" (which generally encompasses most Section 401(k) plans, tax-qualified profit-sharing plans, and Section 423 employee stock purchase plans) are exempt from the operation of Section 16(b) without having to satisfy any specific conditions. Fund-switching transactions or volitional cash withdrawals from an employer securities fund in an employee benefit plan will be exempt if the election to engage in the transaction is at least six months after the last election to engage in an "opposite way" (purchase vs. sale) transaction under any company plan.

Other acquisitions of a company's equity securities by an officer or director from his or her company, including grants of stock options, are exempt from the operation of Section 16(b) if the transaction is approved by the company's board of directors, approved by a committee of two or more non-employee directors, approved or ratified by the company's shareholders, or a six-month holding period requirement is satisfied. While these conditions make it much easier to qualify the grant or award of a company's equity securities, including the stock option grant, for exemptive treatment, the stock plan administrator must make sure that the required approval has been obtained for each grant or award to a corporate insider.

Proxy Statement Disclosure A public reporting company is required to disclose in its annual proxy statement and annual report on Form 10-K under the caption "Section 16(a) Beneficial Ownership Reporting Compliance" a list of any corporate insiders who have been delinquent in filing or failed to file the required Section 16(a) reports with the SEC during the last completed fiscal year. This disclosure is to include (1) the name of the corporate insider who failed to file reports on a timely basis during the fiscal year, (2) the number of late reports by the insider, (3) the number of transactions not reported on a timely basis, and (4) any known failures to file a required report.

This disclosure is based solely on the information contained in the reports furnished to the company during the fiscal year and any written representations delivered to the company by corporate insiders stating that no Form 5 was required. For these purposes, the company is permitted to presume that any report received from a corporate insider within three calendar days of the required filing date was timely filed with the SEC. The company may also rely on any written representation from a corporate insider that no Form 5 was required if the company maintains a file of such representations for two years and makes copies available to the SEC upon request.

Equity Compensation Disclosure

A company is required to disclose in tabular form each year in its annual report on Form 10-K, and in its proxy statement in years in which the company is submitting a compensation plan for shareholder approval, certain information about the number of securities to be issued upon the exercise of outstanding stock options, the weighted-average exercise price of outstanding stock options, and the number of securities remaining available for future issuance under all of the company's equity compensation plans. This disclosure is to be made on an aggregated basis in two categories: plans that have been approved by shareholders, and plans that have not been approved by shareholders. Individual equity compensation arrangements, such as individual stock options that have been granted outside a formal plan, and equity compensation plans that have been assumed in a merger, consolidation, or other acquisition transaction may be aggregated in the appropriate category with the company's plan disclosure.

In addition, where a company has one or more equity compensation plans that have not been approved by shareholders, the company must disclose the material features of each non-shareholder-approved plan and attach a copy of the plan as an exhibit to the Form 10-K, unless the plan is immaterial in amount or significance.

Form S-8 Registration

Following the IPO, the company will need to ensure that the securities issued to employees under the company's employee stock option plans satisfy the requirements of federal and state securities laws. Generally, securities cannot be issued under an employee stock option plan unless a registration statement is in effect or an exemption from registration is available.

Form S-8 is a simplified registration statement that may be used by a company that is subject to the reporting requirements of the Exchange Act to register the securities to be offered and sold pursuant to the company's employee stock option plan. The registration statement reflects an abbreviated disclosure format and incorporates by reference information contained in the company's other publicly available documents.

Unlike other registration statements, the preparation and distribution of a formal prospectus is not required. Instead, the company need only deliver to employees certain required information about the employee stock option plan and a statement of the documents that are available upon request to participants. This information can be provided separately or integrated into the company's customary employee communications. The information must be identified as comprising part of the Form S-8 "prospectus," which is accomplished by including a specific legend at the beginning of each document that contains the required plan information.

A company may use a registration statement on Form S-8 at any time after becoming subject to the reporting requirements of the Exchange Act. In addition, Form S-8 becomes effective immediately upon filing with the SEC.

Form S-8 covers offers and sales of securities under an employee stock option plan to consultants and advisors, as well as to employees, officers, and directors. Transactions by former employees are also covered in certain instances. Form S-8 applies to transactions pursuant to individual written compensatory contracts, as well as actual employee stock plans.

Option shares acquired under a Form S-8 registration statement may be resold by non-affiliates without restriction. Affiliates may sell their Form S-8-registered option shares pursuant to Securities Act Rule 144 (but without regard to the holding period condition).

Section 162(m)

Under Code Section 162, a company is entitled to deduct from gross income all ordinary and necessary expenses paid or incurred during a taxable year in connection with carrying on a trade or business. The expenses contemplated by this provision include a reasonable allowance for salaries or other compensation for personal services actually rendered. Thus, amounts expended by a company to compensate its employees, including equity compensation, are deductible as long as the amounts are "reasonable."

Code Section 162(m) contains a limitation on the deductibility of certain executive compensation. Section 162(m) limits the ability of publicly held corporations to deduct from their corporate income taxes compensation in excess of $1 million paid to certain executive officers. While the limit is clearly aimed at limiting the deductibility of cash compensation, such as salary and bonus, it is also potentially applicable to compensation income realized in connection with the receipt of stock under an employee stock plan. For example, the limit would apply in the case of compensation income realized upon the exercise of a nonqualified stock option, upon the disqualifying disposition of shares of stock acquired upon the exercise of an incentive stock option, and upon the vesting of restricted stock.

The deduction limit of Section 162(m) applies only to "publicly held corporations." For these purposes, a corporation is considered to be "publicly held" if a class of its common equity securities is required to be registered under Section 12 of the Exchange Act as of the last day of the company's taxable year. Thus, companies that voluntarily register under Section 12 are not subject to Section 162(m).

The deduction limit of Section 162(m) applies only to the compensation paid to specific "covered employees." These are (1) the chief executive officer of the company (or the individual acting in that capacity) on the last day of the taxable year, and (2) the four most highly compensated officers of the company (other than the chief executive officer) whose compensation is required to be reported to shareholders under the executive compensation disclosure rules of the Exchange Act.

Whether an individual is a "covered employee" is determined under the executive compensation disclosure rules found in the Exchange Act. In other words, the determination is based on who is covered in the Summary Compensation Table of the company's proxy statement. The "covered employee" definition does not incorporate the 1993 amendment to the executive compensation disclosure rules, which extended disclosure to certain former executive officers. Thus, the deduction limit does not apply to a CEO who leaves the company before the end of the taxable year, nor to an officer who would be among the four most highly compensated officers for the year but for the fact that he or she was not with the company at year-end.

For purposes of the deduction limit, "applicable employee remuneration" with respect to any covered employee includes all otherwise deductible remuneration for services performed by the employee (whether or not such services were performed during the taxable year). Thus, covered compensation can include the compensation income recognized upon the exercise of a nonqualified stock option, the disqualifying disposition of an incentive stock option, or the vesting of restricted stock, even if the option or restricted stock was granted in a prior year.

Certain types of compensation are expressly excluded from the deduction limit of Section 162(m) and thus need not be taken into account in determining whether an employee's total compensation for the year exceeds the $1 million threshold. These include (1) compensation payable solely on a commission basis; (2) certain "fringe" benefits that are not included in the employee's gross income; (3) payments made to or from certain tax-qualified retirement plans; (4) compensation payable under any written binding contract that was in effect on February 17, 1993 (and which has not been subsequently modified in any material respect); and (5) "performance-based" compensation.

Performance-Based Compensation   Certain performance-based compensation is excluded from the deduction limit of Section 162(m) if several conditions are satisfied. To be considered "performance-based," (1) the compensation must be payable solely upon the attainment of one or more performance goals that are determined by a compensation committee of the board of directors comprised solely of two or more "outside" directors; (2) the material terms of the plan or arrangement under which the compensation is to be paid, including the performance goals, must be disclosed to shareholders and approved by a majority of the vote in a separate shareholder vote before the payment of the compensation; and (3) before the payment of the compensation, the compensation committee must certify that the performance goals and any other material terms of the arrangement were in fact satisfied.

Transition for Closely Held Companies   Unless a company has been publicly held for the entire taxable year, the deduction limit of Section 162(m) does not apply to any compensation plan or agreement that was in effect while the company was closely held, as long as the plans and agreements are adequately disclosed at the time of the company's IPO and are not thereafter materially modified. In other words, the deduction limit would not apply to stock options granted under stock option plans that are in existence when a company becomes publicly held, provided that such plans are disclosed as part of the prospectus accompanying the company's IPO.

This exception may be relied upon until the earliest to occur of (1) the expiration or material modification of the plan or agreement, (2) the issuance of all the securities or other compensation that has been allocated under the plan, or (3) the first meeting of shareholders at which the directors are to be elected that occurs after the close of the third calendar year following the calendar year in which the IPO took place. Thus, corporations can rely on the exemption for any compensation received as the result of the exercise of a stock option or the vesting (or receipt) of restricted stock if the grant or award (rather than the exercise or vesting) occurs before the end of the reliance period.

Insider Trading

Under the federal securities laws, any person, including a corporate insider, possessing "material" nonpublic information about a company must refrain from engaging in transactions in the company's securities until adequate public disclosure of this information has been made. The penalties for trading in securities while in the possession of material nonpublic information are severe and include injunctive actions or actions for civil penalties that may be brought by the SEC, actions for monetary damages that may be brought by private parties, and criminal penalties. The federal securities laws also prohibit persons, including corporate insiders, from "tipping" third parties, either by disclosing confidential information to such persons or by making trading recommendations based on such information.

Of the various antifraud provisions found in the federal securities laws, Section 10(b) of the Exchange Act has enjoyed the broadest application. Generally, Section 10(b) makes it unlawful for any person, directly or indirectly, to use or employ, in connection with the purchase or sale of a security (whether or not registered on an exchange), "any manipulative or deceptive device or contrivance" which contravenes such rules and regulations as the SEC may adopt.

Pursuant to this authority, the SEC has adopted Exchange Act Rule 10b-5, which states that it is unlawful for any person, directly or indirectly, to employ any "device, scheme or artifice to defraud," to make any untrue statement of a material fact, to omit to state a material fact necessary to make statements not misleading, or to engage in any "act, practice or course of business which operates" as a fraud or deceit upon any person.

One of the primary uses of Exchange Act Rule 10b-5 over the years has been to prohibit trading in securities by persons having knowledge of material, undisclosed information, thereby promoting full and fair disclosure of material information to all investors. This prohibition on "insider trading" is applied broadly by the courts and covers not only directors, officers, and principal shareholders of the company, but essentially anyone who comes into possession of confidential information and has a duty to disclose (or to abstain from trading), including an insider's spouse and immediate family members. The prohibition covers trading in the equity, debt, and derivative securities of the company.

"Material" Information   While there is no specific definition of what constitutes material information for purposes of the insider trading prohibitions, at least two standards are commonly applied to determine the "materiality" of specific information. First, if the information would be expected to significantly affect the market price of the company's stock, then it is probably material. Alternatively, if the information would influence or affect the investment decisions of a reasonable investor, then, once again, it is probably material. Typical examples of "material" information might include a company's quarterly and annual financial results (or components thereof); major proposed or pending transactions; changes in a company's capital structure; research and development projects or plans; pricing, sales, or market plans or projections; management or other key personnel changes; and litigation developments.

Nonpublic Information   Generally, information is considered to be "nonpublic" until it has been disseminated throughout the securities markets. As construed by the courts, this means that the information must have first been distributed through the media of widest circulation. Typically, this is accomplished by disclosure of the information in one or more of the company's periodic reports or filings under the federal securities laws or through the issuance of a press release.

The prohibitions against insider trading not only restrict a person from making use of the confidential information but also prohibit "tipping," or passing the information on to another person who then trades on the basis of the information (where the person could have reasonably foreseen that the recipient would make use of the information).

Trading Policies   Because of the difficulties associated with determining the materiality of undisclosed information, many companies maintain internal trading policies to prevent inadvertent violations of the insider trading prohibitions. A typical trading policy will restrict transactions in the company's stock to certain designated periods following the release of quarterly financial information about the company. These trading periods are commonly referred to as "window periods." In addition, the company may designate an employee, usually a member of management, to act as a compliance officer. In this capacity, the compliance officer must clear in advance any trade in the company's stock by an employee subject to the policy.

At a minimum, corporate trading policies will be applied to its directors, officers, and other corporate insiders. Some companies extend the policy to several additional levels of employees, while others apply the policy to all employees. Even where a company limits its trading policy to corporate insiders, most companies take steps to ensure that, at a minimum, all employees are aware of their obligations under the federal securities laws.

Exchange Act Rule 10b5-1   Under Exchange Act Rule 10b5-1, for purposes of Section 10(b) of the Exchange Act, an individual will be considered to have traded "on the basis of" material non-public information if he or she was aware of the information at the time he or she made the subject purchase or sale of securities. The rule goes on, however, to provide an affirmative defense to this "awareness" standard for determining insider trading liability. If an individual has (1) entered into a binding contract, provided instructions to another person, or adopted a written trading plan before becoming aware of the material, nonpublic information, (2) the binding contract, instructions, or written plan expressly provides (by amount of formula) the amount, price, and date of the transaction, and (3) demonstrated the transaction in question was pursuant to the binding contract, instructions, or written plan, then the binding contract, instructions, or written plan will act as an affirmative defense to a claim of insider trading.

Because a written program for trading securities may cover any securities owned by an individual, many officers and directors of public reporting companies have taken to adopting written trading plans as a means for implementing liquidity strategies for their employee stock options. Unlike a trading "window" instituted to ensure compliance with Exchange Act Rule 10b-5, a trading plan does not permit any discretion on the part of the individual adopting the plan. It does, however, permit trading at any time, as long as the criteria for trading were established at a previous time when the individual was not aware of any material, nonpublic information about the company. If a trading plan involves the disposition of "restricted securities" for purposes of Securities Act Rule 144, the parties must ensure compliance with the resale conditions of that rule.

Insider Trading Prohibition During Pension Fund Blackouts Section 306(a) of the Sarbanes-Oxley Act of 2002 prohibits the directors and executive officers of public reporting companies from, directly or indirectly, purchasing, selling, or otherwise acquiring or transferring any equity security of the company during a pension plan blackout period that prevents plan participants or beneficiaries from engaging in equity security transactions, if the equity security was acquired in connection with the director or executive officer's service or employment as a director or executive officer. In addition, the company must provide timely notice to its directors and executive officers, as well as to the SEC, of an impending blackout period.

The SEC has adopted rules that clarify the application of this insider trading prohibition, including rules that define when an equity security is acquired "in connection with" service of employment as a director or executive officer. Generally, these rules provide that equity securities, including stock options, acquired under an equity compensation plan maintained by the company are to be considered acquired in connection with service or employment. Accordingly, companies will need to assist their directors and executive officers in identifying the equity securities that are subject to the trading prohibition and in monitoring any pension plan blackout periods to avoid violations of the prohibition.

Where a director or executive officer engages in a prohibited transaction, he or she is subject to possible enforcement action by the SEC. In addition, the company may recover from the director or executive officer any profits that are realized as a result of the purchase, sale, acquisition or transfer that occurred during the blackout period. Similar to Section 16(b) of the Exchange Act, Section 306(a) of the Sarbanes-Oxley Act imposes strict liability on a director or executive officer who violates the trading prohibition. In other words, disgorgement of any profits realized from the prohibited transaction is required whether or not the director or executive officer intended to trade in violation of the statutory provision.

Other Insider Trading Restrictions Over the past 15 years, the existing body of insider trading law has been supplemented by a number of statutory provisions. The adoption of these provisions has been frequently cited as a significant influence in the development of insider trading policies and other internal controls by many publicly held companies. In the mid-1980s, the Insider Trading Sanctions Act of 1984 was enacted by Congress. Among other things, the Act authorized the SEC to seek civil penalties of up to three times the profit gained or the loss avoided where a person purchased or sold securities while in possession of material nonpublic information.

In 1988, Congress enacted the Insider Trading and Securities Fraud Enforcement Act, which added Section 21A to the Exchange Act. Among other things, Section 21A authorizes the SEC to seek civil penalties against employers and other controlling persons who "knew or recklessly disregarded" the fact that a controlled person was likely to engage in insider trading and failed to take appropriate steps to prevent such act before it occurred. While the Exchange Act does not define what constitutes appropriate steps, most companies have concluded it is necessary to communicate regularly with all employees, especially those most likely to have access to confidential information, about their responsibilities under the federal securities laws and to establish some control over trading by directors and officers.

Section 21A retained the civil remedy established by the Insider Trading Sanctions Act against primary traders. In addition, it authorizes the imposition of a penalty against controlling persons of the greater of $1 million or three times the profit gained or loss avoided as a result of the controlled person's violation.

In 1990, the Securities Enforcement Remedies and Penny Stock Reform Act was enacted. The Act substantially increased the enforcement powers of the SEC for violations of the federal securities laws. Among the remedies available under the Act, the SEC has the authority to issue both permanent and temporary cease-and-desist orders to enforce the various federal securities laws, the power to seek in federal district court monetary penalties ranging from $5,000 to $500,000 for securities law violations, and the ability to seek to have individuals who have violated specific provisions of the federal securities laws barred from serving as a director or officer of a public reporting company.

Financial Statement Information

Stock Option Valuation   Following the IPO, the company will need to use the "fair value" method of accounting in order to comply with SFAS No. 123. While previously the "fair value" method was used primarily to meet a company's disclosure obligations under SFAS No. 123, today many companies are adopting SFAS No. 123 for purposes of calculating the expense associated with their stock option programs.

"Fair value" is to be determined using an option-pricing model, such as the Black-Scholes or a binomial model, that takes into account, as of the grant date, the option price and the expected life of the option, the current price of the underlying shares of stock and its expected volatility, expected dividends on the stock, and the risk-free interest rate for the expected option term. The determination of the required assumptions for input into the option-pricing model will be more challenging for the initial years following the offering. This will be the case for the expected option life and stock price volatility assumptions.

One potential problem in formulating the expected option life assumption can arise if there are differences in the terms and conditions of the stock options being valued and the stock options that will form the basis of the historical information to be analyzed to determine the assumption. Where the terms and conditions of the stock options being valued differ from those of the historical option grants (for example, different vesting schedules), the stock plan administrator will need to decide to what degree the historical data is relevant to determining the expected life of the stock options being valued. This issue may be of particular significance if the company has revised or updated the terms and conditions of its stock option plan in connection with the IPO.

In addition, the IPO will likely result in a large number of stock option exercises related to the offering. These transactions should be given less weight in the evaluation of the company's historical data for purposes of establishing the expected option life assumption because the economic conditions that influenced the exercise decisions are not likely to be duplicated in the near future.

With respect to the stock price volatility assumption, because the company will not have a trading history that is commensurate with the expected life of the stock options being valued, it will need to consider the historical volatility of similar companies following a comparable period in their lives. Consequently, the stock plan administrator will need to assist in selecting the group of companies to be compiled for this purpose.

Earnings per Share   Under current generally accepted accounting principles, an earnings-per-share computation must be presented by publicly held corporations. This information is used by investors to assess the profitability and the performance of the company from period to period and to compare the company to other businesses. Simply put, the earnings-per-share (EPS) computation involves spreading the company's earnings for the period being reported over the number of common equity securities outstanding during such period. For purposes of this computation, the company's shares of stock are weighted for the actual time that such shares were outstanding during the period.

The current requirements for calculating earnings per share are set forth in SFAS No. 128. The standard requires the presentation of both "basic" and "diluted" earnings per share. The basic earnings-per-share computation does not take into consideration the effects of dilution. It is calculated by dividing the total income available to common shareholders for the reporting period by the weighted average number of shares of common stock actually outstanding during that period, without factoring in any potentially issuable securities that could have a dilutive effect on the company's outstanding shares of stock, such as employee stock options. Shares of stock issued during the period and shares reacquired during the period are weighted for the portion of the period that they were outstanding.

The diluted earnings-per-share computation reflects the potential dilutive effect of outstanding stock options and other common stock equivalents by treating them as if they were exercised or converted into common stock that then shared in the total income of the company available to shareholders. The calculation of diluted earnings per share is similar to the calculation of basic earnings per share except that the denominator is increased to include the number of additional shares of common stock that would have been outstanding if the dilutive potential common shares had been issued. In addition, the calculation does not take into consideration the exercise of conversion of any securities that would have an antidilutive effect on earnings per share (that is, the exercise or conversion would result in an increase to earnings per share because the acquisition of the shares of stock would result in the payment to the company of more than the current value of the shares). Generally, the dilutive effect of options and warrants is to be reflected in the calculation through the application of the so-called "treasury stock" accounting method. Under this method, (1) the exercise of options and warrants is to be assumed at the beginning of the reporting period (unless actually exercised at a later time during the period) and shares of common stock are assumed to be issued, (2) the proceeds from the assumed exercise are further assumed to be used to repurchase outstanding shares of common stock at the average fair market value of the company's stock for the reporting period, and (3) the incremental shares of common stock (the difference between the number of shares assumed to be exercised and the number of shares assumed to be repurchased) are included in the denominator of the diluted earnings-per-share calculation.

Disgorgement of Bonuses and Profits Upon Financial Restatement Under Section 304 of the Sarbanes-Oxley Act of 2002, if a public reporting company is required to restate its financial statements because of the material noncompliance of the company, due to misconduct, with any financial reporting requirements, the company's chief executive officer and chief financial officer are required to return to the company any bonus or other equity or incentive based compensation, including stock options, received from the company during the one-year period preceding following the issuance of the original financial statements (that are now being restated) and any profits realized from any sale of the company's securities during the same one-year period. This provision became effective on July 30, 2002.

Conclusion

While the reasons for an IPO can be compelling, most companies underestimate the amount of work involved in getting ready to "go public." A fundamental understanding of the process and adequate advance preparation are essential to a successful offering. Because the company's stock option plan will likely be the primary source of equity for the company's employees before and after the IPO, it is important to understand both the impact the plan will have on the offering and the impact the offering will have on the plan. In addition, administering the stock option plan following an IPO can be very complex and challenging. The stock plan administrator must have a thorough familiarity with the applicable legal and other requirements to ensure a smooth transition from a closely held to a public reporting company.

CHAPTER

5

Stock Options and Divorce

Linda A. Olup

*W*HEN COUPLES DECIDE TO SPLIT, it is likely that their stock options will split too. Although the treatment of stock options varies by state, it is important to understand the critical issues and legal trends that could affect a property settlement and any child or spousal support orders.

Stock Options in Divorce

In contrast to the years before 1985, when compensation was largely contained in a base salary, executives and many other employees today are paid in part or even primarily with long- and short-term incentives such as stock options, and the base salary may be incidental.

A few divorce courts, most notably in California, began to examine stock options as part of compensation as early as the late 1960s and into the 1970s. A few more courts began their examination in the early 1980s. However, most courts did not adjust to this trend in compensating executives until the 1990s.

Different state courts have issued different rulings regarding whether to consider stock options as marital assets in the overall property distribution, and, if they *are* marital assets, how to dispose of them.

The law has evolved over the years, and now most courts consider stock options in the overall property distribution. A few courts have also examined long- and short-term incentives as income to be distributed for the purpose of child support or spousal maintenance (i.e., alimony).

This article discusses how options are treated in divorce proceedings. It does not address tax, accounting, or securities issues for such options.

Divorce Law Basics

If you work with a divorce lawyer, the process may go more smoothly if you have a basic understanding of the world of matrimonial law. Stock plan professionals and divorce attorneys speak different languages. For example, courts may use the term "matured" when referring to fully vested options, while a stock plan professional considers a "matured" stock option to be one that has expired. Likewise, if the terms "graded vesting" and "cliff vesting" are used in speaking with a divorce attorney, he or she will probably wonder why you have introduced mountain climbing into the conversation.

That said, there are four basic stages of every divorce: the preliminary stage, discovery, settlement, and finalization. In the preliminary stage, the parties file the pleadings that begin the divorce. They may also appear in court for temporary relief or an order *pendente lite,* which is an order that establishes some ground rules while the case is pending in the court. These interim orders typically address custody, child support, alimony ("spousal maintenance"), payment of existing and future debt, and temporary use of assets.

During the discovery stage, the parties seek information that will help them identify assets and debts and determine the facts for such issues as premarital assets, spousal maintenance, child support, and custody. This second stage is when questions regarding the nature and value of stock options will generally arise.

In the third stage, the parties try to use the information they have gathered to reach a settlement—usually a compromise agreement. As a general rule, 95% of cases settle, although not always quickly.

In the final stage, the parties either file their settlement agreement with the local court and have a divorce decree entered, or they go to trial. In a few states, a jury may hear part of the case.

Legal Analysis of Stock Options in Divorce

Divorce courts tend to use three stages of analysis in assessing the distribution of stock options:

1. Is the option "property" to be distributed in the division of assets (classification)?

2. What is the appropriate method for determining the value of the property (valuation)?

3. What is the appropriate distribution of the property between the parties (distribution)?

While there are discernible trends, each state has its own specific laws as well as cases that interpret those laws.

Certain terms used in a corporate environment to describe stock options are not of much value to a divorce court in characterizing the option as either community or marital property. The phrases "vested," "unvested," "restricted," and "unrestricted" are either corporate definitions or those used in the marketplace. These definitions, by themselves, do not greatly assist a court in deciding whether the options are assets of the marriage. Neither do these terms assist the courts in setting a value for the options. Many of these definitions are driven by the Internal Revenue Code and concern corporate taxes.

Classification

Whether a state is governed by principles of "community property" or "equitable distribution," there must be a preliminary determination of whether the disputed item is "property." Generally, state statutes do not provide a specific, inclusive list of what constitutes an asset. An example is the Colorado statute that defines marital property as "all property acquired by either spouse subsequent to the marriage" but does not further define "property."[1] This is unlike Indiana, which excludes unvested pension plans from consideration as property.[2] No statute or case establishes a rule that all contingent employee benefits can be considered assets of the marriage and distributed.

In the process of classification, there are generally two approaches available to divorce courts in determining whether an asset is property. One is the "mechanical approach," a concept used in workers' compensation cases. This approach provides that future benefits are marital property if the underlying claim occurred during the marriage. Under the mechanical approach, timing is everything. In a stock option case, if the grant of the options occurred during the marriage, the court would find it property of the marriage.

A second approach is the "analytic approach." Under this method, the nature of the claim, its component parts, and the character of the settlement are all analyzed to determine whether the award is marital property, separate property, or both. One court commented that its "analysis of case law from other jurisdictions indicates that this is the modern and prevailing rule on this issue."[3]

Vested Options

Many courts refer to vested options as having "matured." Some say the options are "exercisable" or "vested." Different courts use different terms. There is no uniform legal reference to stock options in divorce law. Courts generally have considered "matured options" a marital asset if granted during marriage.[4]

Vested options are the least troublesome for courts because they most resemble stock or other property. Courts have had little difficulty equitably dividing these options upon dissolution or divorce.

Unvested Options

While most courts have held that matured stock options obtained during marriage are assets divisible at divorce, it is less than clear how courts will handle stock options that are not vested. Courts have had their biggest challenge analyzing stock options that are not vested. There is no prevailing trend among a majority of the courts at this time.

Many divorce courts are reluctant to deprive the non-employee spouse of sharing the future benefit of a stock option that is not vested, especially when the option will vest within a short period after the divorce decree is entered.

In one Arizona case, a husband had been granted options that had not vested. The court held that the accumulated value of the husband's interest in the stock option plan was community property subject to the court's equitable division power.[5]

In a California case involving the division of the community interest in the husband's retirement benefits, which included a contingent stock plan, a California appellate court held that although the plan had not vested, it was a community asset. The court reasoned that a right to future employment benefits is a contractual right and therefore a form of property. It was not a mere expectancy, regardless of whether it was contingent.[6]

Another example illustrating the difficulties the courts have in classifying options is found in a Maryland case in which the Court of Appeals overturned the lower court decision and held that fully vested but unexercised stock options acquired during marriage are marital assets, and their value is subject to equitable division at divorce.[7] In this case, the employee-spouse was granted irrevocable, nontransferable stock options, exercisable only by the employee-spouse or his estate. If the employee-spouse was terminated, all options expired 90 days after termination. By the time the marriage had dissolved, the employee-spouse had purchased 15,000 shares under two distinct stock option plans. Another 2,500 shares were exercisable at the time of the divorce proceedings, and another 2,500 after the divorce was final.

The trial court held that because the latter options had not been exercised before separation or dissolution, the stock was not yet acquired and could not be marital property. Due to the time restrictions under the stock option plans, the court found that the unexercised options had no "fair market value." Absent a value, the trial court concluded the unexercised options could not be considered marital property.

The Court of Appeals disagreed with the trial court, holding that even though these options had no fair market value, they were an economic resource and could be treated like pensions and other employee benefits for which a value could be determined. The court supported its rationale by citing a New Jersey case, *Kruger v. Kruger*, which held the right to receive future compensation was an economic resource.[8]

Some courts have held that employee stock options accruing at some future date are not marital or community property subject to division.[9] A Louisiana court found that unvested stock options were marital property because the options were granted for performance that occurred during the marriage.[10] The fact that the option may have also been given as an incentive for future effort did not remove it from the community. In cases that have similar determinations, the actual date of the stock option grant is not the determinative factor. Rather, the determinative factor is whether work performed during the existence of the community (or marriage) was taken into consideration in granting the option. Along similar lines, a New Jersey appellate court held that unvested options awarded to the wife *after* she filed for divorce were marital property because the options were in recognition of her efforts expended during the marriage.[11]

In a 1994 Colorado case, the husband received stock options that vested over a period of time in equal amounts. The Court of Appeals held that the vesting was a contingency that distinguished the compensation earned during the marriage (i.e., property subject to division) from that earned after the marriage ended (i.e., property not subject to division).[12]

Decisions by the highest courts in Pennsylvania and in Massachusetts in 2001 held that unvested options are part of the marital assets, to be divided when the options are ultimately exercised.[13]

Time Rule Formula

To address unvested options and determine what, if any, portion of the unvested stock options are divisible marital property, a legal fiction known as the "time rule formula" was devised. There are variations, but the formula is designed to calculate the marital interest in unvested options so that the "marital interest" can be divided by the court.

In the case *In re Marriage of Hug*, a California Court of Appeal created the concept of a "time rule formula."[14] The decision is considered a landmark case and continues to be widely examined in states that have not yet adopted a rule of law on the treatment of stock options. The court developed the concept of a "time rule formula" because it believed the determination as to whether unvested stock options were community assets "can be complicated."

There are two different versions of the "time rule formula."[15] While the genesis of the first version was in California, the second originated in the state of Washington.

The California "time rule formula" provides that the marital or community interest in the stock options is a fraction with the number of months on the job from the start date of employment to the date of separation (in some states this point would be the date of divorce, the date of the first pretrial, or another date) over the number of months on the job from the start date of employment to the date when the options could first be exercised, multiplied by the number of shares that could be purchased on the date of exercise.

The Washington state "time rule formula" for unvested options provides a fraction wherein the number of days of the marriage during the year in which the option vests is the numerator and the number of days in the year is the denominator. The fraction is then converted into a percentage, which represents the community/marital interest in the option. Such treatment allows the court to find that a marriage may have an interest in unvested options that will not vest until after the parties' divorce.

The "time rule formula" effectively provides a non-employee spouse with a limited interest in options that are unvested during the period before divorce. The theory is that the options are reflective of the extent of the community/marital effort in earning the right to receive the benefits, and thus the non-employee spouse should retain some interest in the unvested option.

Valuation

Because stock options cannot be sold on the open market by the employee-spouse, the courts are faced with a dilemma: what is the option worth?

The spouse to whom the options were issued typically claims the option, especially if it is not vested, has no value. The following arguments are advanced:

1. The vesting contingencies are such that the "contingent resource" amounts to a "mere expectancy." Thus it cannot be considered an asset with value.

2. No mathematical calculation can be performed to accurately value "contingent resources," and therefore "its value cannot not be ascertained with certainty."

3. Unvested options are not assets of the marriage because they are earned by continued future employment, not past performance.

4. Because the options can usually be terminated by the employer or by the employee leaving the company, the benefits do not really exist. The supplemental argument is that the employee spouse could be hired away by another corporation, be terminated, or retire before the options could be exercised.

The courts tend to view the value to the employee of the stock option as being the "intrinsic" price. The "intrinsic" price is often considered the current market price of the stock less the strike price, multiplied by the number of shares of stock in the options that have been issued.

Under modern marital property law, regardless of whether a state is a community property or equitable property state, most courts are required by statute to divide assets based on a broad mandate of fairness and equity. Thus, unless the law requires an equal division of property acquired before separation, marital property is not necessarily divided in equal shares.

However, unless the court employs a "time rule formula," it must ascertain the value of the options before their value can be divided. Many courts have failed to provide adequate guidance in explaining how the value of stock options should be assessed. Many decisions are silent on how the options were valued.

The method by which judges determine the value of an option is not precise. In one New Jersey case, the court determined the value of the option from the stock price but failed to provide specific guidance as to the date it used as the basis for the valuation.[16]

In one Montana case, the court calculated the value of the stock option as the difference between the cost of an option under the agreement and the market price of the stock.[17]

An Arizona court held, for the purpose of equitable division of the community assets, that the total value of the option is to be calculated as of the date of the divorce decree, without consideration of any impairment in value resulting from the contingencies specified in the option plan.[18]

In Arkansas, the Supreme Court held the value of vested but unexercised stock options was the difference between the cost of exercising the options and the price of the stock on the date of trial.[19]

Courts take a variety of approaches when the market value of a stock contained in the option is incalculable. For example, one court appears to have suggested that the absence of evidence of value means no marital property right exists. In that case, the husband had acquired an option to buy all of the shares of stock in a closely held corporation he was managing. Without exercising the option, he transferred it to the corporation for zero consideration. The corporation exercised the option by repurchasing the company stock. At dissolution, the trial court did not include the option as community property. On appeal, the wife argued that the option should have been included and contended the value of the option was equal to the price paid by the corporation. The Court of Appeals found that the community had paid nothing for the option and held that whatever its value was, the community lost any rights when the option was transferred to the corporation.[20]

The Illinois Court of Appeals held it was improper to take judicial notice of the price at which the stock was traded on a specific date to determine its value. The appellate court, reasoning that an award of an interest in future benefits derived from a spouse's employment was prohibited under Illinois marriage dissolution laws, found that the trial court had acted improperly in taking judicial notice of the trading value of the stock. The Court of Appeals also held the trial court erred in apportioning to the optioned spouse all rights and interest to the stock option at a specific value. The appellate court remanded the matter to the trial court to retain jurisdiction until the options were exercised.[21]

Formulas like Black-Scholes may provide some assistance to the courts, but no court has definitively declared such a formula to be a preferred method of valuing stock options.

An Ohio court summarized the real value of a stock option when it noted that "the true value of the stock option to its owner is the potential for appreciation in stock price without investment risk. If the stock price were to drop, the owner of the option simply would not exercise it, because he could instead buy the stock more cheaply on the market. As stated by Treas. Reg. 1.83-7(b)(3), the value of this type of stock option is risk-free appreciation."[22] "In fact, the only risk to the owner of a stock option is the risk of a potential 'lost opportunity cost'—in other words, the option may peak at a higher spread between the option price and the market price before the owner actually exercises the option, thereby giving the owner a smaller than optimal net gain. However, there is never a risk of loss because the lowest value an option can have is zero."[23]

The process of valuation varies widely and needs to be examined closely when addressed.

Recent events regarding Enron, Global Crossing, and other similarly situated companies do not affect the legal process of classification or division. The issue of valuation is affected if the state in which the options are being addressed endeavors to value the stock at the time of trial.

A concern to divorce lawyers is that companies will be able to redeem options that are "underwater" in exchange for other options that reflect the current and future economic health of their company through repricing the options or devising other, less controversial, means of keeping the compensation intended by the option available to the employee. This issue adds another layer of difficulty to the process of classification and valuation for the divorce attorney representing the non-employee spouse. The issue is how the attorney for the non-employee spouse connects the redeemed or worthless options to the newly issued options, or other compensation, in order to obtain an appropriate share for the client.

Division

States are either equitable property or community property states. The division of assets in community property states is usually based on the date of separation. In equitable property states, the division of marital assets may be based on a point at any time between the time of filing for the dissolution and the time of trial.

Stock options that the court deems to be property are generally not transferable, although some companies are permitting the transfer of options, with the non-employee spouse being subject to the same conditions as the employee spouse.

The court may direct the optioned spouse to exercise the option and transfer the shares derived from the exercise, but the option itself is not something the court can award to the non-optioned spouse unless the company that issued the options permits the transfer. This does not mean that a judge will not elect to do so if he or she is unaware of the restrictions on transferability.

There are several approaches to the division of stock options. Some courts divide the value of the option "if and when" the option is exercised. Other courts place a value on the option during the divorce process and allocate the determined value as part of the marital estate. Yet other courts hold that the parties have a joint interest in the options and that the employee spouse is in essence a trustee of the non-employee's interest in the option. Again, there is no single method that is universally adopted by all states.

In addressing the division of options, a California court held that although an accrued stock option constituted community property to be weighed when making a division of all community assets, it was not necessarily subject to direct division.[24] California law only required that the value each spouse received be equal and that each asset be divided in kind.

Similarly, a Maryland court held that the value of matured and accrued but unexercised stock options obtained during marriage was subject to equitable distribution at divorce, implying direct division was not necessary or required.[25]

A number of courts have held that even if stock options are to be included in the marital estate, distribution of the parties' interest in the options at dissolution will be effected only "if, as, and when" the options are exercised. A few cases have discussed, in very specific terms, the form of distribution of the interest "if, as, and when" the options are exercised. In at least two instances, the court divided the profits from the sale of the exercised stock options based on the proportional terms set out in the decree.[26]

In other cases, courts have indicated that stocks acquired by exercising the option will be distributed in the form of shares.[27]

A number of courts have held that until the options are exercisable and if severance is unfeasible, the parties shall be deemed "tenants in common" in future vesting of the stock option interests of the community.[28]

Other courts have chosen to impose a constructive trust that effected distribution when options were exercised under the established option agreement.[29]

Stock Options As Income

Before 1999 it was generally accepted that stock options were assets, with classification (marital or nonmarital) and value to be determined by the court. Stock options awarded to one spouse became the separate property of that spouse. As such, any profit derived from their sale was considered that spouse's separate property.[30]

However, recently there has been some movement to consider stock options as income for the purpose of awarding child support and spousal maintenance. Stock options granted after the divorce or options classified as marital assets during the divorce are viewed by attorneys as fair game for consideration.

Statistically, there has been a dramatic change in the composition of executive compensation. Articles published in magazines and newspapers note that corporations see stock options as a method of providing additional compensation to employees without incurring an additional capital expense. Small companies see the opportunity to compete with larger companies for the pool of available talent by granting stock options to hire employees. Retaining employees and providing the incentive to perform have long been recognized as the basis for stock option grants. This change renders options an important part of the compensation offered to prospective employees. Thus, the question of options as income is a legitimate one for support issues.

In 1999, an Ohio court found that the stock option package of the husband, an executive with Proctor & Gamble, was the "single most important element" of his compensation package. The court determined that the options were recurring and regular to the extent that the employee could "expect to receive the executive stock options so long as he continued to work." The options were fully vested although not all exercised.[31]

The facts of this case and the definition of gross income under Ohio matrimonial law allowed the court to find that the options were income to be considered by the court in awarding child support. While this case has not yet been widely adopted, it will eventually find a voice in factually similar cases in different states. It is simply a matter of time.

Notes

1. *In re Marriage of Miller*, 915 P.2d 1314, 1316 (Colo. 1996).
2. *Hann v. Hann*, 655 N.E.2d 566 (Ind. Ct. App. 1995).
3. *Lowery v. Lowery*, 23 Fam. L. Rptr. 1163, 1164 (1997) (Md. Ct. Spec. App., January 30, 1997, Harrell, J.).
4. See *Cooper v. Cooper*, 269 Cal. App. 2d 6, 74 Cal. Rptr 439 (1969), *Richardson v. Richardson*, 280 Ark 498, 659 S.W.2d 510 (1983), *Demler v. Demler*, 836 S.W.2d 696 (Tex. App. 1992), and *In re Marriage of Renier*, 854 P.2d 1382 (Colo. App. 1993).

5. *Warren v. Warren*, 2 Ariz. App. 206, 407 P.2d 395 (1965).

6. *In re Marriage of Judd*, 68 Cal. App. 3d 515, 137 Cal. Rptr 318 (1977).

7. *Green v. Green*, 64 Md. App. 122, 494 A.2d 721 (1985).

8. *Kruger v. Kruger*, 73 N.J. 464, 375 A.2d 659 (Sup. 1977).

9. *Ettinger v. Ettinger*, 637 P.2d 63 (Okla. 1981) (Oklahoma Supreme Court found that unvested stock options were not "acquired" and thus could not be subject to division); *Baum v. Baum*, 120 Ariz. 140, 584 P.2d 604 (1978) (the court held that unexercised stock options were lost to the community when they were transferred by the husband for zero consideration to the corporation he managed).

10. *Goodwyne v. Goodwyne*, 639 S.W.2d 1210 (La. App. 1984).

11. *Pascale v. Pascale*, 140 N.J. 583, 660 A.2d 485 (1995).

12. *In re Miller*, 888 P.2d 317 (Colo. App. 1994).

13. *Fisher v. Fisher*, 564 Pa. 586, 769 A.2d 1165 (2001); *Bacanti v. Morton*, 434 Mass. 787 (2001).

14. *In re Marriage of Hug*, 154 Cal. App. 3d 780, 201 Cal. Rptr. 676 (1984).

15. See *In re Marriage of Hug* and *Short v. Short*, 125 Wash.2d 865, 890 P.2d 12 (1995).

16. *Callahan v. Callahan*, 142 N.J. Super. 325, 361 A.2d 561 (1976).

17. *Smith v. Smith*, 682 S.W.2d 834 (Mo. App. 1984).

18. *Warren v. Warren*, 2 Ariz. App. 206, 407 P.2d 395 (1965).

19. *Richardson v. Richardson*, 280 Ark. 498, 659 S.W.2d 510 (1983). See also *Green v. Green*, 64 Md. App. 122, 494 A.2d 721 (1985).

20. *Baum v. Baum*, 120 Ariz. App. 140, 584 P.2d 604 (1978).

21. *In re Marriage of Moody*, 119 Ill. App. 3d 1043, 75 Ill. Dec. 581, 457 N.E.2d 1023 (1983).

22. *Rice v. City of Montgomery*, 104 Ohio App. 3d 776, 663 N.E.2d 389, 392 (1995).

23. Ibid, 663 N.E.2d at 394.

24. *Monitor Technology, Inc. v. Hetrick*, 144 Cal. Rptr. 609, 576 P.2d 92 (1978).

25. *Green v. Green*, 64 Md. App. 122, 494 A.2d 721 (1985). See also *Smith v. Smith*, 682 S.W.2d 834 (Mo. Ct. App. 1984).

26. *In re Marriage of Moody*, 119 Ill. App. 3d 1043, 75 Ill. Dec. 581, 457 N.E.2d 1023 (1983); *Green v. Green*, 64 Md. App. 122, 494 A.2d 721 (1985).

27. *In re Marriage of Hug*, 154 Cal. App. 3d 780, 201 Cal. Rptr. 676 (1984); *Everhart v. Everhart*, 360 So.2d 1319 (Fla. App. 1978).

28. *Smith v. Smith*, 682 S.W.2d 834 (Mo. App. 1984).

29. *Callahan v. Callahan*, 142 N.J. Super. 325, 361 A.2d 561 (1976).

30. *Denley v. Denley*, 38 Conn. App. 349, 661 A.2d 628 (1995).

31. *Murray v. Murray*, 128 Ohio App. 3d 662, 716 N.E.2d 288 (1999).

Handling Death Under a Stock Option Plan

Arthur S. Meyers

*M*ANY WELL-WRITTEN PIECES have been published on general stock option plan administration. These texts provide a wealth of information on matters such as granting options, exercising options, and withholding taxes.[1] Little has been written, however, specifically on the impact of death upon stock options and stock plan administration. This chapter is intended to provide stock plan administrators and others with general guidance on this topic.

Probate Administration

A stock plan administrator and legal counsel should carefully review the terms of all stock option plans as well as each form of grant agreement for provisions relating to the death of option holders. Preferably, this task should be undertaken in the plan design phase. Many issues need to be addressed regarding the impact of death on outstanding options. For example, is the option extinguished or is it transferable pursuant to the optionholder's will or the laws of descent and distribution? Does vesting accelerate? How long is the option exercisable after death—90 days, six months, one year, or more?

If a plan provides for the designation of death beneficiaries, those records should be examined upon notice of the death of the option holder. Unlike tax-qualified or ERISA retirement plans, there is no legal requirement that the optionholder's spouse be named as the beneficiary. If the option survives the death of the optionholder and a beneficiary designation was not executed, then the optionholder's estate would become the beneficiary, subject to any specific bequest in the optionholder's will. In some states, beneficiary designations for stock options may not be valid, and a dispute could arise as to the rightful beneficiary.

In the event of the death of an option holder, the stock plan administrator should obtain a copy of the death certificate and the court order appointing the deceased optionee's personal representative. The personal representative of an estate (the "Representative") has the legal responsibility to take possession of all of the decedent's property that is subject to probate; file an inventory and appraisal of the estate's assets; pay the debts, taxes, and liabilities of the estate; and distribute the remaining assets to the persons entitled to receive them. If the options are to be transferred to the estate, the Representative will need to determine whether he or she has the authority under the will or state law to exercise stock options, hold stock, sell stock, or transfer the option or stock. Other issues may arise, such as whether the Representative has sufficient funds to exercise any options and whether the Representative has the authority to borrow or pledge stock.[2]

Note that the probate process generally requires that following the optionee's death, the stock plan administrator correspond and interact with the Representative, not the surviving spouse or children. (In many cases, however, the surviving spouse will be appointed as the Representative.) A copy of the notice of exercise form, prospectus, a summary of the optionholder's grants and exercises, and related plan materials should be furnished to the Representative.

In community property states, the surviving spouse is deemed to own outright a one-half share of the options granted to the optionholder as of the time of the grant.

Tax Consequences

Incentive Stock Options

Incentive stock options (ISOs) must satisfy certain statutory requirements, including employment and holding requirements. The Internal Revenue Code (the "Code") requires that an optionee be an employee of the company granting the option (or an employee of its parent or a subsidiary) at all times during the period beginning on the date of grant through the day three months before exercise. The Code also requires that stock be held for two years from the date of grant of an ISO and one year from the date of exercise of an ISO. If these requirements are met, the employee will not be taxed until the sale of the shares and will be entitled to long-term capital gains tax treatment on the difference between the sales price and the exercise price. The employer will not be entitled to any compensation deduction.[3]

If an employee fails to meet the employment or holding period requirements, the employee will have a so-called "disqualifying disposition." If the price of the stock has gone up since the exercise, the employee will have ordinary income in the year of disposition equal to the amount by which the fair market value of the stock received (determined as of the time of exercise) exceeds the exercise price. The balance of the gain (e.g., the amount by which the sale price exceeds what the fair market value was at the date of exercise) would be capital gains. If the price of the stock has gone down since exercise (e.g., the exercise price was $10 per share, the fair market value at exercise was $15, and now the market price at which the employee sells is $13), the employee will have ordinary income in the year of disposition equal to the amount by which the sales price exceeds the exercise price.[4] In the case of a disqualifying disposition, the employer would receive a tax deduction equal to the amount that the employee must include in ordinary income as long as the employer reports the income on Form W-2. No withholding is presently required for federal income tax (FIT) or FICA purposes.[5]

The exercise of an ISO also has consequences for the Alternative Minimum Tax (AMT) that must be addressed. AMT is a tax determined under a separate tax system originally designed to require the wealthy to pay their fair share of taxes. The calculations can be quite complex. The calculations start with adjusted gross income minus itemized deductions. That figure is increased by the amount of certain deductions (e.g., state and local property and income taxes), certain items of income (e.g., ISO spread at exercise), and certain items of tax preference to obtain alternative minimum taxable income (AMTI). Next, AMTI is reduced by the applicable AMT exemption amount ($35,750 single, $49,000 married joint filers, but subject to phase-out) to obtain the AMT base. To obtain the amount of AMT owed, apply the 26% AMT rate to up to $175,000 of the AMT base, and apply the 28% AMT rate for amounts above. The taxpayer pays the larger of AMT or "regular tax" liability. Often, the exercise of an ISO will cause the employee to pay AMT because the spread increases the AMT base but not the regular income tax base. In many cases, all or a part of extra taxes owed for the year of exercise of an ISO can be recovered through a tax credit in later tax years when the taxpayer's "regular tax" liability exceeds the AMT liability (but only to the extent of excess). Usually, the bulk of the tax credit cannot be recovered until the sale of the ISO stock. No AMT is owed if the stock is sold in the year of exercise.

If an optionee exercised an ISO before death, then stock acquired by the ISO exercise may be sold by the estate without satisfying the one- and two-year holding periods generally required for long-term capital gains tax treatment on the post-option grant appreciation.[6] Also, the estate will receive a step-up in basis in the stock equal to its fair market value determined at the date of death of the optionee.[7]

If the optionee has not exercised the ISO at the time of death, then the estate receives a step-up in basis in the option itself. When the option is exercised by the estate, the estate will have a basis in the underlying shares equal to the sum of the exercise price and the fair value of the option at the optionee's death.[8] Note that in this case, the holding period of the option does not tack with holding period of the resulting stock for capital gains purposes. So, if the ISO is exercised by the estate, the underlying shares must be held for more than a year to obtain long-term capital gains treatment on the post-grant appreciation.

The exercise of an ISO by an estate raises complicated AMT issues. If an estate exercises an ISO, then there is a positive AMT adjustment equal to the difference between the fair market value of the stock acquired at the date of exercise over the estate's basis in the stock. The basis for this purpose is the sum of the exercise price plus the date of death value of the option.[9] So, if the company's stock has appreciated, the estate may owe AMT tax. A sale of the shares by the estate in the same year could reverse the AMT adjustment.[10] Under certain circumstances (the discussion of which is beyond the scope of this chapter), the AMT may in effect be passed on to beneficiaries through distributions in the same tax year of the estate as the year of exercise.[11] If neither tax event occurs, the estate could be stuck with an AMT bill.

If the ISO is specifically bequested in a will to a beneficiary, then the beneficiary will receive the same regular tax basis as the estate. The beneficiary will also be forced to address the AMT consequences of the ISO upon exercise.

Note that the transfer of an ISO to a beneficiary or estate is not treated as a modification of the option (although an extension of an exercise period to accommodate an estate or beneficiary will be treated as a modification and will disqualify the ISO), and that the transfer of stock to a beneficiary or an estate is not deemed to be a "disqualifying disposition."[12]

The regular ISO requirement that the option be exercised within three months of the optionee's leaving the company does not apply if an employee dies while in service or up to three months later. However, if the optionee dies more than three months after terminating employment, and thereafter the option is exercised by the estate, then the option cannot be treated as an ISO.[13]

The employer would not have any withholding obligations upon the exercise of an ISO or the sale of the underlying stock by the Representative or beneficiary, but the employer must report certain information regarding any ISO exercise to the Representative or beneficiary in January of the following year.[14]

Although a stock option plan administrator is generally not involved with the estate tax aspects of an option, it is worth mentioning here that for estate tax purposes, ISOs are generally given a value equal to the option spread (if any) at date of death.[15]

Nonqualified Stock Options

Nonqualified stock options (NSOs) are options other than statutory stock options. No employment or holding requirements apply as a matter of law. Upon the exercise of an NSO, the optionee realizes ordinary income equal to the spread between the fair market value of the stock at the date of exercise and the exercise price.[16] Any gain over the optionee's adjusted basis upon disposition (i.e., the price paid plus the amount included in income) is treated as capital gain. The capital gain is given favorable tax treatment as long-term capital gains if the shares are held for more than a year.[17] The employer is entitled to receive a deduction upon exercise equal to the amount that the employee includes in income, but only if the employer reports such amount to the Internal Revenue Service (IRS) on Form W-2.[18] The spread at exercise is treated as wages for purposes of FIT and FICA withholding, and FUTA.[19]

Unlike ISOs, NSOs exercised after the death of the optionee constitute an item of "income in respect of the decedent" (i.e., an amount that is not includable on the employee's final tax return as earned compensation, but which retains its character as a gross income item in the hands of the recipient).[20] The estate will not be entitled to a step-up in basis on the value of the option.[21] Consequently, the estate or beneficiary must recognize ordinary income equal to the difference between the fair market value of the option on the date of exercise and the exercise price of the option. The long-term capital gain holding period begins upon the exercise of the option.

If the NSO is specifically bequeathed to a beneficiary, the beneficiary obtains the same tax basis as the estate. Again, there is no step-up in basis.

Similarly, the beneficiary would have ordinary income upon exercise of the NSO.[22]

The employer is entitled to a tax deduction equal to the spread upon exercise. In the case of an NSO exercise following the optionee's death, the employer is not required to withhold for FIT.[23] The employer will be required to withhold for FICA purposes if the exercise of the option occurs in the same calendar year as the optionee's death. If the option exercise occurs thereafter, the income is not considered to be FICA or FUTA wages.[24]

The employer is required to report income realized by the estate or beneficiary attributable to the exercise of the NSOs on Form 1099-MISC and any FICA wages attributable to the exercise of the options during the year of death on the optionee's final Form W-2.

Generally, NSOs are valued for estate tax purposes by reference to the option spread (if any) at the optionee's date of death. However, for vested non-statutory stock options of publicly-traded companies, the IRS has issued safe-harbor guidance that uses a Black-Scholes valuation model with an additional variable involving the underlying stock's expected dividend yield.[25]

Securities Law Considerations

Registration

The Securities Act of 1933 (the "1933 Act") requires all "offers" or "sales" of "securities" to be registered by filing a registration statement with the Securities and Exchange Commission (SEC) unless an exemption is available. The grant of an option is generally exempt from registration because there usually is no sale. The underlying securities are not considered offered until the options are exercisable. At that time, a stock option plan should be registered unless there is an exemption.

Public companies subject to the reporting requirements of the Securities Exchange Act of 1934 (the "1934 Act") usually register a stock option plan for purposes of the 1933 Act on Form S-8. To register a stock option plan on Form S-8, the employer must also deliver a description of the plan and its tax consequences (known as a "prospectus") to the eligible employees, together with a copy of the company's latest annual report to stockholders. The employer must advise the plan participants that certain shareholder information is available upon request. The information provided must be periodically updated. The shares acquired under a plan registered on Form S-8 may be resold without registration or delivery of a prospectus, except that officers, directors, and 10% owners are subject to certain conditions. These "affiliates" may sell securities only in compliance with the applicable limitations of Rule 144 or under another exemption from registration. (Private companies usually rely on Rule 701 for an exemption from the registration requirements for the offer and sale of shares under a stock option plan. Unless a company "goes public," securities issued under Rule 701 may be resold only pursuant to registration or an exemption.) If option grants are limited to a small group of executives, an employer may elect to rely on the private placement exemption of Section 4(2) of the 1933 Act for a registration exemption.

Options granted with respect to public companies that are exercised by Representatives and beneficiaries may be covered by an S-8 registration statement.[26] If an employer is aware of outstanding unexercised options held by an estate or beneficiary, then the employer should deliver a copy of the prospectus and latest company annual report to the Representative or beneficiary.

Reporting

Section 16(a) of the 1934 Act requires "insiders" (generally, officers, directors, and persons who beneficially own more than 10% of any class of securities) to report various securities transactions. Option grants are to be reported on Form 4 by the end of the second business day following the day of grant. Option exercises and resales must be reported on Form 4 by the end of the second business day following the day on which the option is exercised. Form 5 is used to annually report certain other changes in beneficial ownership within 45 days of the end of the company's fiscal year.

The transfer of an option or the resulting shares held by an executive to the executive's estate or beneficiary is not reportable. The exercise of a stock option and the sale of the underlying stock by the executive's estate would not be reportable under Section 16 unless the estate is a 10% owner or the Representative is an insider and such transactions occurred more than 12 months after the executive's death.[27]

An insider who acquires additional shares as a beneficiary of another person's estate must report the acquisition on Form 5 or a voluntary Form 4.

Short-Swing Profit Recovery

Any profits resulting from the purchase and sale (or sale and purchase) of stock of a company registered under the 1934 Act within a period of less than six months by any insider may be recovered by an action brought by the company, or on behalf of the company by another stockholder, against the insider under Section 16(b) of the 1934 Act. This disgorgement provision is intended to discourage the unfair use of inside information. Rule 16b-3 provides an exemption for certain transactions between officers or directors and the company. Option grants and exercises of options are exempt from the matching of purchases and sales if the grants are authorized by the company's board of directors or by a committee composed of two or more non-employee directors.[28] Sales of stock acquired by exercises of options can be matched with other purchases.

An executive or director ceases to be an insider upon death. Thus, the transfer of an option or the resulting shares held by an executive to an insider's estate or beneficiary is not subject to short-swing profit recovery. The exercise of a stock option and the sale of the underlying stock by the insider's estate would not be subject to Section 16(b) if it occurs during the first 12 months after the insider's death. Thereafter, such sales would be subject to Section 16 only if the estate is a 10% owner or the Representative is an insider.[29]

In the event that an heir is already an insider, the acquisition of shares as a beneficiary is not deemed to be a purchase for purposes of Section 16(b) of the 1934 Act.[30] If a beneficiary is an insider or receives sufficient stock to become an insider following the executive's death, then the individual would be required to comply with Section 16 following the transfer.

Conclusion

Stock plan administration is often a thankless task. When mistakes are made, management complains. If administrative matters are properly handled, no one is praised. The author hopes this chapter provides those involved with administering stock option plans with a sufficient understanding of the complex issues that may be encountered upon death so that material problems may be avoided.

Notes

1. E.g., Mark A. Borges, "Administering an Employee Stock Option Plan," chapter 1 of this book.

2. When borrowing funds to exercise options, an institutional fiduciary may be restricted by Regulation U of the Board of Governors of the Federal Reserve System.

3. Code §§ 421(a) and 422(a).

4. Code §§ 421(b) and 422(c)(2).

5. Under Notice 2002-47, dated June 25, 2002, the IRS extended the moratorium on FICA and FUTA taxes for statutory options. The IRS will not assess FICA or FUTA taxes upon exercise, or impose federal income tax withholding upon any disposition of the acquired stock, until the calendar year beginning two years after the final rule is issued by the IRS. Notice 2002-47 does not relieve employers of their reporting obligations with respect to income arising from disqualifying dispositions.

6. Code § 421(c)(1); Prop. Reg. § 1.421-8(d).

7. Code § 1014(a).

8. Treas. Reg. § 1.421-5(d)(4)(ii); Code § 421(c)(3).

9. Rev. Rul. 78-182, 1978-1 C.B. 265.

10. Code § 56(b)(3).

11. Code §§ 661-663.

12. Code § 424(c)(1)(A); Prop. Reg. § 1.421-8(b)(2); Code § 421(c)(1); Prop. Reg. § 1.421-8(c)(1); Prop. Reg. § 1.421-8(d).

13. Id.

14. Code § 6039(a).

15. Rev. Rul. 53-196, 1953-2 C.B. 178.

16. Treas. Reg. § 1.83-7(a).

17. Code § 1222(3).

18. Code § 83(h); Treas. Reg. § 1.83-6.

19. Rev. Rul. 78-185, 1978-1 C.B. 304.

20. Code § 691(a); Treas. Reg. 1.691(a)-1; Treas. Reg. 1.83-1(d).

21. Code § 1014(c).

22. Code § 691(a); Treas. Reg. 1.83-1(d).

23. Rev. Rul. 86-109, 1986-2 C.B. 196; PLR 8113058 (December 31, 1980); PLR 9738009 (June 17, 1997).

24. Id.

25. Rev. Proc. 98-34, 1998-1 C.B. 983.

26. General Instruction A1 to Form S-8.

27. Rule 16a-2(d).

28. Rule 16b-3(d)(1).

29. Rule 16a-2(d); See also, SEC No-Action Letter, American Soc. of Corp. Secretaries (Dec. 11, 1996).

30. Rule 16b-5.

Evergreen Provisions for Stock Plans

Thomas LaWer

*S*TOCK OPTION and employee stock purchase plans typically reserve a fixed number of shares for issuance under the plan. To add more shares to a plan, the company's board of directors must amend the plan, and in most cases, the company's shareholders must approve the amendment. If a company's stock option or employee stock purchase plan (throughout this chapter, these will be referred to as "stock plans" or "plans") runs out of shares, there is often significant time, expense, and uncertainty involved in receiving shareholder approval of share increases.

To avoid the issues involved with frequent shareholder approval of share increases, a company can incorporate an automatic replenishment feature (commonly referred to as an "evergreen" provision) into its stock plans. The evergreen provision automatically increases the number of shares reserved under the company's stock plans at regular intervals. The evergreen provision can eliminate the expense and difficulty of seeking frequent shareholder approval of a plan share increase. In addition, a company may plan its option grants for several years with greater certainty because it has a reliable supply of reserved shares. Finally, the evergreen provision detaches equity compensation strategies from the vagaries of the company's stock price. Companies may have a more difficult time obtaining shareholder approval for share reserve increases when the stock has performed poorly. Because employers often need to motivate people more in a downturn, this can be the worst time for a company to curtail its option grants.

This chapter discusses the issues involved with designing and implementing an evergreen provision.

Evergreen Design

The simplest evergreen provision is an annual increase in the number of shares reserved under the stock plan by a percentage of the outstanding shares of the company on the date of increase (see example 1 below). This evergreen provision allows the stock plan to continue to grow as the company's outstanding capital stock increases. Unfortunately, this design does not meet the requirements of the tax laws for incentive stock options (ISOs) and tax-qualified employee stock purchase plans (ESPPs). (Thus, such a plan cannot be used for plans granting ISOs or as an ESPP.) However, a "percentage of the outstanding" evergreen provision does work for non-employee director plans and for stock plans that grant nonqualified stock options rather than ISOs.

> *Example 1.* The maximum number of shares reserved under the Plan is 1,000,000 shares, plus an annual increase to be added on each anniversary date of the adoption of the Plan equal to four percent (4%) of the outstanding Common Stock on such date.

To qualify for preferential tax treatment, ISOs and ESPPs must comply respectively with the requirements of Sections 422(b) and 423(b) of the Internal Revenue Code of 1986, as amended (the "Code"). One of the conditions for preferential tax treatment is that the option must be granted under a plan specifying "the aggregate number of shares which may be issued."[1] The maximum aggregate number of shares that may be issued under a plan must be determinable at the *time the plan is adopted.* That is, on the date the board of directors adopts the plan, the total number of shares that can possibly be granted under the plan must be calculable. For companies that wish to grant ISOs or have an ESPP, this requirement limits the flexibility of the evergreen provision. The evergreen must provide for periodic increases of a fixed number of shares (see example 2 below).

> *Example 2.* The maximum number of shares reserved under the Plan is 1,000,000 shares, plus an annual increase to be added on each anniversary date of the adoption of the Plan equal to 400,000 shares.

However, many companies would prefer to add an amount determined as a percentage of the outstanding shares on a specified date each year, such as each anniversary date of the plan adoption. As discussed above, such a provision, by itself, violates the determinable-number-of-shares requirement of ISOs and ESPPs. One way to remedy this problem is to draft a tiered evergreen provision that provides that the number of shares to be added each year is equal to the *lesser* of (1) a fixed number of shares or (2) a percentage of the outstanding shares on each anniversary of the plan adoption (see example 3 below).[2] In drafting this provision, it is important to select a fixed number of shares that will be greater than the anticipated percentage of the outstanding shares necessary to restore the maximum reserve amount. In the example, the tiered evergreen provision satisfies the maximum-determinable-number-of-shares condition because the maximum number of shares reserved under the plan is equal to the initial reservation of 1,000,000 shares plus 1,000,000 (the fixed number to be added each year) multiplied by the term of the plan.

> *Example 3.* The maximum aggregate number of shares that may be optioned and sold under the Plan is 1,000,000 shares, plus an annual increase to be added on each anniversary date of the adoption of the Plan equal to the lesser of (1) 1,000,000 shares, or (2) four percent (4%) of the outstanding shares on such date.

A company may retain even greater control over the number of shares being added to the plan by adding to the formula a third variable, a lesser "amount determined by the Board," to the tiered evergreen provision described above (see example 4 below). If either the fixed number of shares or the number of shares equal to a percentage of the outstanding shares provides more generous benefits than is required or appropriate, this refinement lets the board of directors limit the number of shares that would otherwise be added to the plan.

> *Example 4.* The maximum aggregate number of shares which may be optioned and sold under the Plan is 1,000,000 shares, plus an annual increase to be added on each anniversary date of the adoption of the Plan equal to the lesser of (1) 800,000 Shares, (2) four percent (4%) of the outstanding shares on such date, or (3) an amount determined by the Board.

A final variation is to reload the option grants made in the prior year (a "top-up" evergreen provision). The number of shares to be added to the plan is still determinable: it is the total number of shares reserved under the plan. In example 5 below, the evergreen provision will add the number of shares granted in options in the prior year up to the maximum number of shares reserved under the plan of 400,000. There are further refinements possible for the top-up provision. One refinement allows for topping up the shares based on the number of shares originally reserved under the plan. In all these refinements, the basic concept of the top-up is the same.

> *Example 5.* The maximum aggregate number of shares that may be optioned and sold under the Plan is 400,000 shares, plus an annual increase to be added on each anniversary date of adoption of the Plan equal to (1) the optioned stock underlying options granted in the immediately preceding year or (2) a lesser amount determined by the Board.

Shareholder Approval Considerations

Shareholder approval is needed to add an evergreen provision to the same extent shareholder approval would be required to add any increase in shares to a stock plan. This means that shareholder approval is required to add an evergreen provision to a stock plan that issues ISOs or to a tax-qualified employee stock purchase plan. In addition, generally for private companies granting options in California,[3] Nasdaq-listed companies that grant options to officers and directors,[4] and New York Stock Exchange (NYSE)-listed companies that do not meet one of the NYSE's exceptions,[5] shareholder approval will be required to add an evergreen provision to a stock plan, whether or not the stock plan will be qualified to issue ISOs or be an ESPP. In addition to the general shareholder approval requirements, there are several other shareholder approval issues.

Section 162(m)

Section 162(m) of the Code, the $1 million compensation deduction limitation rule, does not require shareholder approval specifically for the addition of shares and thus does not directly affect an evergreen provision. However, Section 162(m) does require that if a stock plan is approved while a company is "private" (i.e., the company does not have to comply with the Securities and Exchange Act of 1934, as amended), shareholder approval will be required to the extent the company wishes to exempt options from the deduction limitations after the company is "public."[6] The maximum time period until Section 162(m) requires shareholder approval is the shareholder meeting in which members of the board of directors are elected that occurs in the fourth calendar year following the calendar year in which the initial public offering (IPO) occurs.[7] Until this time, the provisions of Section 162(m) are not applicable (assuming the material terms of the plan were described in the IPO prospectus).[8] Shareholder approval for purposes of Section 162(m) may be required before the annual meeting in the fourth calendar year upon the occurrence of any of the following events: (1) the expiration of the plan or agreement, (2) the material modification of the plan or agreement within the meaning of Section 162(m), or (3) the issuance of all stock that has been allocated under the plan.[9]

This means that a company that adopts an evergreen provision immediately before its IPO and has enough shares at the end of the Section 162(m) exemption period will still have to submit its plan for shareholder approval if it wants future option grants exempt from the Section 162(m) compensation deduction limitations. Implementing an evergreen provision while a company is private delays seeking approval from the company's public shareholders for several years, but does not entirely avoid all need for it.

Voting Issues

For public companies, implementing an evergreen provision also may affect the ability of brokers to vote the shares held in street name (i.e., shares owned by a client of the broker but registered under the broker's name to facilitate trading) without instructions from the beneficial holders.[10] This may affect the company's ability to obtain shareholder approval of the evergreen feature. Rule 452 of the New York Stock Exchange states that brokers may not vote shares on a matter without instruction from the beneficial owner when such matter authorizes issuances of stock, or options to purchase stock, to directors, officers, or employees in an amount that exceeds 5% of the total amount of the class of shares outstanding.[11] For purposes of calculating whether the shares reserved under the plan exceed 5% of the total outstanding stock, the maximum annual increase for each year of the plan must be considered (see example 6 below). Under both California and Delaware law, while broker non-votes may be counted for purposes of determining the presence or absence of a quorum, broker non-votes are not counted as votes cast with respect to the proposal. Most Nasdaq-listed companies also follow the NYSE rule.

> *Example 6.* Company A is publicly held and has 50 million shares authorized and outstanding. Company A adopts a stock option plan for which it has reserved 2 million shares for issuance and submits it for shareholder approval. In this case, the broker would be able to vote the shares to approve the plan since the number of shares reserved under the plan, 2 million shares, is less than 5% of the issued and outstanding shares.

Example 7. Same as Example 6 except that the number of shares reserved under the plan includes an annual increase of 500,000 shares and the term of the plan is 10 years. In this case, the broker would not be able to vote the shares to approve the plan because the total number of shares reserved under the plan totals 7 million shares (2 million + 5 million), which exceeds 5% of the issued and outstanding shares.

Shareholder Reaction

Institutional investors generally do not favor evergreen provisions because they want to retain control of any increases in the shares reserved under the stock plans and thereby limit the dilution of their ownership. Although in the past, where the share increase proposed in the evergreen has been reasonable, institutional investors have approved evergreen provisions. However, in the current post-Enron and post-WorldCom environment, institutional investors are far less likely to approve an evergreen provision. Historically, it appears that there is less resistance to approving evergreen provisions in (1) employee stock purchase plans, which by their broad based, non-discretionary nature appear to require less shareholder oversight, and (2) not surprisingly, for companies whose stock price has performed well.

Institutional Shareholder Services (ISS) judges stock option plans based on the shareholder value transfer (the estimate of the cost of the shareholder's equity transferred to optionees upon exercise of their options) and the voting power dilution.[12] By increasing the number of shares reserved under a plan, an evergreen provision negatively affects both these calculations. Therefore, by increasing the potential dilution from the stock options, an evergreen can make a stock plan too "expensive" to the shareholders, in ISS's opinion. This may result in ISS recommending that shareholders vote against the evergreen provision.

Often, to make an evergreen provision more palatable to institutional investors, a company will limit the evergreen provision to a specified period of years. For example, the evergreen may last for three or four years, after which it expires and the company must go back to the shareholders for any further increase in the shares reserved under the plan (see example 8 below). This modification can help avoid the broker non-vote issue described above under "Voting Issues." However, this tactic somewhat undercuts the purpose of the evergreen by limiting the number of shares it can add to the plan.

Example 8. The maximum aggregate number of shares that may be optioned and sold under the Plan is 1,000,000 shares, plus an annual increase to be added on each anniversary date of the adoption of the Plan for the next three years beginning in the year 2003 equal to the lesser of (1) 800,000 Shares, (2) four percent (4%) of the outstanding shares on such date, or (3) a lesser amount determined by the Board.

Securities Issues

Each year, when the evergreen provision replenishes the stock plan, the S-8 registration statement under which the stock plan shares are registered must be amended to register the annual increase. This is an important administrative matter that needs to be completed each year in order to ensure that shares may be validly issued under the stock plan.

Stock Splits, Dividends, and Tracking Stock

The stock option or employee stock purchase plan should contain a provision to adjust the shares reserved under the plan, including the evergreen provision, for any stock split or stock dividend, or for the creation of tracking stock. With such a provision incorporated into the plan at the time the evergreen provision is adopted, the evergreen provision can automatically be adjusted for the split, dividend, or change in class of shares without any concern about obtaining shareholder approval.

Conclusion

An evergreen provision can be a useful tool for a company. It reduces the administrative expense involved with adding shares to a stock plan, provides a company with a reliable supply of reserved shares for option grants, and is easily implemented (especially for private companies). Shareholder reaction to an evergreen provision, while it may be unfavorable, is generally not insurmountable for a well-drafted and justified evergreen provision.

Notes

1. Section 422(b)(1) of the Code, Treasury Regulation ("Treas. Reg.") § 1.423-2(c)(3), and Proposed Treas. Reg. § 1.422A-3(i) and (ii).

2. See Private Letter Ruling 9531031, which specifically approves of this design structure for an automatic replenishment feature.

3. California Code of Regulations § 260.140.41.

4. Rule 4350(i)(1) of *the NASD Manual for The Nasdaq Stock Market* (update date). Please note that Nasdaq has proposed amendments to this rule that would require shareholder approval for any addition of shares to a plan regardless of whether officers and directors participate.

5. Rule 312.03(a) of the *NYSE Listed Company Manual.* Please note that the NYSE has proposed amendments to this rule that would severely limit any exceptions to shareholder approval.

6. Treas. Reg. § 1.162-27(f).

7. Treas. Reg. § 1.162-27(f)(2)(iv).

8. Treas. Reg. § 1.162-27(f)(1).

9. Treas. Reg. § 1.162-27(f)(2).

10. As of the date of this revision, the NYSE has proposed eliminating the broker non-vote rule with respect to stock plans. Should this proposal be implemented, the issue discussed in this section will disappear. The shareholder voting requirements will be the same regardless of the number of shares being added to the stock plan.

11. Rule 452 of the *NYSE Listed Company Manual.*

11. *Institutional Shareholder Services Proxy Voting Manual,* Chapter 10.

8

Underwater Stock Options and Repricing Strategy

Daniel N. Janich

GREAT DEAL OF public attention has been focused over the past decade upon the use of stock options to compensate employees instrumental to a company's future success. Although stock options have been part of the compensation package of members of the highest reaches of management for quite some time, particularly in public companies, it has been the cash-starved Internet startups and emerging high-tech companies who have led the way in making broad-based stock options popular among rank-and-file employees in more recent years. One of the lasting effects that these companies, including the dot-coms, may have had on the workplace is a greater awareness, if not understanding, of the role that stock options play in the total compensation package of employees and independent contractors.[1] In fact, the reality today is that many rank-and-file employees consider stock options to be an essential part of their total compensation package. From a company's perspective, stock options have been particularly attractive as a compensation device under Financial Accounting Standards Board (FASB) APB (Accounting Principles Board) Opinion 25 ("APB 25"), where the compensation cost, if any, is measured when the exercise price and the number of shares are "fixed and determinable." Typically, this cost would be fixed and determinable when the option is granted. If a company reports stock-based compensation under APB 25, the option grant does not result in a compensation charge to the income statement if the exercise price is not less than the fair market value of the underlying stock on the date of grant.[2]

Although the problem of underwater options is widespread and easily understood, an appropriate solution may not at all be clear for many companies that are now faced with considerable pressure to develop an effective strategy to revive their option programs before losing valuable talent to a competitor. Until recently, most employees were able to exercise their vested options at a market price that was greater than its exercise price. However, due to a downturn in the U.S. economy, in many cases this is no longer true, and companies that issued options that are now underwater are often confused in their quest to find the most effective solution. Companies that have historically resorted to "repricing" their underwater stock options may no longer be willing to undertake this approach due to adverse accounting treatment that repricing entails today.[3] However, the alternatives to repricing may carry their own baggage. Therefore, if a company is to develop and implement an effective strategy that deals with this problem, then the advantages and disadvantages of repricing and its alternatives must be clearly understood and carefully considered.

Repricing

What Is Stock Option Repricing?

Stock option repricing generally refers to a company's decision to effectively lower the exercise price of its outstanding options whose underlying shares have declined in value. In addition to amending the existing options to lower the exercise price, a repricing also may be accomplished by means of a cancellation of the existing option and granting to the optionee one or more new options at a lowered exercise price.[4] Under a recent interpretation of the accounting rules, a repricing will be deemed to have occurred if the grant of a new option at a lower exercise price and cancellation of the underwater option occurs within six months of each other.[5] This six-month look-back/look-forward period cannot be avoided by otherwise agreeing to compensate the employee for any stock price increases until a new stock option is granted. If the company takes any action that has the effect of either lowering the exercise price on the underwater option, such as payment of a cash bonus to the optionee upon exercise of the option or a below-market interest loan to facilitate option exercise, a repricing will be deemed to have occurred for accounting purposes.[6] Furthermore, an effective cancellation will be deemed to have occurred if the stock option is modified or an agreement is reached to reduce the likelihood of option exercise. This would include a modification of the outstanding stock option to reduce the exercise period, restart or extend the vesting period, increase the exercise price, or reduce the number of shares of the award.[7] Of course, any adverse change to the outstanding option would require the optionee's consent.

Accounting Treatment of Stock Options After FIN 44, and the Consequences of Repricing

Until recently, companies simply repriced their underwater stock options in order to permit optionees to "profit" by any subsequent increase in share value. The repricing did not entail any adverse accounting treatment until FASB Interpretation No. 44, "Accounting for Certain Transactions Involving Stock Compensation" ("FIN 44"), was adopted by FASB on March 31, 2000.[8] Under FIN 44, which applies retroactively to December 15, 1998, repricing causes the exercise price to be treated as "variable" for the life of the option, resulting in "variable accounting treatment" for the remaining life of the repriced option.[9] When the exercise price is subject to variable accounting treatment, the difference between the revised (lower) exercise price and the value of the underlying stock when the repriced option is exercised (or forfeited or expires unexercised) must be recognized as a compensation expense for financial reporting purposes. Under variable accounting, as the company's stock price increases, a periodic charge to earnings must be reported.[10] This new accounting treatment alone has discouraged many companies from repricing their underwater stock options and has caused them to consider alternatives that may hold relatively less onerous consequences.

Federal Income Tax Considerations

The federal income tax rules treat a repriced stock option as an option exchange, i.e., a cancellation and regrant, regardless of the actual form of repricing.[11] Generally, there are no federal income tax consequences for option holders on their exchange of underwater stock options because repricing is not a taxable event. However, the decision to reprice may still involve several significant income tax considerations for the five highest officers of a public company as well as holders of incentive stock options.

Five Highest Paid Officers In many instances, the participation in a repricing by the five highest paid officers of a public company will trigger Code Section 162(m) considerations. Under Section 162(m) of the Internal Revenue Code (the "Code"), a publicly held company may deduct no more than $1 million in compensation paid to any of its five highest paid officers unless the options are considered to be "performance-based compensation" that has been approved by at least two "outside directors" of the company's full board of directors.[12] Stock options may be treated as compensation includible for purposes of this limitation under Section 162(m). For repriced options to continue to be exempt from the deduction limits of Section 162(m), they must also be approved in this same manner.

For the Section 162(m) exemption to apply, the option plan must also specify the maximum number of shares for which options may be granted to any employee during a specified period of one or more years.[13] If the option is repriced during the same period in which it was granted, in order to be able to determine the maximum number of shares for which options may be granted to an employee during the specified period, the plan would include the number of shares subject to the option after the repricing as well as the number of shares subject to the option before the repricing.[14] If repricing causes the individual limit to be exceeded, the Section 162(m) exemption would no longer apply to that individual.[15]

Incentive Stock Options (ISOs) Whether publicly or privately held, companies repricing their incentive stock options must consider the holding period and share value dollar limitations of Code Section 422. To retain their status as incentive stock options, repriced options will be required to satisfy the two-years-after-grant and one-year-after-exercise holding period applicable to incentive stock options for such options to continue to defer tax recognition.[16] Repricing will start over the capital gains tolling period again. Therefore, to obtain incentive stock option treatment, shares subject to the repriced option may not be disposed of within two years from the date of the repricing, nor within one year from the date of exercise of the repriced option. Also, to retain incentive stock option treatment, the aggregate fair market value (determined as of the grant date) of stock that is bought by exercising an incentive stock option may not exceed $100,000 in a calendar year.[17] Repricing may cause the number of shares subject to the option to increase. These additional shares would be counted against the $100,000 limit when the repriced options are exercisable.[18] Any repriced options exceeding this limit would be treated for tax purposes as nonqualified stock options.

Securities Law Issues

The securities laws treat option repricing as an option exchange. In the case of a repricing where the exercise price of stock options held by "named executive officers" (generally the five highest-paid executives) was revised during the preceding fiscal year, the company must disclose (in reasonable detail) the repricing and its basis in its proxy statements.[19] Additionally, the repricing may trigger extensive 10-year reporting for all officers and directors in the proxy statement.[20] As part of this report, the company must describe repricing of options held by any executive officer during the last 10 fiscal years.[21] Therefore, companies should consider whether to include "named executive officers" in a repricing of the company's stock options.

On March 21, 2001, the SEC issued an order under the Exchange Act "for issuer exchange offers that are conducted for compensatory purposes." The effect of this order is stricter advance filing requirements for public companies that reprice their stock options because exchange plans are considered to be tender offers (bids to buy company shares, usually at a premium), which require added disclosure.[22] However, they are exempt from the tender-offer requirement that they must be offered to all stockholders as long as the stock options are issued under the company's employee plans and are used for compensation purposes.[23]

In addition to the foregoing, the securities laws provide that the repricing of options is to be treated as a disposition of the existing options and the acquisition of new ones for purposes of Section 16 of the Exchange Act.[24] As such, repricing will trigger short-swing liability on gains, unless at least two "non-employee directors" or the full board approved both the cancellation and regrant.[25] Repricing must also be reported by a person who is subject to Section 16 as the disposition of the existing option and the acquisition of new options.[26]

A repricing effected by an options exchange may trigger the registration requirements of Section 5 of the Securities Act, if the repriced option includes terms that are less advantageous than the original option (such as a new vesting schedule or a decrease in the number of shares subject to the new options).[27] An exemption from this registration may be available under Section 3(a)(9) of the Securities Act if no commission or other remuneration is paid or given for the exchange of options.[28] Notice filings may also be necessary in connection with repriced options under some state blue-sky laws.[29]

Timing the Repricing: Excess Parachute Payment Considerations

When a company is in a "change of control" situation, a repriced stock option may be treated as a "change-in-control stock option" for purposes of the excess parachute payment rules under Code Section 280G.[30] A change in control stock option is usually granted during the one-year period preceding the event.[31] As a result of the repricing, the entire option spread might be treated as a parachute payment, subjecting the company to loss of a tax deduction and the optionee to additional tax payments.[32]

Is Stock Option Repricing Fair to Shareholders?

An often-stated rationale for issuance of stock options is its ability to foster an "ownership" culture among employees. By aligning their interests with those of the company, employees benefit by any increase in the value of the company as a result of their individual and collective performance. During an economic downturn that depresses the value of the company's stock, however, it may be logical to presume that these same employees might also be expected to suffer the declining share values along with the company's shareholders. At least this is the thinking of many shareholders, in particular institutional shareholders, who believe that option holders should be subject to the same risks in the volatility of the underlying share price as the shareholders themselves.[33] Since the shareholders do not in any way benefit from the repricing, they feel that repricing allows option holders to "change the rules" of the game when the game itself changes, an advantage they obviously do not enjoy. Companies that undergo an option repricing should anticipate shareholder protest and therefore may want to avoid putting this issue up for a shareholder vote.

The Alternatives to Repricing: How Viable Are They?

How can a company effectively deal with their underwater stock options without incurring the problems and complexities of repricing? Although there is no one sure-fire approach, a company may find that one of the following alternatives to repricing provides an appropriate solution. These alternatives have advantages because they return value to the option holders, but they must be carefully considered because they may contain their own drawbacks.

Extend the Expiration Date of the Underwater Options

By extending the option exercise period, a company allows additional time for the share price to bounce back in order to self-correct the problem. The extension may be implemented by amending the underwater options without incurring adverse accounting treatment. However, if incentive stock options are involved, due to statutorily imposed restrictions under the Internal Revenue Code, an amendment of the expiration period to permit exercise of the option beyond three months following termination of employment will cause the option to be treated as a nonqualified stock option for tax purposes.[34]

Grant/Cancellation of Options More Than Six Months Apart

The grant of new options and cancellation of underwater options in two separate and independent transactions spaced more than six months apart is a popular alternative to repricing among many companies. With this six-months-and-a-day approach ("six-and-one"), if the higher priced option is cancelled with the optionee (foregoing any increase in the share price of the cancelled option) and a new option is granted six months and one day later at the then-current fair market value, repricing will not be deemed to have occurred and, therefore, variable accounting treatment is avoided.[35] The exchange ratio may be 1:1, but it often is less, allowing the company to lessen shareholder dilution by having the new grant issue fewer options than the number of underwater options that were exchanged. The company cannot compensate the optionee for any appreciation in the stock price during the six-month period.[36] Option holders who terminate their employment with the company prior to the six-month waiting period before receiving reissued options will not be eligible to receive the new grant.

This approach clearly puts the optionee at risk, in that the value of the shares, and hence the exercise price of the new options, may increase over the six-month period, perhaps to a point that is even higher than the previously cancelled options. To offset this risk, the company may provide for a shorter vesting period or larger award when the new options are granted. Before using this approach, a company should be mindful that it might actually create a disincentive for employees to want the stock price to rise before they get their new grant in six months. As with any option exchange program, the option holder must agree to the cancellation of his option. A grant/cancellation that is spaced more than six months apart may be appropriate for companies whose options are so deeply underwater that there is little likelihood that the share value will recover or that a change of control will occur within six months. However, if the value of the shares is volatile, the "six-and-one" approach may not be the most effective approach to use.

Accelerate Next Grant or Make Additional Grant

A company may issue a grant of options at current fair market value either as a new grant ahead of schedule or as an extra grant of options. The optionee gets the advantage of a low exercise price, and if the additional grant involves issuance of fixed options, there is no adverse accounting treatment for the company under APB 25. This may be the simplest alternative. However, the danger of this approach is two-fold: (1) a continued downturn in the economy or volatile market conditions may effectively strip the additional option grant of any increased incentive if it joins the old options underwater, and a rapid stock price rebound may result in an unexpected and unintended windfall for the option holders who receive this additional grant; and (2) the grant of additional options will increase shareholder dilution,[37] perhaps beyond competitive levels, may accelerate depletion of the pool of reserved shares under the shareholder approved option plan, and may also result in an excessive option overhang.[38] Therefore, this strategy is most appropriate when the company has sufficient shares in the option plan and dilution and potential windfall gains are not major considerations for the company. The frequent grant of options periodically throughout the year may be particularly appropriate for volatile stock, in that it reduces the problem of fixing an exercise price based solely on the value of the shares on the grant date.

Increase Option Grant Frequency and Decrease Size of Option Grants

Companies may be able to minimize the effects of a volatile stock market by increasing the frequency of its option grants while decreasing the size of each grant. Each grant would be having the exercise price fixed to the prevailing market conditions. Of course, if the stock's value continues to decline, the employee may still be holding underwater stock options, though the total impact may tend to minimize the number of options that are underwater as well as the degree of disparity between the exercise price and current fair market value when the pool of options granted over the course of the year is "averaged" for market value and exercise price. In conjunction with an increase in stock option grants, a company may also consider shortening the option term.

Grant "Paired" Options with Six-Month-Plus Expiration Period

Companies may want to grant options that expire at least six months and a day after the market value of the stock reaches the exercise price of the original options. Due to use of the "six-and-one" approach, this would not be considered a repricing and therefore would not trigger variable accounting treatment.[39] Although the additional grant has the negative effect of increasing share dilution, if the value of the company's shares increase to the original exercise price, the dilution caused by issuance of "paired" options will be limited due to the relatively short period for exercise of the additional grant. This is an effective way of restoring value to holders of underwater options while minimizing shareholder dilution.

Issue Restricted Stock in Exchange for Cancelled Options

This alternative requires the company to issue restricted stock in exchange for the cancelled underwater options. In such cases, fixed accounting applies to the new stock award, and the compensation expense that is recognized for accounting purposes will equal the value of the restricted shares on the grant date, less the price paid for the shares, allocated over the vesting period.[40] Under this approach, the company cannot grant options to the same optionees (within six months of cancellation) at a price lower than the exercise price of cancelled options.[41] Absent a prior election under Code Section 83(b),[42] as the restrictions on such shares lapse, the grantee would be subject to income tax measured by the difference between the price paid for the shares and their value at the time the restriction lapses.[43]

A complication may arise if the exchange ratio used is less than a 1:1 ratio of new shares to canceled options. The excess of options that were issued within the six-month look-back/look-forward period over restricted shares granted may receive variable accounting treatment if those options were granted at a lower exercise price within six months before or after the cancellation.[44] This approach may be most useful where the value of the shares has dropped significantly since the options were issued and would result in a reduction of the company's option overhang. Shareholders may protest the company's decision to grant restricted stock insofar as such an award has immediate value, notwithstanding the restrictions. Perhaps not surprisingly, few companies to date have opted for this alternative.

Buy Out Options with Cash

This alternative requires the company to buy out the underwater options with cash, perhaps at a discount from the options' Black-Scholes value.[45] For accounting purposes the payment will be recognized as an expense on the company's financial statements. To avoid variable accounting treatment, the company must not make any option grants to the same optionees within six months of the cancellation (before or after) that have a lower exercise price than the bought-out options.[46] The company could make a new, fair-value option grant after a six-month waiting period; however, as with canceling and replacing, the company cannot compensate the employees for increases in the market price of the stock. This approach may be most feasible for companies willing to spend cash and incur a fixed accounting expense that the payment entails. The employee receives compensation for surrendering the options, which offset the risk of waiting for six months before receiving a new option grant. By redeeming the options, the company helps control stock dilution. This approach may be the most effective solution for a company that decides to no longer offer stock options as compensation.

Sell Options to a Third Party

An employee may sell the underwater options to a third party, provided that the option plan or agreement permits it.[47] In this fashion, the employee recoups some value from the sold option, but permitting this alternative will create a new class of non-employee option holders. Obviously, this alternative would not be possible if incentive stock options are involved.[48] However, for nonqualified options, this approach might work if the company is willing to have outside investors holding their stock options. A company willing to consider this approach should have other incentives to use to attract, motivate, and retain employees.

Offer Non-Stock Incentives

A company may want to consider offering its key employees who are holding underwater stock options additional cash, in the form of a lump-sum bonus or increased salary, as compensation for their loss. In addition, employers should not overlook the value of non-cash perks (such as flextime, increased vacation benefits, and other similar benefits) as viable ways to "re-incentivize" a work force. Under this approach, neither additional stock dilution nor excessive option overhang is likely to occur. Furthermore, the scope of eligibility for this program (whether cash, non-cash or a combination of the two) may be as broad or as limited as company expense may allow.

As previously discussed, the decline in stock prices has forced companies with underwater stock options to address how they will retain top talent, appease shareholders, and avoid potential regulatory traps. Any company in search of an appropriate solution should be prepared to address the considerations outlined in the following checklists. The first addresses repricing considerations while the second considers repricing alternatives.

Checklist of Repricing Considerations

__ **Mechanics of Repricing:** Are there any impediments under state law to option repricing? Does either the option plan or agreements restrict repricing? Will the company amend existing options or cancel existing options and grant new options? The grant of new options may entail a new vesting schedule and expiration date.

__ **Exclusion of Officers:** Should repricing include or exclude company officers? This is a reporting consideration for securities law purposes. Repricing of the options held by the top five executives of the company may trigger extensive 10-year reporting for all officers and directors in the company's proxy statement.

__ **Repriced Option Terms:** Should the repriced options include new vesting schedules, set the exercise price above current fair market value, or grant fewer options in exchange for the cancelled options?

__ **Optionees Subject to Repricing:** The company should determine whether senior executives and directors would participate in a repricing. Institutional shareholders may have less opposition to repricing that excludes options held by company's senior executives or directors. Note that extensive proxy statement disclosure obligations may be avoided if the repricing is not applicable to options granted to any executive officer named in the proxy statement.

__ **Timing of Repricing:** When should repricing occur? What should be the new exercise price of repriced options—current fair market value or less? How long is the downturn in the market expected to last?

__ **Exercise Moratorium:** Should there be a moratorium on exercising after an option repricing? What "black-out" period is most appropriate?

__ **Ramifications of Repricing:** Consider the accounting, tax and securities law issues when repricing, as well as the pooling of interests and excess parachute payment considerations.

__ **Company Performance:** Determine why the options are underwater. Has the depressed market price for company stock occurred because of a general downturn in the economy, because of company performance, or both?

__ **Share Dilution:** What impacts will the repricing have on shareholder dilution? Should you anticipate negative shareholder reaction to repricing?

__ **Communicating the Repricing to Option Holders:** How best can the repricing be communicated to optionees and other shareholders? What impact will a repricing have on morale of option holders or on the company's ability to retain key personnel?

Checklist of Repricing Alternatives for Consideration

__ **Self-Correction:** Will the value of the shares be expected to bounce back in the foreseeable future? If so, perhaps a simple extension of the expiration date for the underwater stock options will effectively address the problem. This approach anticipates that the company is fairly certain of a rebound of the value of the company's shares.

__ **Six Months and a Day for Option Exchange:** Will the new grant and cancellation be spaced more than six months apart? Are these transactions independent of each other or tied together in some fashion? Will the option exchange occur in a ratio of 1:1 or something less? Be careful about inadvertently creating a disincentive for option holders to increase the value of the shares before setting the exercise price on the new option grant. This approach may work best when the company believes that the share value is not likely to rebound at any time in the foreseeable future.

__ **Grant of Additional Options:** If the company grants additional options at current fair market value, how will this affect shareholder dilution? Will such an additional grant accelerate the depletion of the option plan's share reserve? How will the option overhang be affected? What will be the overall effectiveness of this approach if the shares have not yet bottomed out in value? If the company has sufficient shares and is not concerned with share dilution or option overhang, this approach may be effective—and perhaps particularly appropriate if the share price is volatile.

__ **Increase Grant Frequency and Decrease Grant Size:** In a volatile market, this approach may be an attractive course of action, since it tends to minimize the effects of a stock's decline in value. By combining an increase in frequency with a decrease in size, the company may also be able to minimize the dilutive effects of this approach as well as the danger of an excessive option overhang.

__ **Grant Paired Options with Six Months-Plus Expiration Period:** The company may "pair" a new option with the original grant, causing the former to expire when the exercise price of the latter recovers. To avoid variable accounting treatment, the new option must expire more than six months after the share value reaches the exercise price of the original option. This approach works best when share dilution is not a principal concern.

__ **Issue Restricted Shares in Exchange for Cancellation of Options:** This approach may be appropriate where share dilution is not a concern and the company is willing to accept a compensation expense measured by the value of the restricted stock on the date of issue. Will an option exchange occur in a ratio that is 1:1 or less? The company may be required to exercise special care if it intends to avoid variable accounting treatment when issuing restricted stock in a ratio that is less than 1:1 ratio with cancelled options. Unlike options, restricted shares have immediate value, notwithstanding their restrictions. Therefore, the company that adopts this approach should anticipate and be prepared to address potential shareholder objections.

__ **Buy Out Options with Cash:** A company purchase of the options with cash will require the payment to be recognized as an expense on the company's financial statements. Does the company have sufficient liquidity to adopt this approach? Is the company willing to accept the charge to earnings that this approach entails? Does the company have an issue with excessive shareholder dilution? If the company is not going to offer options as compensation in the future, a buyout with cash would appear to make the most sense. A company must be mindful not to issue a new grant with a lower exercise price within six months preceding or following the buyout if it wants to avoid variable accounting treatment.

__ **Sell Options to Third Party:** A sale of the options to a third party must be permitted by the option plan or agreement for this alternative to be a viable one. Does the company's option plan or agreements permit such a sale since it creates a new class of optionees (and potential shareholders) who are not employees? A sale would allow the optionee to recoup some value for a non-qualified option. This approach would not work for incentive stock options that cannot be transferred as a matter of law.

__ **Offer Non-Stock Incentives:** A company should not overlook the value of making cash payments (whether in the form of a salary increase or cash bonus or non-cash perks, such as flextime or increased vacation benefits) to make up for the lost value of underwater stock options. What are the cash incentives and non-cash perks that the company can offer in lieu of additional options or restricted shares? Is stock dilution and/or excessive overhang a problem? These non-stock incentives avoid stock dilution and option overhang concerns. The company may restrict the total cost of this approach by limiting program participation to key employees holding underwater stock options.

Conclusion

Stock options will continue to be a major component of compensation for employees in many companies. These companies will once again face the problem of underwater stock options during the next downturn in the U.S. economy. Such companies will need to develop and implement an effective stock option strategy that is based upon a thorough understanding of the ramifications of repricing and its alternatives. The sooner a company can rid itself of the confusion as to what must be done to effectively respond to the difficulties posed by underwater stock options, the greater its chances will be that it can retain talent critical to its success in today's competitive business environment.

Notes

1.   Employees are eligible to receive either incentive stock options or nonqualified stock options. Non-employee service providers, such as independent contractors, however, are eligible to receive nonqualified stock options, but are not eligible under the requirements of Code Section 422 to receive incentive stock options.

2.   Since October 1995, companies have been permitted to elect to report their stock based compensation under Statement No. 123, "Accounting for Stock-Based Compensation." However, from the financial reporting perspective, the accounting treatment provided under Statement No. 123 is not as favorable to a company issuing stock options as APB 25. For this reason, many companies that adopted APB 25 treatment have continued to use the accounting treatment thereunder to report their stock-based compensation. Under

APB 25, compensation cost is measured using the "intrinsic value method." FASB requires that all companies that continue to use APB 25 disclose in a footnote to their financial statement net income and earnings per share as if they had implemented Statement No. 123.

3. See FASB Interpretation No. 44, "Accounting for Certain Transactions Involving Stock Compensation" ("FIN 44"), which was adopted by FASB on March 31, 2000. According to a recent survey conducted on behalf of PricewaterhouseCoopers, almost 43% of 113 companies had repriced their options since 1988.

4. The grant of a new option in tandem with the cancellation of the underwater option may involve more than just a lowering of the exercise price, and may also affect the vesting and expiration terms of the new option.

5. FIN 44.

6. Id.

7. Id.

8. Id.

9. Id. Variable accounting occurs when the exercise price at grant is not certain. The grant must be expensed against the company's earnings in each quarter, based on the spread between the exercise and market price of the stock.

10. FIN 44. If the company's stock price decreases rather than increases after repricing, variable accounting treatment may result in periodic credits to earnings as the stock price decreases.

11. Treas. Reg. 1.162-27(e)(2)(vi)(B). For the purposes of this chapter, "options exchange" refers to a repricing by means of a cancellation of outstanding underwater options in exchange for the regrant of a new option at the then-current fair market value.

12. Code Section 162(m), Treas. Reg. 1.162-27(e)(2). The definition of an "outside director" for this purpose differs from that used for Section 16 of the Securities Exchange Act of 1934.

13. Treas. Reg. 1.162-27(e)(2)(vi)(A) requires that the plan under which the option is granted state the maximum number of shares that may be granted during a specified period to any employee in order for the performance-based compensation Section 162(m) exception to apply.

14. Treas. Reg. 1.162-27(e)(2)(vi)(B) provides that in the case of a repricing, "both the option that is deemed to be canceled and the option that is deemed to be granted reduce the maximum number of shares for which options may be granted to the employee under the plan."

15. Treas. Reg. 1.162-27(e)(2)(vi)(B).

16. See Temp. Reg. 14A.422A-1.

17. Code Section 422(d) provides that to the extent that the aggregate fair market value of the underlying shares of stock are exercisable by the optionee in any

calendar year exceeds $100,000, such options are not be treated as incentive stock options.

18. Code Section 422(d)(2) discusses the ordering rule for purposes of applying the $100,000 per year limitation.

19. See Item 402 of Regulation S-K issued by the Securities Exchange Commission.

20. Id.

21. Id.

22. See Press Release 2001-32 at *www.sec.gov/news/press/2001-32.txt.*

23. See Rule 13e-4 of the Securities Exchange Act of 1934.

24. See "Option Exchange Offers" discussed at *www.sec.gov/divisions/corpfin/repricings.htm.*

25. Rule 16b-3(d)1. A "non-employee director" is defined as a director who: (a) is not currently an officer or otherwise employed by the issuer or a parent or subsidiary of the issuer; (b) does not receive within the fiscal year compensation in excess of $60,000 for services as a consultant or in any capacity other than as a director of the issuer, or a parent or subsidiary of the issuer; (c) does not have an interest in any other transaction for which disclosure would be required in the issuer's proxy statement; and (d) is not engaged in a business relationship that would require disclosure under Item 404(b) or Regulation S-K. Rule 16b-3(b)(3)(i).

26. Section 16(a) of the Securities Exchange Act of 1934.

27. Section 5 of the Securities Act of 1933.

28. Section 3(a)(9) of the Securities Act of 1933.

29. The state blue-sky laws should always be checked for each state where the stock option plan is offered.

30. Code Section 280G(b)(2).

31. Code Section 280G(b)(2)(C).

32. Code Section 280G(a). An excise tax of 20% of an "excess parachute payment" is imposed on the person who receives such a payment, as provided under Code Section 4999(a). For this purpose, an "excess parachute payment" is defined under the rules that deny a deduction to the corporation that makes an excess parachute payment. Code Section 4999(b).

33. Institutional shareholders may insist upon no repricing if additional option grants are issued and may actually seek to add language that prohibits a repricing of new grants.

34. Code Section 422.

35. FIN 44.

36. Id.

37. Shareholder dilution generally refers to the effect that the grant of stock options has upon the other shareholders. When options are issued, an existing shareholder's ownership interest is potentially reduced to the extent that the value of the stock is greater than the exercise price of the option.

38. Option overhang refers either to the stock reserved for stock option plans or to unexercised options outstanding as a percentage of total company shares outstanding. Excessive overhang dilutes earnings per share and may result in shareholder opposition to new or amended stock option plans. Overhang is determined by a fraction whose numerator is option shares reserved or actually granted and the denominator is the number of total company shares outstanding.

39. FIN 44.

40. APB No. 25.

41. FIN 44.

42. An election under Code Section 83(b) must be filed within 30 days of the date the options was exercised. Code Section 83(b)(2), Treas. Reg. 1.83-2(b). No special form is required.

43. Code Section 83(a).

44. FIN 44.

45. Companies must establish the current "fair value" of their options when they are granted. FASB requires that companies use an option pricing model for valuing employee stock options that takes into consideration six specific variables. The most common option pricing model used by public companies is the Black-Scholes method, a mathematical formula that considers such factors as the volatility of returns on the underlying securities, the risk-free interest rate, the expected dividend rate, the relationship of the option price to the price of the underlying securities, and the expected option life.

46. FIN 44.

47. Option plans and agreements may and often do restrict the transfer of options. Code Section 422(b)(5) generally prohibits incentive stock options from being transferred during the optionee's lifetime.

48. Code Section 422(b)(5).

A Layperson's Glossary of Employee Stock Option Terminology

Alisa J. Baker

$\mathcal{A}$S WITH ANY SPECIALIZED FIELD, the world of employee stock options has its own vernacular. Stock options and related plans are governed, as well as influenced, by a wide array of laws, regulations, rules, and standards, including tax laws and concepts, securities laws, and accounting principles. Following is a glossary of many of the more commonly used words and phrases in this field. All references to the "Code" in this glossary refer to the Internal Revenue Code (which itself is defined below).

10% Owner

An employee who, at the time an incentive stock option is granted, owns stock possessing more than 10% of the total combined voting power of all classes of stock of the employer corporation or of its parent or subsidiary corporation. Under Section 422(b)(6) of the Code, such an employee is not eligible to receive an incentive stock option unless, as provided in Section 422(c)(5) of the Code, at the time such option is granted the option price is at least 110% of the fair market value of the company's stock subject to the option and such option by its terms is not exercisable after the expiration of five years from the date such option is granted.

Also refers to a beneficial owner of more than 10% of a class of equity securities of an issuer that is registered under Section 12 of the Securities Exchange Act of 1934.

Accounting Principles Board (APB)

A group established by the American Institute for Certified Public Accountants (AICPA) to help formulate generally accepted accounting principles. The predecessor of the Financial Accounting Standards Board (FASB).

Administrator

See "Plan Administrator."

Alternative Minimum Tax (AMT)

A federal tax imposed to ensure that taxpayers with large amounts of economic income pay at least a threshold amount of federal tax. The difference, if any, between the option price and the fair market value of the stock of the corporation on the date of exercise of an incentive stock option is an adjustment that is added to an employee's regular taxable income for purposes of computing alternative minimum taxable income (AMTI). Alternative minimum tax paid as a result of the exercise of an incentive stock option may result in a tax credit that may be applied against the employee's regular federal income tax liability in future years.

AMEX (American Stock Exchange)

The second largest organized stock exchange, on which corporate securities are traded. Because the listing requirements of this exchange are considered to be less stringent than those of the New York Stock Exchange, the exchange generally trades the securities of small-to-medium-sized corporations.

Amount Realized

A tax concept that represents the difference between what was paid for property and the amount received upon the sale or exchange of the property.

Annual Meeting

A meeting of a corporation's directors, officers, and shareholders/stockholders, held for the purpose of communicating the operating and financial results of the business for the prior fiscal year, the corporation's prospects for the future, and major decisions of management, and for deciding matters requiring the approval of the corporation's shareholders/stockholders. Generally, the election of the corporation's board of directors occurs at the annual meeting. Shareholders/stockholders who are not able to physically attend the annual meeting may vote on the election of directors and other matters brought before the meeting by submitting a proxy before the meeting authorizing a third party to vote their shares of stock.

Anti-dilution Adjustment

A change to the terms, conditions, and/or price of a security to prevent a diminution in value as the result of a change in the capital structure of a corporation. Typically, an employee stock option plan will provide for an appropriate adjustment in the number and kind of securities subject to the plan and to all outstanding employee stock options in the event of a change in the capitalization of the corporation.

Authorized but Unissued

The difference between the number of securities of a given class authorized for issuance under a corporation's charter documents and the number of securities of that class that have been issued and are presently outstanding.

Available for Grant

The incremental difference between the number of shares of stock authorized for issuance under a corporation's employee stock option plan and the number of shares of stock that have already been granted under option to optionees. Cancelled shares that are added back to the employee stock option plan and any increase in the number of shares of stock available for issuance pursuant to the plan are included in the calculation of shares "available for grant."

Basis

See "Tax Basis."

Beneficial Owner

For purposes of Section 13(d) of the Securities Exchange Act of 1934, a person who, directly or indirectly, through any contract, arrangement, understanding, relationship or otherwise, has or shares voting power (which includes the power to vote or to direct the voting of) a security and/or investment power (which includes the power to dispose of or to direct the disposition of) such security. For purposes of determining which equity securities are subject to reporting and liability under Section 16 of the Securities Exchange Act of 1934, a person who, directly or indirectly, through any contract, arrangement, understanding, relationship, or other means has or shares a direct or indirect pecuniary interest in equity securities.

Beneficial Ownership

For purposes of Section 16 of the Securities Exchange Act of 1934, a proprietary interest in securities based upon the holder's entitlement to the economic benefits resulting from a transaction in the subject securities, whether or not the holder is the record, or registered, owner of the securities.

Blackout Period

The period, as determined by a corporation, during which the securities of the corporation cannot be sold by certain designated individuals, typically the corporation's insiders. Generally, the period runs from some predetermined time following the release of the corporation's quarterly or annual financial results until 24 to 48 hours following the release of the subsequent period's financial results.

Also, a period during which the ability of participants or beneficiaries in a corporation's pension plan to direct or diversify assets credited to their accounts, to obtain loans from the plan, or to obtain distributions from the plan is temporarily suspended, limited, or restricted.

Black-Scholes Option Pricing Model

A mathematical formula used for valuing employee stock options that considers such factors as the volatility of returns on the underlying securities, the risk-free interest rate, the expected dividend rate, the relationship of the option price to the price of the underlying securities, and the expected option life. Developed by Fisher Black and Myron Scholes, the model was originally created to value options traded on European commodity exchanges.

Blue Sky Laws

State statutes that regulate the offer and sale of securities within a state's jurisdiction and which also are designed to prevent fraudulent activities in connection with such offers and sales. The relevant statutes vary from state to state. The phrase "blue sky" originates from a federal case that described such laws as aimed against "speculative schemes which hold no more basis than so many feet of blue sky."

Board of Directors

A group of individuals elected by a corporation's shareholders to set the policies and oversee the affairs of the corporation. The board of directors generally does not get involved in the day-to-day management of the corporation. The board of directors may also discharge other responsibilities as set forth in the corporation's charter documents or bylaws. The members of the board of directors are usually elected on an annual basis.

Broker/Brokerage Firm

An individual or a company that acts as an intermediary between a buyer and seller of securities. A broker receives compensation, in the form of a commission, for assisting in or effecting the purchase or sale of securities. A broker is "registered" with the National Association of Securities dealers and the exchange on which the securities are traded. Brokers are also regulated under federal and state securities laws.

Broker-Assisted Same-Day Sale

See "Same-Day Sale."

Cancellation

In the context of an employee stock option plan, a transaction (usually triggered by a specific event, such as an optionee's termination of employment) in which an outstanding employee stock option is declared void and inactive and the unexercised shares of stock subject to the stock option are returned to the pool of shares of stock reserved for issuance under the plan.

Capital Asset

Tax term used to describe property that is eligible for certain preferential tax treatment under the Code upon its sale or exchange. Historically, favorable tax treatment was afforded to this category of property in recognition of the fact that it constituted an investment reflecting accrued appreciation over an extended period of time (sometimes several years) and that, upon its sale or other disposition, the progressive tax rate structure would operate to penalize the recognition of this accrued appreciation all at one time. Much of this objective has been lost over the years, however, as a result of the multitude of regulatory changes to the original statutory provisions.

Defined in Section 1221 of the Code as property held by a taxpayer, other than (1) stock in trade, inventory or property held primarily for sale to customers in the ordinary course of business, (2) real property or depreciable property used in a trade or business, (3) a copyright, a literary, musical, or artistic composition or similar property of a taxpayer who created such property, (4) accounts or notes receivable acquired in the ordinary course of a trade or business, or (5) publications of the United States government received at a discount.

Capital Gain

The increase in value, or profit, realized from the sale or exchange of a capital asset; that is, the excess of the proceeds received from the transaction over the basis of the asset. Capital gains can be short-term (where the capital asset was held for one year or less) or long-term (where the capital asset was held for more than one year). Generally, long-term capital gains are taxed at rates more favorable than those applicable to ordinary income.

Capital Loss

The decrease in value realized from the sale or exchange of a capital asset; that is, the excess of the basis of the asset over the proceeds received from the transaction.

Capital Stock

The common equity securities of a corporation that confer the right to vote, select directors, receive dividends, and share in the residual assets upon the dissolution or winding up of the business. Generally, represents the basic ownership interest in the corporation. The term is often used interchangeably with "common stock" when the corporation has only one class of securities outstanding.

Capitalization

The total types and amount of the outstanding securities that have been issued by a corporation. A corporation's capitalization may include both equity securities and debt securities.

Cash Exercise

Form of exercise of an employee stock option where the option price for the number of shares of stock being purchased is paid with cash. Typically, this payment will be made with a cashiers' check or a personal check.

Cashless Exercise

Form of exercise of an employee stock option where the option price for the number of shares of stock being purchased is paid with consideration other than cash. Common cashless exercise methods include a stock swap exercise, delivery of a promissory note, and a broker-assisted same-day-sale transaction. Frequently used to refer to an arrangement between a corporation and a third party, such as a securities brokerage firm or a financial institution, whereby the third party will provide funds, on a temporary basis, to an employee to exercise an employee stock option, immediately upon which some or all of the shares of stock acquired upon exercise of the employee stock option will be sold to repay the funds advanced to initiate the transaction.

Certificate

A document that evidences ownership of a specific number of securities of a corporation. The certificate typically contains an alphanumeric identifier, the name of the issuing corporation, the number of securities represented by the certificate, and the name and address of the shareholder/stockholder.

Change in Capitalization

An adjustment to the capital structure of a corporation, such as a stock dividend, stock split, or reverse stock split, that results in either an increase in the number of outstanding securities, with a corresponding reduction in the value of each security, or a decrease in the number of outstanding securities, with a corresponding increase in the value of each security.

Change in Control

A transaction that alters the ownership of a corporation. Such transactions include mergers and consolidations, stock sales, and asset sales. Typically, an employee stock option plan will provide for the disposition of outstanding stock option grants in the event of a "change in control" of the issuer. Such dispositions may include assumption of the outstanding stock options by the acquiring corporation, substitution of an equivalent benefit by the acquiring corporation, acceleration of vesting with respect to some or all of the shares of stock subject to the outstanding stock option, and/or termination of the outstanding stock option (to the extent not previously exercised) as of the date of the "change in control" transaction.

"Cliff" Vesting

Term used to describe the vesting schedule for an employee stock option where all of the shares of stock subject to the stock option vest (or are earned) on the same date.

Code

The Internal Revenue Code, with such modifications, revisions, and additions, as in effect from time to time.

Commission

The Securities and Exchange Commission. See "Securities and Exchange Commission."

Common Stock

The basic ownership interest of a corporation that typically confers on the holder of the security the right to vote, select directors, receive dividends, and share in the residual assets upon the dissolution or winding up of the business. Unlike preferred stock, common stock has no preference to dividends or to any distribution of assets by the corporation.

Compensation Deduction

Expense for compensation paid or accrued by a corporation that is deductible by the corporation for income tax purposes.

Compensation Expense

For financial reporting purposes, the "cost" recognized by a corporation for the issuance of its securities in connection with a stock-based compensation plan or arrangement. Under APB Opinion No. 25, the amount of compensation expense associated with an employee stock option represents the "intrinsic value" of the employee stock option (the excess of the fair market value of the shares of stock subject to the option over the amount, if any, payable by the employee to purchase the shares of stock) calculated as of the "measurement date" of the option (typically, the date of grant of the employee stock option). Under SFAS No. 123, the amount of compensation expense associated with an employee stock option represents the "fair value" of the employee stock option calculated as of the date of grant of the option using a mathematical option pricing model (such as the Black-Scholes Option Pricing Model).

For federal income tax purposes, the amount that is potentially deductible by a corporation as a trade or business under Section 162 of the Code (subject to the application of Section 162(m)) in connection with the exercise of a non-qualified stock option or upon the disqualifying disposition of shares of stock acquired upon the exercise of an incentive stock option. Generally, the amount of deductible compensation expense is equal to the amount of compensation income recognized by the employee for federal income tax purposes.

Compensation Income

For federal income tax purposes, the amount of income recognized by an optionee in connection with the exercise of a non-qualified stock option or by an employee in connection with the disqualifying disposition of shares of stock acquired upon the exercise of an incentive stock option. For federal income tax purposes, this income is subject to taxation at ordinary income rates.

Confirmation of Exercise

A written statement issued by a corporation to an optionee setting forth specific information about a stock option exercise transaction. In the case of an exercise of an incentive stock option, this statement is sometimes used to provide the information required by Section 6039 of the Code to be provided to an employee.

Constructive Receipt

A tax concept applicable to cash-basis taxpayers. Where income is unreservedly subject to the demand of the taxpayer, so that he or she could have received payment, but chose not to do so, the income is regarded as having been constructively received and is taxed currently as if it had been received (even though actual payment does not take place until a later time).

Corporate Tax Deduction

For federal income tax purposes, the amount of compensation expense that is potentially deductible by a corporation as a trade or business under Section 162 of the Code (subject to the application of Section 162(m)) in connection with the exercise of a non-qualified stock option or upon the disqualifying disposition of shares of stock acquired upon the exercise of an incentive stock option. Generally, the amount of deductible compensation expense is equal to the amount of compensation income recognized by the employee for federal income tax purposes.

Corporation

Generally, an artificial entity formed for the purpose of conducting a business. A corporation is a legal entity that is separate from, and independent of, the persons who formed and/or own the business. A corporation possesses the attributes of (1) limited liability (that is, its shareholders/stockholders are not personally liable for the debts of the corporation), (2) centralized management (that is, responsibility for managing the business and affairs of the corporation resides with designated directors and officers rather than with the owners, the shareholders/ stockholders), (3) continuity of life (that is, the corporation has a perpetual existence that is not affected by the death or departure of its shareholders/stockholders), and (4) free transferability of interest (that is, the shareholders/stockholders have the ability, subject to any contractual limitations, to freely transfer or otherwise dispose of their shares of stock without affecting the corporation's status).

Derivative Security

A security that takes, or "derives," its value from another instrument. For purposes of Section 16 of the Securities Exchange Act of 1934, a derivative security includes any option, warrant, convertible security, stock appreciation right or similar right with an exercise or conversion privilege at a price related to an equity security, or similar securities with a value derived from the value of an equity security.

Date of Exercise

The date on which an employee stock option is exercised and some or all of the shares of stock underlying the stock option are purchased by the optionee.

Date of Grant

The date upon which an employee stock option is formally extended to an individual and becomes effective. The grant gives rise to certain contractual rights and obligations on the part of the optionee and the corporation.

Deduction

An expense item associated with the production of income that can be used to reduce revenue for purposes of determining taxable income.

Director

An individual elected by the shareholders/stockholders of a corporation to serve on the corporation's board of directors who performs the functions of a director set forth in the corporation's charter documents and bylaws.

Discount Stock Option

An employee stock option granted with an option price that is less than the fair market value of the corporation's stock on the date of grant. By virtue of the requirement under Section 422 (b)(4) of the Code that an incentive stock option must have an option price that is not less than the fair market value of the corporation's stock on the date of grant, a discount stock option will necessarily be a non-qualified stock option. Under APB Opinion No. 25, a discount stock option will result in compensation expense that must be calculated and recorded by the corporation. The amount of such compensation expense will be equal to the excess of the fair market value of the shares of stock subject to the option over the amount payable by the optionee to purchase the shares of stock calculated as of the date of grant.

Disposition

The relinquishment or transfer of property (such as shares of stock) by a person.

Disqualifying Disposition

The sale or other disposition of shares of stock acquired upon the exercise of an incentive stock option or Section 423 ESPP option before the satisfaction of the two holding period requirements for preferential tax treatment set forth in Section 422(a)(1) of the Code (that is, preferential tax treatment under Section 421(a) of the Code is available only if no disposition of such shares of stock occurs within two years from the date of grant of the incentive stock option nor within one year after the date of transfer of such shares of stock to the employee). In the year of the disqualifying disposition, the employee recognizes compensation income equal to the difference, if any, between the option price and the fair market value of the stock of the corporation on the date of exercise. Any post-exercise appreciation recognized by the employee as a result of the disposition is taxable as capital gain. Under Section 422(c)(2) of the Code, if the amount realized upon the disqualifying disposition that is treated as a sale or exchange with respect to which a loss (if sustained) would be recognized by the employee is less than the fair market value of the stock of the corporation on the date of exercise, the amount of compensation income recognized by the employee (and the amount deductible by the corporation) is limited to the amount realized on such sale or exchange over the adjusted basis of such shares of stock (generally, the aggregate option price plus any fees or other costs associated with the sale or exchange).

Double Trigger Provision

In a stock option plan, a provision stating that upon a change of control coupled with a termination of employment, the options vest fully and can be immediately exercised. See "Single Trigger Provision."

EDGAR (Electronic Data Gathering, Analysis, and Retrieval System)

An automated computer system developed and implemented by the Securities and Exchange Commission for the filing of registration statements, periodic reports, and other filings mandated under the federal securities laws by issuers registered under Section 12 of the Securities Exchange Act of 1934.

Employee

An individual who is subject to the will and control of an employer both as to what work will be done and as to how the work will be performed. Employee status is distinct from that of an independent contractor. For income tax purposes, withholding of income taxes on wages applies only to employees.

Employee Stock Option

See "Option" or "Stock Option."

Employee Stock Option Agreement

See "Option Agreement."

Employee Stock Option Plan

A formal arrangement, typically in writing, that provides for the granting of employee stock options to eligible participants in the plan upon the terms and conditions set forth in the plan.

Employee Stock Purchase Plan (ESPP)

See "Section 423 Plan."

Employer

Person who directs and controls the performance of services by an employee.

Employment Taxes

Generally, a term used to describe taxes imposed under the Federal Insurance Contributions Act and the Federal Unemployment Tax Act. These taxes are assessed against employers and, in the case of Federal Insurance Contributions Act taxes, employees with respect to the wages paid to such employees.

Equity

Term that refers to an ownership interest in a corporation. Equity also represents the amount of capital invested by the shareholders/stockholders plus the retained earnings of the business. The term is also used to denote the capital stock of a corporation.

Equity Compensation

Amounts paid by an employer to an employee or independent contractor for services rendered and work performed that take the form of an equity interest in the corporation.

Equity Security

A stock or similar security, or a security that is convertible, with or without consideration, into such a security, which provides an equity interest in the corporation.

Evergreen Provision

A replenishment feature in a stock plan that automatically increases at regular intervals the number of shares reserved under the plan.

Exercisablity

The ability to convert an employee stock option into the underlying shares of stock through their purchase or other acquisition.

Exercisable Date

The first date upon which an employee stock option may be converted into the underlying shares of stock through their purchase or other acquisition.

Exercise

The transaction in which an optionee elects to purchase some or all of the shares of stock underlying an employee stock option.

Exercise Date

The date on which an employee stock option is exercised and some or all of the shares of stock underlying the stock option are purchased by the optionee.

Exercise Notice

Form completed by an optionee and submitted to a corporation notifying the corporation of the optionee's desire to exercise his or her employee stock option and purchase all or a portion of the shares of stock subject to the stock option. Generally, an exercise notice requires the optionee to identify the employee stock option being exercised, indicate the number of shares of stock being purchased, provide payment of the aggregate option price for the shares of stock being purchased in a form permitted under the option agreement, make certain representations to the corporation concerning the optionee's investment intent, and agree to certain restrictions imposed on the shares of stock.

Exercise Price

The consideration in money or property that, pursuant to the terms of an employee stock option agreement, is the price at which the shares of stock subject to an employee stock option may be purchased. The exercise price is typically expressed on a per share basis. See also "Option Price."

Expiration Date

The last date on which an employee stock option may be exercised by an optionee. This date is typically set forth in the option agreement for the

employee stock option and usually ranges from five to ten years following the date of grant of the employee stock option. Also refers to the date
on which an employee stock option plan expires.

Fair Market Value

The value of a corporation's equity securities. In the case of a publicly
traded corporation, fair market value is typically based upon the price
at which the corporation's stock is traded. For purposes of an employee
stock plan, this is usually the closing price if the stock is traded on a major
exchange, or the average of the bid and ask price if the stock is traded
over-the-counter. In the case of a privately held corporations, fair market value is typically based upon an independent appraisal conducted
by one or more third parties or determined by the board of directors based
on all of the relevant facts and circumstances.

Federal Insurance Contributions Act (FICA)

A series of employment taxes imposed on employees and employers with
respect to the wages paid to employees. Presently consists of Social Security and Medicare taxes.

Financial Accounting Standards Board (FASB)

The private sector organization recognized by the Securities and Exchange Commission as the source for generally accepted accounting principles for corporations that offer and sell securities in the United States.

Fiscal Year

The annual accounting period for a corporation. A fiscal year is a period
of 12 consecutive months. It frequently coincides with the calendar year,
but can conclude at the end of a different month. For example, a fiscal
year can run from October 1 to September 30.

Form 3

The initial ownership report for directors, officers, beneficial owners of
more than 10% of a class of an issuer's registered equity securities, and
any other person subject to Section 16 of the Securities Exchange Act of

1934. A Form 3 requires information on the number of non-derivative securities and derivative securities beneficially owned at the time the reporting person becomes subject to Section 16 and, except in the case of an issuer's first registration of a class of equity securities pursuant to Section 12 of the Securities Exchange Act of 1934, must be filed with the Securities and Exchange Commission within 10 days of that date. A Form 3 must be filed with the Securities and Exchange Commission even if the reporting person does not own any securities of the issuer at the time the filing is required.

Form 4

Change in beneficial ownership report for directors, officers, beneficial owners of more than 10% of a class of an issuer's registered equity securities, and any other person subject to Section 16 of the Securities Exchange Act of 1934. A Form 4 requires information on any change in beneficial ownership of non-derivative securities and derivative securities by a reporting person that is not eligible for deferred reporting. With limited exceptions, a Form 4 must be filed with the Securities and Exchange Commission within two business days after the date of execution of the transaction that results in a reportable change in beneficial ownership.

Form 5

Annual change in beneficial ownership report for directors, officers, beneficial owners of more than 10% of a class of an issuer's registered equity securities, and any other person subject to Section 16 of the Securities Exchange Act of 1934. A Form 5 requires information on holdings and changes in beneficial ownership by a reporting person of non-derivative securities and derivative securities that are exempt from current reporting. A Form 5 must be filed with the Securities and Exchange Commission within 45 days after the end of the issuer's fiscal year.

Form 1099

A tax report that must be provided to a non-employee who received compensation income from a corporation and to the Internal Revenue Service describing the amount of compensation income earned or received during the taxable year covered by the report.

Form 10-K

An annual disclosure report for issuers subject to the reporting requirements of Section 13(a) or 15(d) of the Securities Exchange Act of 1934.
The report contains information about the business and management of
the issuer, legal proceedings involving the issuer, management compensation, and the issuer's latest audited financial statements. Form 10-K
must be filed within 90 days after the end of an issuer's fiscal year in 2003,
75 days after the end of an issuer's fiscal year in 2004, and 60 days after
the end of an issuer's fiscal year in 2005 and thereafter.

Form 10-Q

A quarterly report for issuers subject to the reporting requirements of
Section 13(a) or 15(d) to the Securities Exchange Act of 1934. The report
contains information about the business and management of the issuer,
and other specified information. In 2003, Form 10-Q must be filed within
45 days after the end of an issuer's first three fiscal quarters. In 2004, Form
10-Q must be filed within 40 days after the end of an issuer's first three
fiscal quarters. In 2005 and thereafter, Form 10-Q must be filed within 35
days after the end of an issuer's first three fiscal quarters.

Form S-8

Form of registration statement under the Securities Act of 1933 that may
be used by issuers subject to the reporting requirements of Section 13(a)
or 15(d) of the Securities Exchange Act of 1934 to register securities issuable to participants in an employee benefit plan, such as an employee
stock option plan.

Form W-2 Income

Income recognized by an individual in connection with the acquisition
of shares of stock upon the exercise of a non-qualified stock option or
upon the disqualifying disposition of shares of stock acquired upon the
exercise of an incentive stock option. For federal income tax purposes,
this income is subject to taxation at ordinary income rates.

Federal Unemployment Tax Act (FUTA)

An employment tax imposed on employers with respect to the wages paid
to employees.

Gain

The excess of the proceeds received over the amount originally paid for securities. In the context of an employee stock option, it is the difference between either the fair market value or sale price of shares of stock of the corporation acquired upon the exercise of the stock option on the date of exercise and the option price. This is also sometimes known as the "spread" on exercise.

Generally Accepted Accounting Principles (GAAP)

Substantive rules for the practice of accounting as established by the body of opinions and decisions issued by the FASB.

Grace Period

Period of time provided under an option agreement for the exercise of an employee stock option following termination of the optionee's employment. Typically, this period of time ranges from 30 days until the expiration of the original option term, may vary depending upon the reason for the termination of employment, and is limited to the exercise of shares of stock that were vested as of the date of termination.

Grant

A contractual right granted to an individual to purchase a specified number of shares of stock of the granting corporation at a specified price for a specified period of time. Also known as an "option."

Grant Agreement

See "Option Agreement."

Grant Date

The date upon which an employee stock option is formally extended to an individual and becomes effective. The grant gives rise to certain contractual rights and obligations on the part of the optionee and the corporation.

Grant Price

See "Exercise Price" and "Option Price."

Holding Period

A period of time during which an employee stock option has no exercisable shares and, consequently, cannot be exercised.

For an incentive stock option, the period of time that shares of stock acquired upon the exercise of the stock option must be held by the employee in order for the employee to be eligible for preferential tax treatment. Under Section 422(a)(1) of the Code, these holding periods are two years from the date of grant of the incentive stock option and one year after the date of transfer of such shares of stock to the employee.

For federal securities law purposes, the period of time that "restricted securities" must be beneficially owned by the holder before such securities may be resold in reliance on the exemption provided by Rule 144. Generally, this holding period is one year in order to satisfy the requirements of Rule 144(d) and two years in order to satisfy the requirements of Rule 144(k).

Incentive Stock Option (ISO)

An employee stock option that meets the requirements of Section 422(b) of the Code and, therefore, qualifies for the preferential tax treatment under Section 421 of the Code. Generally, an incentive stock option does not give rise to federal income tax consequences for the employee either at the time of grant or at exercise. Instead, the employee is subject to taxation at the time of disposition of the shares of stock acquired upon the exercise of the incentive stock option.

Income Tax Regulations

Rules promulgated by the Internal Revenue Service implementing and interpreting the statutory provisions of the Code. Congressional authority for the issuance of regulations is set forth in Section 7805 of the Code. While such rules are not law, they represent the Internal Revenue Service's interpretation of the proper application of the law and are presumed to be valid.

Income Taxation

System for taxing the annual earnings of individuals, corporations, and other persons. Income taxes are imposed at the federal. State, and local government levels.

Indexed Stock Option

A stock option with an option price that is periodically adjusted in relation to a market, industry or peer group performance (such as the Standard & Poor's 500). Economically, for the stock option to have value to the optionee, the corporation's stock must outperform the designated performance indicator. While it is possible that the stated option price can be decreased if the designated performance indicator declines over the option term, many employee stock option plans do not permit the option price to drop below the fair market value of the corporation's stock on the date of grant.

Since the option price for this type of employee stock option changes over time, for financial reporting purposes it is considered a "variable" award that results in periodic compensation expense until the option price is finally fixed.

Initial Public Offering (IPO)

A corporation's first offering of securities to the general public under a registration statement prepared and filed with the Securities and Exchange Commission in accordance with the Securities Act of 1933. The offering must also be made in compliance with the requirements of the securities laws of the various states where the securities will be offered for sale and sold.

Insider

A general term referring to persons who, by virtue of their positions within a corporation, have access to confidential information about the corporation. Frequently used to denote the directors, officers, beneficial owners of more than 10% of a class of an issuer's registered equity securities, and persons otherwise subject to Section 16 of the Securities Exchange Act of 1934.

Insider Trading

A person's wrongful use or wrongful communication, whether directly or indirectly, of confidential information to purchase or sell a security, if the person knows, or is reckless in not knowing, that such information has been obtained wrongfully, such as through theft, conversion, misap-

propriation or a breach of fiduciary, contractual, employment, personal
or other relationship of trust or confidence.

Internal Revenue Code

Federal statutes that provides for the taxation of individuals, corporations, and other persons.

Internal Revenue Service (IRS)

Agency of the federal government, under the supervision of the Department of the Treasury, that is responsible for administering the federal
tax laws, including the Code.

In-the-Money

Term used to describe an employee stock option where the current fair
market value of the shares of stock subject to the stock option is greater
than the option price.

ISO Amount Limitation

A dollar limitation to the amount of stock that can receive preferential
tax treatment under an incentive stock option grant. As set forth in Section 422(d) of the Code, to the extent that the aggregate fair market value
of the shares of stock with respect to which incentive stock options are
exercisable for the first time by an employee during any calendar year
(under all plans of the employee's employer corporation and its parent
and subsidiary corporations) exceeds $100,000, such stock options shall
be treated as non-qualified stock options to the extent of the amounts in
excess of $100,000. For purposes of applying this rule, options are to be
taken into account in the order in which they were granted. In addition,
for purposes of applying this rule, the fair market value of any shares of
stock is to be determined as of the time the incentive stock option with
respect to such shares of stock was granted.

Issuer

A corporation that is issuing, or that has issued, securities. Frequently
used to describe an entity that has issued securities that is subject to the
requirements of the federal securities laws.

Leave of Absence

A temporary, approved absence from employment. For purposes of applying the incentive stock option rules, a leave of absence is not considered an interruption of the employment relationship if the leave is shorter than 91 days or the employee's right to reemployment is guaranteed by statute or contract.

Legend

Statement printed on a stock certificate to indicate that the securities represented by the certificate are subject to limitations or restrictions on transfer. Generally, used to denote that the securities were issued in a private placement and, therefore, are "restricted securities" for purposes of the federal securities laws. May also reflect a contractual restriction that has been placed on the securities by the issuer as a condition to their original issuance.

Legended Stock

Securities that are subject to one or more limitations or restrictions on transfer. Generally, these restrictions are reflected in a written statement placed on the stock certificate. Also called "lettered stock."

Lettered Stock

Securities that are subject to one or more limitations or restrictions on transfer. Generally, these restrictions are reflected in a written statement placed on the stock certificate. Also called "legended stock."

Loan Exercise

An exercise of an employee stock option in which the corporation loans the optionee sufficient funds to cover the cost of the exercise. Generally, the ability to exercise an employee stock option using a loan is authorized in the employee stock option plan and set forth in the option agreement.

"Lock-Up" Restrictions

Transfer restrictions imposed by the underwriters of a public offering of securities on the directors, officers, principal shareholders, and, possibly, others associated with the issuer in order to maintain an orderly trading market in the issuer's securities.

"Mature" Shares

For financial reporting purposes, shares of stock that have been held by an employee for at least six months after purchase or other acquisition. Under Emerging Issues Task Force Issue No. 84-18, to avoid "variable" plan accounting treatment for a stock swap exercise, the swapped shares must be "mature" shares. If the shares of stock are considered to be "immature" shares, the transaction is viewed as the settlement of a stock appreciation right that triggers a compensation expense to the corporation.

Measurement Date

For financial reporting purposes, the date on which compensation expense is measured for an employee stock option grant under APB Opinion No. 25.

Medicare

An employment tax for hospital and medical insurance imposed on employees and employers under the Federal Insurance Contributions Act with respect to wages paid to employees.

Merger

A combination of two or more corporations into a single entity. Generally, a merger is effected pursuant to a statutory provision under state corporation law.

National Association of Securities Dealers, Inc. (NASD)

A self-regulatory organization subject to the Securities Exchange Act of 1934 comprised of brokers and dealers in the over-the-counter securities market. The NASD was established in the late 1930s to regulate the over-the-counter securities market.

National Association of Securities Dealers, Inc., Automated Quotations System (NASDAQ)

A computerized network showing quotations and transaction information with respect to securities traded in the over-the-counter market which meet the size and trading volume requirements to be quoted on the system. NASDAQ tends to reflect prices for the more active OTC-traded securities.

New York Stock Exchange (NYSE)

The oldest and largest organized stock exchange on which securities are traded. Issuers listed on the NYSE must meet more stringent requirements as to net earnings, assets, and trading volume than those required by other stock exchanges.

No-Action Letter

Interpretive letter issued by the SEC to a specific requestor, indicating the SEC staff's advice regarding the application of specific securities forms or rules. No-action letters are available to the general public when they are issued.

Nonqualified Stock Option (NSQO, NSO)

An employee stock option that does not satisfy the requirements of a statutory stock option under the Code. Consequently, this type of employee stock option gives rise to federal income tax consequences on the date of exercise. In addition, this type of employee stock option typically requires payment of withholding taxes at the time of exercise on the difference, if any, between the option price and the fair market value of the stock of the corporation on the date of exercise. Such taxes may include both income and employment taxes. Also known as a "nonstatutory stock option."

Non-Recourse Loan

Term used to describe a loan or other obligation that does not provide for personal liability against the debtor. In the event of a default on the obligation, the creditor is limited to recovery on the collateral provided for in the loan.

Nonstatutory Stock Option (NSO)

See "Non-Qualified Stock Option."

Nontransferability Restriction

Term used to describe a restriction imposed on a security that precludes its transfer or conveyance to a third party.

Notice of Exercise

Form completed by an optionee and submitted to a corporation notifying the corporation of the optionee's desire to exercise his or her employee stock option and purchase all or a portion of the shares of stock subject to the stock option. Generally, an exercise notice requires the optionee to identify the employee stock option being exercised, indicate the number of shares of stock being purchased, provide payment of the aggregate option price for the shares of stock being purchased in a form permitted under the option agreement, make certain representations to the corporation concerning the optionee's investment intent, and agree to certain restrictions imposed on the shares of stock.

Offering Period

With respect to an ESPP, the period starting with the grant, or offering date and ending with the exercise date.

Officer

Corporate officials responsible for managing the day-to-day operations of a corporation. For purposes of Section 16 of the Securities Exchange Act of 1934, an issuer's president, principal financial officer, principal accounting officer (or if there is no such accounting officer, the controller), any vice-president of the issuer in charge of a principal business unit, division or function, any other officer who performs a policy-making function or any other person who performs similar policy-making functions for the issuer.

Option

A contractual right granted to an individual to purchase a specified number of shares of stock of the granting corporation at a specified price for a specified period of time. Also known as a "grant." As set forth in the Income Tax regulations, the term "option" includes the right or privilege of an individual to purchase stock from a corporation by virtue of an offer of the corporation continuing for a stated period of time, whether or not irrevocable, to sell such stock at a pre-determined price, such individual being under no obligation to purchase. Such a right or privilege, when granted, must be evidenced in writing. The individual who has such right or privilege is referred to as the "optionee."

Option Agreement

A written contract setting forth the terms and conditions of an employee stock option grant. While no particular form of words is necessary, the written agreement should express, among other things, an offer to sell at the option price and the period of time during which the offer shall remain open. Typically, the written agreement also contains the complete name of the individual receiving the stock option, the effective date of the stock option, the type of stock option granted, such as ISO or NSO, the number of shares of stock covered by the option, the option price, and the vesting schedule for the shares of stock covered by the option.

Option Date

See "Grant Date."

Option Plan

A formal program adopted by a corporation, often in writing, that provides for the grant of employee stock options to one or more individuals upon the terms and conditions set forth in the plan document and the issuance of shares of stock of the corporation upon the exercise of such stock options.

Option Price

The consideration in money or property which, pursuant to the terms of an employee stock option agreement, is the price at which the shares of stock subject to an employee stock option may be purchased. The exercise price is typically expressed on a per share basis. See also "Exercise Price."

Option Term

The period of time granted to an individual to exercise an employee stock option. Generally, the term of an employee stock option ranges from five to 10 years.

Optionee

The recipient of an employee stock option. In the case of an incentive stock option, the optionee must be an employee of the granting corporation or a parent corporation or subsidiary corporation of the granting corporation at both the time of grant of the stock option and the time of exercise of the stock option (or have been an employee within three months of the date of exercise). In the case of a non-qualified stock option, the optionee may be either an employee of the granting corporation or, if provided in the employee stock option plan, a non-employee (such as a non-employee director or a consultant or other independent contractor providing services to the granting corporation or a parent corporation or subsidiary corporation of the granting corporation.

Ordinary Income

Income that does not qualify for preferential tax treatment under the federal income tax laws, such as wages, dividends, and interest income. Under Section 64 of the Code, any gain from the sale or exchange of property which is neither a capital asset nor property described in Section 1231 of the Code.

Out-of-the-Money

Term used to describe an employee stock option where the option price is greater than the current fair market value of the shares of stock subject to the stock option. The term "underwater" also refers to this situation.

Outstanding Option

An employee stock option which has been formally granted by a corporation and is not cancelled, exercised or expired. The shares of stock underlying an employee stock option have their own status, which is affected by exercise and expiration of the stock option as well as cancellation.

Overhang

Used as a measure of dilution, this is the percentage of company stock represented by all potentially grantable shares under the plan. It is calculated by adding the total number of shares represented by outstanding, unexercised stock options to the number of additional shares available for grant and then dividing that sum by the total number of shares of common stock outstanding.

Over-the-Counter Market

The public trading market for securities which are not traded on either the AMEX or the NYSE. It is composed of brokerage firms making a market and executing transactions in non-listed securities. The over-the-counter market operates primarily through telephone transmissions rather than through the auction-style market found at the exchanges.

Par Value

A dollar amount assigned to shares of stock by the corporation's charter documents. It may be used to compute the dollar accounting value of common shares on a corporation's balance sheet. Many corporations issue no-par stock. Par value has no relation to fair market value.

Parent Corporation

A corporation that owns a controlling interest in the securities of another corporation. For purposes of the incentive stock option rules, any corporation (other than the employer corporation) in an unbroken chain of corporations ending with the employer corporation if, at the time of grant of the employee stock option, each of the corporations other than the employer corporation owns stock possessing 50% or more of the total combined voting power of all classes of stock in one of the other corporations in such chain.

Performance-Based Stock Option

An employee stock option granted with terms that provide that the stock option will be exercisable as to the shares of stock subject to the stock option only upon the attainment of one or more performance-based objectives (that is, objectives other than merely continued service with the corporation). For financial reporting purposes, a performance-based stock option is considered a "variable" award that results in a periodic compensation expense for the corporation until the stock option vests or is settled.

Plan

A formal program adopted by a corporation that provides for the issuance and distribution of equity securities of the corporation, such as shares of stock, to one or more individuals upon the terms and conditions set forth in the plan document.

Plan Administrator

An individual or committee of individuals authorized under an employee stock option plan to administer and carry out the objectives, purposes, terms, and conditions of an employee stock option plan. The plan administrator usually selects the individuals to whom stock option grants are to be made, determines the number of shares of stock to be covered by a particular grant, sets the option price at which the grant is made, approves the form or forms of written agreement to accompany each grant, and determines all other terms and conditions of the grant (consistent with the employee stock option plan). Typically, the plan administrator will have the power to establish, amend, and rescind rules and policies deemed necessary or appropriate for the proper administration of the employee stock option plan, to make all necessary determinations under the plan, to construe and interpret the provisions of the plan, and to amend or terminate the plan and, under certain circumstances, outstanding stock option grants. Often a corporation's board of directors will act as the administrator of the employee stock option plan or will delegate responsibility for administering the plan to a subcommittee of the board of directors.

For purposes of Section 16 of the Securities Exchange Act of 1934, the plan administrator of an employee stock option plan of an issuer with a class of equity securities that has been registered under Section 12 of the Securities Exchange Act of 1934 will often be composed of individuals who qualify as "non-employee" directors for purposes of Rule 16b-3.

For purposes of Section 162(m) of the Code, the plan administrator of an employee stock option plan of a "publicly-held corporation" (as that term is defined under Section 162(m)(2)) must be comprised of individuals who qualify as "outside" directors (as that term is defined in the income tax regulations) in order for compensation to be eligible for the "performance-based compensation" exception to that provision.

Plan Expiration Date

The date after which shares of stock may no longer be granted, awarded, or issued pursuant to the terms and conditions of a stock plan.

Post-Termination Exercise Period

Period of time provided under an option agreement for the exercise of an employee stock option following termination of the optionee's employment. Typically, this period of time ranges from 30 days until the expiration of the original option term, may vary depending upon the reason for the termination of employment, and is limited to the exercise of shares of stock that were vested as of the date of termination.

Preferential Tax Treatment

Tax benefits available to an employee through an incentive stock option, which include deferral of the recognition of income in connection with the acquisition of the shares of stock upon the exercise of the stock option and the potential recharacterization of the pre-exercise appreciation in such shares of stock as capital gain rather than ordinary income.

Preferred Stock

Equity securities of a corporation that carry certain rights, preferences, and privileges superior to the common stock. Preferred stock generally receives an investment return at a specific rate whenever dividends are declared by a corporation. Preferred stock has priority to the earnings and assets (in the event of a liquidation) of the corporation before distributions may be made to the common shareholders.

Premium-Priced Stock Option

An employee stock option with an option price that is greater than the fair market value of the corporation's stock on the date of grant.

Private Letter Ruling (PLR)

A ruling issued by the IRS to a specific taxpayer, indicating the IRS interpretation of the tax law with respect to a stated set of facts. PLRs include private letter rulings and National Office Technical Memoranda. PLRs bind the IRS only as to the taxpayer requesting the ruling and under Section 6110(j) of the Code may not be cited as precedent.

Privately Held Company

A corporation the securities of which are not publicly traded. Also termed "closely held." Because there is no public market for the corporation's stock, typically the corporation's board of directors will determine the fair market value of the corporation's stock.

Promissory Note

A written promise to pay a specific amount of money owed at a specified time in the future. A promissory note may be unsecured or may be secured by collateral acceptable to the holder of the note.

Prospectus

A written document used as a selling piece in an offering of securities that contains certain specified information about the issuer, its business and financial condition, and the terms and conditions of, and risks associated with, the offering. A prospectus is a condensed version of the registration statement filed with the Securities and Exchange Commission in connection with the offering of securities.

Proxy

A grant of authority to vote the securities of another person. Also refers to the person authorized to vote the securities on behalf of another and/or the written document granting the authority.

Proxy Notice

A written notice to a shareholder/stockholder providing notification of the date, time, and place of a corporation's annual meeting of shareholders/stockholders and describing the matters to be submitted for the approval of the shareholders/stockholders at such meeting.

Proxy Solicitation

A request to be empowered to vote the securities of another person. Typically, a corporation will solicit the authority to vote the securities of its shareholders/stockholders at the corporation's annual meeting of shareholders/stockholders.

Proxy Statement

Solicitation materials relating to an issuer's annual meeting of shareholders, which must be delivered in advance of the meeting. Generally, these materials describe the agenda items for the meeting and contain certain specific information about the directors and principal shareholders/stockholders of the corporation, the compensation of management, and detailed information on proposals to be submitted to the shareholders/stockholders for approval.

Public Offering

An offering of securities to the general public under a registration statement prepared and filed with the Securities and Exchange Commission in accordance with the Securities Act of 1933. The offering must also be made in compliance with the requirements of the securities laws of the various states where the securities will be offered for sale and sold.

Pyramid Exercise

A transaction in which an optionee exercises a minimum number of shares of stock underlying an employee stock option for cash and then immediately tenders such shares of stock back to the corporation at their appreciated value to exercise additional shares of stock under the stock option. Through a series of successive stock swaps in this manner, the optionee is able to fully exercise the shares of stock subject to the employee stock option. In this manner, the employee stock option can be fully exercised with a minimum cash investment. This results in the optionee receiving shares of stock with an aggregate value equal to the total amount of appreciation in value inherent in the stock option at the time that the transaction is initiated. For purposes of APB Opinion No. 25, a pyramid exercise is viewed as a cash settlement of a stock appreciation right and will result in recordable compensation expense for financial reporting purposes.

Qualifying Disposition

A sale of statutory option stock in accordance with the applicable statutory holding periods.

Readily Ascertainable Fair Market Value

Required characteristic for an employee stock option in order for the stock option to be subject to taxation under Section 83 of the Code at the time of grant. In order to have a readily ascertainable fair market value, the Income Tax regulations require that the stock option either be actively traded on an established securities market or, if not actively traded on an established securities market, the fair market value of the stock option be measurable with reasonable accuracy. The Income Tax regulations further provide a series of conditions that must be satisfied in order for an employee stock option to meet the "reasonably accurate measurement" test, including, among other things, free transferability of the stock option and the absence of restrictions that could significantly affect the value of the stock option or the underlying shares of stock. Since employee stock options are virtually always non-transferable and subject to vesting restrictions, such stock options seldom would have a readily ascertainable fair market value at the time of grant. As a result, the compensatory element of the acquisition of the employee stock option will not be subject to taxation under Section 83 of the Code until the stock option is exercised.

Realize

Tax concept that describes when gain accruing to a taxpayer will be considered income for taxation purposes. Generally, a gain is considered "realized," and therefore subject to taxation, when it has been received by a person for such person's use, benefit or disposal. For example, the exercise of an employee stock option to purchase shares of stock that have appreciated in value will be considered a realization of gain since the optionee has taken the final steps to obtain the benefits of economic gain that had previously accrued to the optionee.

Recapitalization

An internal reorganization of the capital structure of the corporation. Typically, a reorganization involves a change to the type or number of securities outstanding. Sometimes the transaction will involve an amendment to the corporation's charter documents.

Recognize

Tax concept that describes when a realized gain will be subject to taxation. Most realized gains are to be reported, and taxes on the resulting income are to be paid, currently. In some instances, however, a realized gain may not be immediately subject to taxation by virtue of a specific statutory provision that overrides the general treatment of the transaction and relieves the taxpayer of the obligation of reporting the gain(possibly until a later time). For example, Section 1036 of the Code is a non-recognition provision that provides that any gain realized from an exchange of shares of stock of a corporation for other shares of stock of the same corporation (such as in a stock swap exercise of an employee stock option) is not to be recognized at the time of the exchange. Instead, typically an adjustment to the basis of the property involved is made to preserve any unrecognized gain or loss, which may eventually be subject to taxation at a later time.

Record Date

The date on which an individual must officially own securities in order to derive an adjustment resulting from a change in capitalization, such as a stock split, a stock dividend or a reverse stock split. As provided in an employee stock option plan, typically employee stock options that are outstanding as of the record date will be adjusted to retain their relative value to the corporation's other outstanding securities. Employee stock options granted after the record date are adjusted.

Recourse

Term used to describe a loan or other obligation that provides for personal liability against the debtor. In the event of a default on the obligation, the creditor can seek to foreclose on the personal assets of the debtor.

Registration

Formal process for the issuance of securities under the federal and/or state securities laws that permit the public sale of securities. Also, the name or names that appear on a stock certificate indicating ownership of the shares of stock.

Regrant

The reissuance or replacement of a previously granted employee stock option, often with terms and conditions that differ from those in the original stock option.

Regulation D

Exemption promulgated by the Securities and Exchange Commission under the Securities Act of 1933 for the private placement of securities which permits limited offerings of securities made in compliance with the conditions of the regulation and exempts such offerings from the registration requirements of the Securities Act of 1933.

Regulation G

Provision promulgated by the Board of Governors of the Federal Reserve System to regulate the extension of credit by persons other than banks or brokers and dealers in connection with the purchase or carrying of marginable securities. Generally, this provision would apply to the extension of credit by certain corporations in connection with the purchase of shares of stock under an employee stock option plan.

Regulation T

Provision promulgated by the Board of Governors of the Federal Reserve System to regulate the extension of credit by brokers and dealers in connection with the purchase or carrying of securities.

Reload Stock Option

A stock option granted to an individual who has exercised another stock option, typically by means of a stock swap exercise. Typically, the number of shares of stock granted under the reload stock option is equal to the number of shares of stock tendered to the corporation in the stock swap exercise. The option price of the reload stock option is equal to the fair market value of the corporation's stock on the date of grant.

Replacement Grant

A new employee stock option grant that is intended to replace a previously granted stock option, often with terms and conditions that differ in some respect from those contained in the original stock option. Frequently, when an employee stock option is "repriced," the transaction will take the form of a cancellation of the original employee stock option and the grant of a new "replacement" stock option.

Reporting Person

A general term referring to directors, officers, beneficial owners of more than 10% of a class of an issuer's registered equity securities, and any other person otherwise subject to Section 16 of the Securities Exchange Act of 1934.

Repricing

The adjustment of the option price of an outstanding employee stock option to reflect a decline in the value of the corporation's stock subject to the stock option. Typically, a stock option "repricing" takes the form of either an amendment of an outstanding stock option to reduce the exercise price or a cancellation of an outstanding employee stock option in exchange for the grant of a new stock option that has an option price equal to or greater than the current fair market value of the corporation's stock. The repricing of employee stock options is subject to extensive regulation and may trigger, among other things, significant income tax, securities law, and accounting consequences.

Repurchase

The reacquisition of shares of stock from an individual by a corporation. Depending on the nature of a corporation's repurchase rights, the corporation may pay the original cost of the shares of stock to the individual or the fair market value of the shares of stock at the time of repurchase.

Repurchase Rights

Contractual agreement in which a corporation has the right to repurchase shares of stock which have been acquired by an individual through the exercise of an employee stock option upon the occurrence of a specified event (such as termination of employment). In publicly traded corporations, these repurchase rights typically apply to shares of stock that were acquired upon the exercise of an employee stock option prior to vesting. In privately-held corporations, these repurchase rights may apply to all shares of stock acquired upon the exercise of an employee stock option, regardless of whether the shares of stock are vested or unvested. Many forms of repurchase rights will expire when a corporation's securities are publicly traded.

Restricted Securities

For securities law purposes, shares of stock issued in a transaction that was not registered under the Securities Act of 1933 (usually because of reliance on an exemption from the registration requirements of such laws). The resale of these securities must be made under a registered offering or pursuant to an exemption from registration, such as Rule 144.

Revenue Ruling

A ruling published by the Internal Revenue Service (IRS), stating the IRS position (and establishing precedent for audit positions by taxpayers) on the application of the tax law to specific facts.

Reverse Stock Split

Generally, a change in the capitalization of a corporation that decreases the number of securities outstanding and adjusts the value of the securities upward.

Right of First Refusal

Contractual restriction imposed on shares of stock that entitles a corporation to match any third party offer to purchase the shares of stock subject to the restriction on the same terms and conditions as the third party offer.

Right of Repurchase

Contractual agreement in which a corporation has the right to repurchase shares of stock which have been acquired by an individual through the exercise of an employee stock option upon the occurrence of a specified event (such as termination of employment). In publicly-traded corporations, these repurchase rights typically apply to shares of stock that were acquired upon the exercise of an employee stock option prior to vesting. In privately-held corporations, these repurchase rights may apply to all shares of stock acquired upon the exercise of an employee stock option, regardless of whether the shares of stock are vested or unvested. Many forms of repurchase rights will expire when a corporation's securities are publicly traded.

Rule 144

Rule promulgated by the Securities and Exchange Commission as a "safe harbor" for the resale of "restricted securities" (that is, securities that were acquired other than in a public offering) and "control securities" (that is, securities owned by affiliates of the corporation).

Rule 16b-3

Rule promulgated by the Securities and Exchange Commission that provides that transactions between an issuer that has registered a class of equity securities under Section 12 of the Securities Exchange Act of 1934 (including an employee benefit plan sponsored by the issuer) and a director or officer of the issuer that involve equity securities of the issuer will be exempt from the operation of the "short-swing profits" recovery rule of Section 16(b) of the Securities Exchange Act of 1934 if the transaction satisfies the applicable conditions set forth in the rule.

Run Rate

Used as a measure of dilution, this is the number of options granted annually (less option cancellations) as a percentage of total shares issued and outstanding.

Sale

A transaction involving the disposition of property, such as shares of stock, in exchange for the receipt of consideration for such property.

Same-Day Sale

A form of "cashless exercise" of an employee stock option in which an individual sets the sale price with a broker on the exercise date (in the case of options) or the purchase date (in the case of a purchase under a Section 423 plan), has the shares delivered directly to the broker, and, on delivery of the shares, receives payment for the shares sold.

Section 12 Registration

Registration of a class of an issuer's equity securities under Section 12 of the Securities Exchange Act of 1934. Registration under Section 12 is required if securities of the class are listed on a national securities exchange or are held by 500 or more individuals and the issuer has total assets exceeding $10 million, as of the last day of the issuer's most recent fiscal year.

Section 16

Provision of the Securities Exchange Act of 1934 that, among other things, requires the directors and officers of an issuer that has registered a class

of its equity securities under Section 12, as well as the beneficial owners
of more than 10% of any class of the issuer's registered equity securities,
to file periodic reports with the Securities and Exchange Commission disclosing their holdings and changes in beneficial ownership of the issuer's
equity securities and further requires such directors, officers, and beneficial owners to turn over to the issuer any profits realized from the
purchase and sale, or sale and purchase, of the issuer's equity securities
made within a period of less than six months.

Section 16(a)

Provision of the Securities Exchange Act of 1934 that requires the directors and officers of an issuer that has registered a class of its equity securities under Section 12, as well as the beneficial owners of more than 10%
of any class of the issuer's registered equity securities, to file periodic
reports with the Securities and Exchange Commission disclosing their
holdings and changes in beneficial ownership of the issuer's equity securities.

Section 16(b)

Provision of the Securities Exchange Act of 1934 that requires the directors and officers of an issuer that has registered a class of its equity securities under Section 12, as well as the beneficial owners of more than 10%
of any class of the issuer's registered equity securities, to return over to
the issuer any profits realized from the purchase and sale, or sale and
purchase, of the issuer's equity securities within a period of less than six
months.

Section 162(m)

Provision of the Code that limits the ability of publicly-traded corporations to deduct as an ordinary and necessary business expense certain
employee remuneration in excess of $1 million paid to specified "cov-
ered employees" of the corporation.

Section 423 Plan

An employee stock purchase plan (ESPP) that qualifies under Section 423
of the Code.

Section 83

Provision of the Code that governs the taxation of property (other than cash) received in connection with the performance of services. Section 83 governs the federal income tax consequences of the grant and exercise of a non-qualified stock option.

Section 83(b) Election

A written statement filed with the appropriate Internal Revenue Service Center under which a taxpayer elects to include in gross income in the year of transfer the fair market value of property (such as shares of stock) acquired subject to transfer restrictions and a substantial risk of forfeiture on the date of transfer over the amount (if any) paid for such property, rather than the fair market value of such property on the date when such property is transferable or not subject to a substantial risk of forfeiture, whichever is applicable, over the amount (if any) paid for such property. In the case of an employee stock option, where the shares of stock acquired on exercise are subject to transfer restrictions and a substantial risk of forfeiture, the filing of a Section 83(b) election enables an employee to calculate and pay taxes, if any, arising in connection with the acquisition of such shares of stock as of the exercise date rather than as of the date such shares of stock vest. If the employee does not make the election, the taxes will be based on the fair market value of the shares of stock acquired on exercise on the date such shares vest. A Section 83(b) election must conform to the requirements set forth in the Income Tax regulations and must be made not later than 30 days after the date of such transfer of property.

Section 6039

Provision of the Code that requires corporations to provide, by January 31 of the following year, certain specified information to employees who have exercised an incentive stock option.

Securities Act of 1933

Federal statutes that govern the offer and sale of securities through the channels of interstate commerce. The Securities Act of 1933 requires full disclosure in the offer of securities and prohibits fraud in the sale of securities. Full disclosure is achieved through the registration process, whereby issuers of securities must file a formal registration statement with the Securities and Exchange Commission before securities are distributed and must disclose in a formal prospectus material information concerning the security offered and the risks involved in the investment. Th Securities Act of 1933 also exempts certain securities and certain transactions from the registration requirements of the Act.

Securities and Exchange Commission (SEC)

Agency of the federal government created under the Securities Exchange Act of 1934 that administers the federal laws regulating the offer and sale of securities within the United States.

Securities Exchange Act of 1934

Federal statutes that require securities exchanges to register with the Securities and Exchange Commission or to obtain an exemption from registration as a prerequisite of doing business. Issuers must register their securities with the Securities and Exchange Commission before they can be traded on an exchange or, in many instances, in the over-the-counter market. The Securities Exchange Act of 1934 contains a variety of requirements concerning periodic reporting, proxy solicitations, the Foreign Corrupt Practices Act, tender offers, and insider trading.

Security

General term, used to describe instruments, such as shares of stock, bonds, and debentures, as well as other instruments that have one or more characteristics of a security. The traditional definition of a security is an instrument that involves an investment where the return is primarily or exclusively dependent on the efforts of a person or persons other than the investor.

Sequential Exercise Rule

A restriction imposed on incentive stock options granted before January 1, 1987 that did not allow the stock options to be exercised in a sequence different from the order in which they were granted.

Share

An individual unit of a class of equity securities that represents the basic ownership interest of a corporation, usually denoted by a share certificate.

Share Certificate

A document that evidences ownership of a specific number of securities of a corporation. The certificate typically contains an alpha-numeric identifier, the name of the issuing corporation, the number of securities represented by the certificate, and the name and address of the shareholder/stockholder.

Shares Outstanding

The equity securities of a corporation that have been issued to, and are currently held by, the shareholders/stockholders of the corporation. In the context of an employee stock plan, the shares of stock of a corporation that have been sold and issued to, and are currently held by, the participants in the plan.

Share Reserve

The number of shares of stock that have been authorized and reserved by a corporation's board of directors for issuance pursuant to an employee stock option plan.

Shareholder

A person who owns one or more of the outstanding shares of stock of a corporation. These shares of stock may be either shares of common stock or shares of preferred stock. Also referred to as a "stockholder."

Shareholder/Stockholder Approval

Authorization of the shareholders/stockholders of a corporation to the occurrence of a specific event or transaction. Generally, shareholder/stockholder approval is sought in connection with the adoption of an employee stock option plan and, in certain instances, with the amendment of such plans.

Shares Swapped

The number of shares of stock tendered to the corporation in a stock swap exercise. The swapped shares are assigned a value, typically the fair market value of the corporation's stock on the date of exercise. To complete the transaction, the optionee must deliver to the corporation a certificate or certificates covering enough previously-issued and presently-owned shares of stock to pay the aggregate option price for the share of stock being acquired through the stock option exercise.

"Short-Swing Profits Recovery" Rule

Section 16(b) of the Securities Exchange Act of 1934. The rule requires the directors and officers of an issuer that has registered a class of its equity securities under Section 12, as well as the beneficial owners of more than 10% of any class of the issuer's registered equity securities, to return over to the issuer any profits realized from the purchase and sale, or sale and purchase, of the issuer's equity securities within a period of less than six months.

Single Trigger Provision

In a stock option plan, a provision stating that upon a change of control, the options vest fully and can be immediately exercised, regardless of whether the optionee has been terminated. See "Double Trigger Provision."

Social Security

An employment tax for retirement income imposed on employees and employers under the Federal Insurance Contributions Act with respect to the wages paid to employees.

Spread

Term used to describe the difference, if any, between the option price and the fair market value of the corporation's stock on the date of exercise. Typically, in the case of a non-qualified stock option, the "spread" on exercise represents the compensation income recognizable by the optionee for income tax purposes and, in the case of an incentive stock option, the "spread" on exercise represents the adjustment item for purposes of computing the employee's alternative minimum taxable income.

Statutory Holding Period

Holding period established by Sections 422 and 423 of the Code for ISOs and ESPP options: one year from exercise, two years from grant.

Statutory Option

A stock option described in the Code. Includes incentive stock options (ISOs) and employee stock purchase plan options (ESPPs) qualifying under Section 423 of the Code.

Stock

Shares that represent an ownership interest in a corporation.

Stock Appreciation Right (SAR)

A contractual right granted to an individual in which the recipient has the right to receive an amount equal to the appreciation on a specified number of shares of stock over a specified period of time. Generally, the recipient controls the timing of exercise of the right, which may be payable in cash or in shares of stock of the corporation.

Stockbroker

An individual that acts as an intermediary between a buyer and seller of securities. A stock broker receives compensation, in the form of a commission, for assisting in or effecting the purchase or sale of securities. A stock broker is "registered" with the National Association of Securities dealers and the exchange on which the securities are traded. Brokers are also regulated under federal and state securities laws.

Stock Certificate

A document that evidences ownership of a specific number of securities of a corporation. The certificate typically contains an alpha-numeric identifier, the name of the issuing corporation, the number of securities represented by the certificate, and the name and address of the shareholder/stockholder.

Stock-for-Stock Exercise

See "Stock Swap Exercise."

Stock Option

A contractual right granted to an individual to purchase a specified number of shares of stock of the granting corporation at a specified price for a specified period of time. Also known as a "grant." As set forth in the Income Tax regulations, the term "option" includes the right or privilege of an individual to purchase stock from a corporation by virtue of an offer of the corporation continuing for a stated period of time, whether or not irrevocable, to sell such stock at a pre-determined price, such individual being under no obligation to purchase. Such a right or privilege, when granted, must be evidenced in writing. The individual who has such right or privilege is referred to as the "optionee."

Stock Option Agreement

See "Option Agreement."

Stock Option Committee

Committee of the board of directors of a corporation responsible for decisions pertaining to employee stock option grants under the corporation's employee stock option plan.

Stock Option Plan

A formal program adopted by a corporation, often in writing, that provides for the grant of employee stock options to one or more individuals upon the terms and conditions set forth in the plan document and the issuance of shares of stock of the corporation upon the exercise of such stock options.

Stock Option Repricing

See "Repricing."

Stock Option Term

The period of time granted to an individual to exercise an employee stock option. Generally, the term of an employee stock option ranges from five to 10 years.

Stock Split

A change in the capitalization of an issuer that increases or decreases the number of securities outstanding, and adjusts the value of the securities accordingly, without a corresponding change in the assets or capital of the issuer. Generally, used to denote a change in capitalization that increases the number of securities outstanding and adjusts the value of the securities downward.

Stockholder

A person who owns one or more of the outstanding shares of stock of a corporation. These shares of stock may be either shares of common stock or shares of preferred stock. Also referred to as a "shareholder."

Stock Swap Exercise

A transaction in which already-owned shares of stock are exchanged in lieu of cash to pay the option price for the exercise of an employee stock option. Also referred to as a "stock-for-stock" exercise.

Street Name Issuance

The registration of a security in the name of a securities brokerage firm as a nominee for the beneficial owner of the securities. Securities are often held in "street name" to expedite transfers of the securities when the securities are sold, since no delivery of the certificate or signature of transfer by the beneficial owner is required.

Subsidiary Corporation

A corporation that is majority owned or wholly owned by another corporation. For purposes of the incentive stock option rules, any corporation (other than the employer corporation) in an unbroken chain of corporations beginning with the employer corporation if, at the time of grant of a stock option, each of the corporations other than the last corporation in the unbroken chain owns stock possessing 50% or more of the total combined voting power of all classes of stock in one of the other corporations in such chain.

Substantial Risk of Forfeiture

Tax concept under Section 83 of the Code that describes a situation in which an individual's rights to the full enjoyment of property is conditional upon the future performance of substantial services.

Swap Share Value

The value assigned to a share of stock surrendered to the corporation to offset the total option price of an exercise. Commonly the swap share value is equal to the fair market value of the corporation's stock on the date of exercise.

TAMRA

Technical and Miscellaneous Revenue Act of 1988.

Tandem Stock Option

An employee stock option that also provides the optionee with a related right, such as a stock appreciation right, covering an equivalent number of securities. Generally, the exercise of one right affects the holder's ability to exercise the other right. For example, to the extent that an optionee exercises the employee stock option portion of a tandem employee stock option/stock appreciation right, the related stock appreciation right is cancelled, and vice versa.

Tax Basis

Tax concept representing the actual and constructive "cost" of property to a taxpayer. For purposes of calculating gain or loss under the Code upon the sale or exchange of property (such as shares of stock), the amount of cash actually expended to acquire the property as well as the amount of any income previously recognized in connection with the property for income tax purposes.

Tax Deferral

The ability to postpone the payment of taxes from the date of a specific transaction until a later date. For example, assuming that a stock option designated as an incentive stock option satisfies the conditions of Section 422(b) of the Code, upon exercise of such incentive stock option the employee is permitted to defer the recognition of taxable income in connection with the acquisition of the shares of stock received upon exercise of the stock option until the disposition of such shares of stock.

Tax Offset Bonus

A cash bonus payable to an employee upon the exercise of a non-qualified stock option to cover, or "offset," the withholding taxes due as a result of the exercise. Generally, the amount of the bonus will be based upon a percentage of the total amount of compensation income recognized by the optionee plus additional amounts needed to "gross up" the bonus to fully offset the tax effect of the transaction on an after-tax basis.

For financial reporting purposes, the use of a tax offset bonus to reimburse an employee for the withholding taxes due on the exercise of a non-qualified stock option will result in "variable" accounting treatment for the transaction. That is, the corporation will record a compensation expense for financial reporting purposes equal to the amount of the cash bonus plus the entire difference between the option price and the fair market value of the corporation's stock on the date of exercise.

Tax Regulations

Rules promulgated by the Internal Revenue Service implementing and interpreting the statutory provisions of the Code. Congressional authority for the issuance of regulations is set forth in Section 7805 of the Code. While such rules are not law, they represent the Internal Revenue Service's interpretation of the proper application of the law and are presumed to be valid.

Tax Withholding

The retention of certain amounts from an employee's wages or compensation by a corporation to satisfy the income tax and/or employment tax obligations of the employee that arise in connection with the exercise of a non-qualified stock option.

Term

The period of time granted to an optionee in which to exercise an employee stock option. Generally, the term of an employee stock option will be a period of up to 10 years. Also may refer to the duration of an employee stock option plan, during which time the plan administrator may grant stock options to eligible participants in the plan.

Termination

When an individual ceases to be an employee of a corporation, typically, unvested shares of stock (or, in the case of a stock option, any right to acquire unvested shares of stock) are normally cancelled. Termination of employment can trigger other rights and obligations for the individual and/or the corporation under the terms and conditions of the employee stock plan or the individual grant or award agreement.

Termination of Employment

The act of an optionee terminating his or her employment with a corporation. Generally, upon termination of employment any unvested shares of stock (or, in the case of an employee stock option grant, any right to acquire unvested shares of stock) will be cancelled as of the date termination. A termination of employment may trigger other rights and obligations for the employee and/or the corporation under the terms of the corporation's employee stock option plan and/or individual option agreement.

Termination of Plan

The conclusion of an employee stock option plan resulting from either the affirmative decision of the plan administrators to wind up the plan, the exhaustion of the plan share reserve or the expiration of the stated plan term.

Time-Accelerated Stock Option

A form of employee stock option that provides for a fixed, service-based vesting schedule with certain vesting accelerators tied to the achievement of specified performance criteria. If properly structured, for financial reporting purposes, the amount of compensation expense associated with the stock option is measured at the date of grant. This type of arrangement enables a corporation to grant an employee stock option that, from a practical standpoint, operates as a performance-based award but which receives "fixed" accounting treatment rather than the "variable" accounting treatment that is typically associated with performance-based arrangements.

Time-Accelerated Restricted Stock Award Plan (TARSAP)

A form of restricted stock purchase award that provides for a fixed, service-based vesting schedule with certain vesting accelerators tied to the achievement of specified performance criteria. If properly structured, for financial reporting purposes, the amount of compensation expense associated with the award is measured at the date of grant. This type of arrangement enables a corporation to grant an award that, from a practical standpoint, operates as a performance-based award but which receives "fixed" accounting treatment rather than the "variable" accounting treatment that is typically associated with performance-based arrangements.

Trade for Taxes

An exercise feature that allows the optionee to request that the corporation withhold some of the shares of stock being acquired upon the exercise of the stock option in order to satisfy the optionee's withholding tax liability arising in connection with the transaction. The traded shares are assigned a value, usually the fair market value of the corporation's stock on the date of exercise. This value is divided into the total taxes due to determine the number of shares of stock required to be withheld. The number of shares of stock exercised is then reduced by the number of shares of stock to be withheld and only the net balance is issued to the optionee.

Trade Share Value

The value assigned to an exercised share that is traded back to the corporation to satisfy a withholding tax liability arising in connection with a stock option exercise. Commonly the trade share value is equal to the fair market value of the corporation's stock on the date of exercise.

Transfer

Conveyance of property, such as shares of stock, from one individual to another individual, followed by recording the ownership of the property on the records of the issuer.

Transfer Agent

An institution selected by an issuer to issue and transfer share certificates representing the ownership of the outstanding securities of the issuer. An agent of the corporation responsible for registering shareholder/stockholder names on the corporation's records. The transfer agent maintains a current list of shareholders/stockholders for purposes of distributing dividends, reports, and other corporate communications.

Transferable Stock Option

A non-qualified stock option that permits the optionee, under the terms and conditions set forth in the option agreement, to transfer the option to one or more third parties. Because of the limitation on transferability set forth in Section 422(b)(5) of the Code, an incentive stock option cannot be a transferable stock option. Most corporations that permit transferable stock options limit the group of permissible transferees to immediate family members of the optionee or to entities (such as trusts or partnerships) for the benefit of immediate family members. A number of federal income and gift tax issues must be considered in connection with the implementation and use of transferable stock options.

Transfer Date

The date upon which securities are considered to have been transferred from one person to another.

Transfer of Control

See "Change in Control."

Treasury Shares (Treasury Stock)

Shares of the capital stock of a corporation that were previously issued by the corporation and have been reacquired and are being held in "treasury" rather than retired. Substantively, treasury shares are equivalent to authorized but unissued shares. However, the corporation may reissue treasury shares without having to satisfy the minimum consideration requirements of state corporate law. Several states do not recognize the concept of treasury shares.

Underwater

Term used to describe an employee stock option where the option price is greater than the current fair market value of the shares of stock subject to the stock option.

Unvested Share Repurchase Option

Contractual restriction placed on shares of stock acquired upon the exercise of an employee stock option that permits the corporation to repurchase any unvested shares of stock at their original purchase price upon the optionee's termination of employment with the corporation.

Unvested Shares

Shares of stock that an individual has not yet earned and, therefore, may not transfer to a third party. Entitlement to the shares of stock is subject to the satisfaction of one or more contingencies (generally service-based) that are attached to the receipt of the shares of stock.

Vesting

The process of earning shares of stock granted under an employee stock option; the process by which rights under an option become nontransferable or not subject to a substantial right of forfeiture. Typically, vesting is achieved by satisfying one or more specific service- or performance-based conditions.

Vest Date

The date on which shares of stock are no longer subject to repurchase by a corporation, or the date on which an individual can exercise the shares.

Vesting Period

An individual increment of a vesting schedule during which a portion of the shares of stock subject to an employee stock option are earned by the optionee. Each increment vests on a different date.

Vesting Schedule

A series of dates on which a specified number of option shares become vested and eligible for exercise or release to the optionee. This schedule is represented in the option record by a chart which defines units of time called periods. Some percentage of the total option shares vests either regularly throughout the period or in full at the end of the period.

Vested Share Repurchase Option

Contractual restriction placed on shares of stock acquired upon the exercise of an employee stock option that permits the corporation to repurchase any vested shares of stock at the then-current fair market value of the corporation's stock upon the optionee's termination of employment with the corporation.

"Window" Period

A period of time during which, under a corporation's trading policy, it is permissible for a director, officer or employee to trade in the corporation's securities if the individual is in compliance with the terms of the policy (that is, the individual is not in actual possession of material, non-public information concerning the corporation). Typically, these periods run from ten days to two months following the release of quarterly or annual financial information by the corporation.

Withholding

The retention of certain amounts from an employee's wages or compensation by a corporation to satisfy the income tax and/or employment tax obligations of the employee that arise in connection with the exercise of a non-qualified stock option.

Withholding Tax

The retention of certain amounts from an individual's wages or compensation by a corporation to cover the tax obligations of an individual that arise in connection with the grant, exercise, vesting, or receipt of an employee stock option or the shares of stock subject to an employee stock option.

W-2 Income

See "Form W-2 Income."

About the Editor and Authors

Editor **Scott Rodrick** is the director of publishing and information technology at the National Center for Employee Ownership (NCEO). He is the author, co-author, or editor of various publications on ESOPs and stock options, such as *An Introduction to ESOPs* and *Employee Stock Purchase Plans;* additionally, he edits the NCEO's *Journal of Employee Ownership Law and Finance*. He also created the NCEO's Web sites at *www.nceo.org* and *www.nceoglobal.org.* Mr. Rodrick served at the U.S. Department of Labor as an attorney-advisor before coming to the NCEO.

Alisa J. Baker is a partner at the California law firm of General Counsel Associates LLP (*www.gcalaw.com*), where she specializes in counseling companies and professionals with respect to employee benefits and compensation matters, including equity and executive compensation, strategic stock planning and plan design, executive contract negotiation, ERISA issues, and option litigation consulting. She speaks and writes frequently on issues related to her practice, and is the author of *The Stock Options Book*, 5th ed., also published by the NCEO.

Mark A. Borges formerly was the general counsel for ShareData, Inc., a provider of equity compensation administration software. He is currently a Special Counsel with the U.S. Securities and Exchange Commission.

Daniel N. Janich is a principal in the law firm of Janich Benefits Group in Chicago, Illinois. His law practice is concentrated in representing corporations and executives in the areas of employee benefits and executive compensation. He has extensive experience in designing and administering stock-based compensation plans, in counseling and negotiating compensation packages for executives, and in representing clients in benefits litigation. Mr. Janich frequently writes and speaks about stock-based compensation issues, and his articles appear in professional journals, books, and treatises. He is a former chair of the Employee Benefits Committee of the Chicago Bar Association.

Thomas LaWer is an associate at the law firm of Cooley Godward LLP in Palo Alto, California. His law practice is concentrated in the areas of employee compensation, and he has worked extensively with both public and private companies in the design and implementation of equity compensation.

Arthur S. Meyers is a partner with the law firm of Palmer & Dodge LLP in Boston, MA. He advises public and closely held companies on executive compensation and the tax, corporate law, accounting, and securities law aspects of equity and quasi-equity corporation plans, including nonqualified stock options, incentive stock options, restricted stock, employee stock purchase plans, and phantom stock plans.

Linda A. Olup is a divorce attorney who routinely handles cases involving equity compensation. She is the principal in Olup & Associates, a St. Paul-Minneapolis-based law firm working exclusively in the area of divorce and family law. She graduated from Rutgers University in 1972 and William Mitchell College of Law in 1977. In 1992, Linda coauthored the book *Family Law,* which is currently in its second edition (St. Paul, Minn.: West Publishing Co., 2000). She has been profiled and quoted in many publications, including the *Wall Street Journal, Minnesota Monthly,* and *Minnesota Law and Politics.*

William R. Pomierski and **William J. Quinlan, Jr.,** are partners in the international law firm of McDermott, Will & Emery, resident in its Chicago office. Mr. Pomierski is a member of the firm's Executive Compensation Group and its Tax Department. Mr. Quinlan is a member of the firm's Executive Compensation Group and its Corporate and Securities Department. Both have worked extensively with both public and private companies in the design and structuring of executive compensation packages, including stock and stock-based compensation plans.

Matthew Topham is an associate in the business department of Preston Gates & Ellis LLP. He has experience in mergers and acquisitions involving both public and private companies, initial public offerings, state and federal securities law filings, and venture capital financings. He has counseled firm clients on a variety of employment-related issues and has experience drafting employment contracts, independent contractor agreements, nondisclosure agreements, and equity incentive plans for both public and private corporations and limited liability companies.

About the NCEO and Its Other Publications

The National Center for Employee Ownership (NCEO) is widely considered to be the leading authority in employee ownership in the U.S. and the world. Established in 1981 as a nonprofit information and membership organization, it now has well over 3,000 members, including companies, professionals, unions, government officials, academics, and interested individuals. It is funded entirely through the work it does. The staff includes persons with backgrounds in academia, law, and business.

The NCEO's mission is to provide the most objective, reliable information possible about employee ownership at the most affordable price possible. As part of the NCEO's commitment to providing objective information, it does not lobby or provide ongoing consulting services. The NCEO publishes a variety of materials—such as this book—explaining how employee ownership plans work, describing how companies get employee owners more involved in making decisions about their work, and reviewing the research on employee ownership. In addition, the NCEO holds dozens of seminars and conferences on employee ownership annually. These include seminars on stock options and on employee stock ownership plans (ESOPs), meetings on employee participation, international programs, and a large annual conference. The NCEO's work also includes extensive contacts with the media, both through articles written for trade and professional publications and through interviews with reporters. The NCEO has written or edited five books for other publishers. Finally, the NCEO maintains an extensive Web site at *www.nceo.org*, plus a site on global equity-based compensation at *www.nceoglobal.org*.

The following pages have information on NCEO membership and NCEO publications. To join or to order publications, see the order form at the end of this section, visit *www.nceo.org*, or telephone 510-208-1300.

Membership Benefits

NCEO members receive the following benefits:

- The bimonthly newsletter, *Employee Ownership Report*, which covers ESOPs, stock options and related plans, and employee participation.
- Access to the members-only area of the NCEO Web site, including the NCEO's Referral Service, a searchable database of over 200 service providers.
- Substantial discounts on publications and events produced by the NCEO (such as this book).
- The right to contact the NCEO for answers to general or specific questions regarding employee ownership.

An introductory NCEO membership costs $80 for one year ($90 outside the U.S.) and covers an entire company at all locations, a single office of a firm offering professional services in this field, or an individual with a business interest in employee ownership. Full-time students and faculty members who are not employed in the business sector may join at the academic rate of $35 for one year ($45 outside the U.S.).

Selected NCEO Publications

The NCEO offers a variety of publications on all aspects of employee ownership and participation. Following are descriptions of our main publications.

We publish new books and revise old ones on a yearly basis. To obtain the most current information on what we have available, visit our extensive Web site at *www.nceo.org* or call us at 510-208-1300.

Stock Options and Related Plans

- *The Stock Options Book* is a straightforward, comprehensive overview covering the legal, accounting, regulatory, and design issues involved in implementing a stock option or stock purchase plan, including "broad-based" plans covering most or all employees. It is our main book on the subject and possibly the most popular book in the field.

    $25 for NCEO members, $35 for nonmembers

- This book, *Stock Options: Beyond the Basics,* is more detailed and specialized than *The Stock Options Book,* with chapters on issues such as underwater options, securities issues, and evergreen options. It ends with an exhaustive glossary of terms used in the field.

  $25 for NCEO members, $35 for nonmembers

- *The Employee's Guide to Stock Options* is a guide for the everyday employee that explains in an easy-to-understand format what stock is and how stock options work.

  $25 for both NCEO members and nonmembers

- *Model Equity Compensation Plans* provides examples of incentive stock option, nonqualified stock option, and stock purchase plans, together with brief explanations of the main documents. A disk is included with copies of the plan documents in formats any word processing program can open.

  $50 for NCEO members, $75 for nonmembers

- *Current Practices in Stock Option Plan Design* is a highly detailed report on our survey of companies with broad-based stock option plans conducted in 2000. It includes a detailed examination of plan design, use, and experience broken down by industry, size, and other categories.

  $25 for NCEO members, $35 for nonmembers

- *Communicating Stock Options* offers practical ideas and information about how to explain stock options to a broad group of employees. It includes the views of experienced practitioners as well as detailed examples of how companies communicate tax consequences, financial information, and other matters to employees.

  $35 for NCEO members, $50 for nonmembers

- *Employee Stock Purchase Plans* covers how ESPPs work, tax and legal issues, administration, accounting, communicating the plan to employees, and research on what companies are doing with their plans. The book includes sample plan documents.

  $25 for NCEO members, $35 for nonmembers

- *Stock Options, Corporate Performance, and Organizational Change* presents the first serious research to examine the relationship between broadly granted stock options and company performance, and the extent of employee involvement in broad option companies.

$15 for NCEO members, $25 for nonmembers

- *Equity-Based Compensation for Multinational Corporations* describes how companies can use stock options and other equity-based programs across the world to reward a global work force. It includes a country-by-country summary of tax and legal issues as well as a detailed case study.

$25 for NCEO members, $35 for nonmembers

- *Incentive Compensation and Employee Ownership* takes a broad look at how companies can use incentives, ranging from stock plans to cash bonuses to gainsharing, to motivate and reward employees. It includes both technical discussions and case studies.

$25 for NCEO members, $35 for nonmembers

Employee Stock Ownership Plans (ESOPs)

- *The ESOP Reader* is a general overview of the issues involved in establishing and operating an ESOP. It covers the basics of ESOP rules, feasibility, valuation, and other matters, and then discusses managing an ESOP company, including brief case studies.

$25 for NCEO members, $35 for nonmembers

- *Selling to an ESOP* is a guide for owners, managers, and advisors of closely held businesses. It explains how ESOPs work and then offers a comprehensive look at legal structures, valuation, financing (including self-financing), and other matters, especially the tax-deferred section 1042 "rollover" that allows owners to indefinitely defer capital gains taxation on the proceeds of the sale to the ESOP.

$25 for NCEO members, $35 for nonmembers

- *Leveraged ESOPs and Employee Buyouts* discusses how ESOPs borrow money to buy out entire companies, purchase shares from a retiring owner, or finance new capital. Beginning with a primer on leveraged ESOPs and their uses, it then discusses contribution limits, valuation, accounting, feasibility studies, financing sources, and more.

$25 for NCEO members, $35 for nonmembers

- The *Model ESOP* provides a sample ESOP plan, with alternative provisions given to tailor the plan to individual needs. It also includes a section-by-section explanation of the plan and other supporting materials.

  $50 for NCEO members, $75 for nonmembers

- *ESOP Valuation* brings together and updates where needed the best articles on ESOP valuation that we have published in our *Journal of Employee Ownership Law and Finance,* described below.

  $25 for NCEO members, $35 for nonmembers

- The *Employee Ownership Q&A Disk* gives Microsoft Windows users (any version from Windows 95 onward) point-and-click access to 500 questions and answers on all aspects of ESOPs in a searchable hypertext format.

  $75 for NCEO members, $100 for nonmembers

- *How ESOP Companies Handle the Repurchase Obligation* is a short publication with articles and research on the subject.

  $10 for NCEO members, $15 for nonmembers

- *The ESOP Committee Guide* describes the different types of ESOP committees, the range of goals they can address, alternative structures, member selection criteria, training, committee life cycle concerns, and other issues.

  $25 for NCEO members, $35 for nonmembers

- *Wealth and Income Consequences of Employee Ownership* is a detailed report on a comparative study of ESOP companies in Washington State that found ESOP companies pay more and provided better benefits than other companies.

  $10 for NCEO members, $15 for nonmembers

- The *ESOP Communications Sourcebook* is a publication for ESOP companies with ideas and examples on how to communicate an ESOP to employees and market employee ownership to customers.

  $35 for NCEO members, $50 for nonmembers

Employee Involvement and Management

- *Ownership Management* draws upon the experience of the NCEO and of leading employee ownership companies to discuss how to build a culture of lasting innovation by combining employee ownership with employee involvement programs. It includes specific ideas and examples of how to structure plans, share information, and get employees involved.

$25 for NCEO members, $35 for nonmembers

- *Front Line Finance Facilitator's Manual* gives step-by-step instructions for teaching business literacy, emphasizing ESOPs.

    $50 for NCEO members, $75 for nonmembers

- *Front Line Finance Diskette* contains the workbook for participants in electronic form (so a copy can be printed out for everyone) in the Front Line Finance course.

    $50 for NCEO members, $75 for nonmembers

- *Cultural Diversity and Employee Ownership* discusses how companies with employee stock plans deal with diversity and communicate employee ownership.

    $25 for NCEO members, $35 for nonmembers

Other

- *Section 401(k) Plans and Employee Ownership* focuses on how company stock is used in 401(k) plans, both in stand-alone 401(k) plans and combination 401(k)–ESOP plans ("KSOPs").

    $25 for NCEO members, $35 for nonmembers

- *A Conceptual Guide to Equity-Based Compensation for Non-U.S. Companies* helps companies outside the U.S. think through how to approach employee ownership.

    $25 for NCEO members, $35 for nonmembers

- The *Journal of Employee Ownership Law and Finance* is the only professional journal solely devoted to employee ownership. Articles are written by leading experts and cover ESOPs, stock options, and related subjects in depth.

    One-year subscription (four issues):
    $75 for NCEO members, $100 for nonmembers

To join the NCEO as a member or to order any of the publications listed on the preceding pages, use the order form on the following page, use the secure ordering system on our Web site at *www.nceo.org*, or call us at **510-208-1300**. If you join at the same time you order publications, you will receive the members-only publication discounts.

Order Form

To order, fill out this form and mail it with your credit card information or check to the NCEO at 1736 Franklin Street, 8th Floor, Oakland, CA, 94612; fax it with your credit card information to the NCEO at 510-272-9510; telephone us at 510-208-1300 with your credit card in hand; or order securely online at our Web site, *www.nceo.org.* If you are not already a member, you can join now to receive member discounts on any publications you order.

Name

Organization

Address

City, State, Zip (Country)

Telephone   Fax   E-mail

Method of Payment: ❑ Check (payable to "NCEO") ❑ Visa   ❑ M/C   ❑ AMEX

Credit Card Number

Signature   Exp. Date

Checks are accepted only for orders from the U.S. and must be in U.S. currency.

Title	Qty.	Price	Total

Tax: California residents add 8.25% sales tax (on publications only, not membership)	Subtotal $
Shipping: In the U.S., first publication $5, each add'l $1; elsewhere, we charge exact shipping costs to your credit card, plus (except for Canada) a $10 handling surcharge; no shipping charges for membership or Journal subscriptions	Sales Tax $
	Shipping $
	Membership $
Introductory NCEO Membership: $80 for one year ($90 outside the U.S.)	TOTAL DUE $

Quantity Purchase Discounts

If your company would like to buy this book in quantity (10 or more) for its employees, a client company's employees, or others, we can sell it to you at a discount below the $25 members/$35 nonmembers price given above. Contact us by e-mail at *nceo@nceo.org* or by phone at 510-208-1300 to work out the details.